Effortless Mindfulı

Effortless Mindfulness: Genuine Mental Health Through Awakened Presence promotes genuine mental health through the direct experience of awakened presence—an effortlessly embodied, fearless understanding of and interaction with the way things truly are. The book offers a uniquely modern Buddhist psychological understanding of mental health disorders through a scholarly yet clinically useful presentation of Theravada, Mahāyāna and Vajrayāna Buddhist teachings and practices. Written specifically for Western psychotherapeutic professionals, the book brings together traditional Buddhist theory and contemporary psycho-neuro-bio-social research to describe the conditioned and unconditioned mind. This in-depth exploration of Buddhist psychology includes complete instructions for psychotherapists in authentic yet clinically appropriate Buddhist mindfulness/heartfulness practices and Buddhist psychological inquiry skills. The book also features interviews with an esteemed collection of Buddhist teachers, scholars, meditation researchers and Buddhist-inspired clinicians.

Lisa Dale Miller, LMFT, LPCC, SEP, is a private practice psychotherapist in Los Gatos, California. She specializes in mindfulness psychotherapy and Buddhist psychology and is a certified Somatic Experiencing practitioner. Lisa trains clinicians in the application of mindfulness interventions and practical Buddhist psychology and is trained in Mindfulness-Based Relapse Prevention (MBRP), Mindfulness-Based Cognitive Therapy (MBCT), and Mindfulness-Based Stress Reduction (MBSR). Lisa has been a dedicated yogic and Buddhist meditation practitioner for almost four decades. For more information on the material presented in this book please visit: www.awakenedpresence.com. More information on Lisa's private practice can be found at: www.lisadalemiller.com

Effortless Mindfulness

Genuine Mental Health Through Awakened Presence

Lisa Dale Miller

NEW YORK AND LONDON

First published 2014
by Routledge
711 Third Avenue, New York, NY 10017

and by Routledge
27 Church Road, Hove, East Sussex BN3 2FA

Routledge is an imprint of the Taylor & Francis Group, an informa business

Library of Congress Cataloging-in-Publication Data

Miller, Lisa Dale.
Effortless mindfulness : genuine mental health through awakened presence / by Lisa Dale Miller. — 1 Edition.
pages cm
Includes bibliographical references and index.
1. Mental illness—Alternative treatment. 2. Mindfulness-based cognitive therapy. I. Title.
RC480.5.M535 2014
616.89—dc23 2013040167

ISBN: 978-0-415-63731-2 (hbk)
ISBN: 978-0-415-63733-6 (pbk)
ISBN: 978-0-203-08465-6 (ebk)

Typeset in Minion
by Apex CoVantage, LLC

To my precious teachers (listed in order of their appearance in my life)

Maharishi Mahesh Yogi
Barbara G. Walker
Jack Kornfield
Phillip Moffitt
Venerable Ajahn Sumedho
Tsoknyi Rinpoche
Mingyur Rinpoche
Anam Thubten Rinpoche

Contents

Foreword

Anam Thubten Rinpoche

It seems that the modern world has become more transient and fleeting than ever in all aspects. What is popular this year might not be in the next. Also, many of the traditional religions are in decline. People have less appetite for any form of draconian doctrine or rigid dogma and are uninterested in adhering to a fixed structure. Nevertheless, the need for spirituality is alive and expressing itself in ever new and exciting ways.

Buddhism has been going through a surprising and interesting evolution in the West. Today, many Westerners from all walks of life practice some form of Buddhism. You'll find businessmen praying inside colorful Tibetan temples, a politician attending a *vipassanā* retreat, and celebrities in gray robes trying to solve koans in a zendo.

One of the wonderful new trends manifesting right now is the integration of Buddhism with psychology and science. *Effortless Mindfulness* is an expression of these new ways, which are opening up for modern seekers who are on the path of healing and transformation on all levels of being. When Albert Einstein stated that Buddhism is the only religion that can cope with modern scientific need, he was certainly thinking about the nontheistic aspects of Buddhism. I wonder how much he was aware of the fact that there are so many areas where Buddhism and science can be integrated. We have come a long way since then. Buddhism has found its friendship with physics, neuroscience and psychology.

Such integration is needed to alleviate human suffering and bring about wellness. This has to do with the fact that a holistic approach comes from integrating a variety of disciplines.

We need a holistic approach to treat the whole person in body, mind and spirit. Let's say someone is dealing with a mental problem, which can have its root in very complex factors. We cannot always expect the person's problem to go away just by practicing Buddhism. His or her problem can be physiological and require medical treatment. Here, my friend Lisa Dale Miller did an extraordinary job in showing the beautiful meeting between those ancient and modern disciplines and how effective they are together.

Another matter is that many selective Eastern disciplines, such as yoga, have been popularized. These days, many people are practicing yoga without connecting to its spiritual root. No longer the esoteric property of Buddhist monks, mindfulness meditation has been introduced to all quarters of society as well as the corporate world. We can take delight in how mindfulness meditation is changing the collective consciousness of the masses in the West, helping so many people become calmer, more centered and healthier. But, at the same time, we must remember that mindfulness meditation lies at the root of the Buddhist tradition. It has a transcendent dimension. Those who have gone before us practiced it as a path to enlightenment. This is still open to everyone too. It depends on how deep one wants to dive in. This point is clearly addressed in Lisa's book with a great deal of care and thoughtfulness.

You will find that the author's scholarship and many years of meditation practice are reflected on every page. It is intellectually satisfying and also serves as a rich contemplative guide for mindfulness meditation and Buddhism in general. No matter what your background might be, as scholar, meditator, seeker, or clinician, you will find many valuable insights in this work. It is such a joy to see Lisa's gift in presenting many essential Buddhist thoughts in contemporary language and making them come alive. I hope this book helps many people find clarity and wholeness on their inner journey.

Foreword

Ronald D. Siegel

Some years ago my colleagues and I had the privilege of being joined by the Dalai Lama at a Harvard Medical School psychotherapy conference. We thought it would be particularly inspiring to have His Holiness lead all 1,100 of us psychotherapists in a brief meditation. When at the appointed time we asked him to conduct the meditation, he began laughing and said, "I think some of you may want just one single meditation. And a simple one. And 100 percent sort of positive. That, I think, impossible." He went on to suggest that there are countless states of mind that lead to suffering; consequently, countless meditation practices are needed to work skillfully with them. What a given person needs at a given time is a very complicated matter, not amenable to one-size-fits-all solutions. He concluded, "Some other sort of companies, they always advertise some simple thing, or something effective, something very cheap. My advertising is just opposite. How difficult, and complicated!"

As mindfulness practices increasingly find their way into Western culture generally, and medicine and psychotherapy in particular, we run the danger of thinking that we all should just learn to follow our breath and relax to alleviate our various symptoms. And while breath-focused concentration practice can be quite useful, it's only one of many different meditative techniques, each of which was refined to develop a different aspect of the heart and mind. Whether choosing practices for ourselves or choosing them for our patients as clinicians, deciding which meditative practice will be most useful at a given moment for a particular individual is indeed a complex matter. Western health care professionals and researchers are just beginning to map this territory, without much scientific data to guide us. In contrast, the Buddhist traditions from which many mindfulness practices derive have been developing complex, nuanced understandings of these techniques' potential to cultivate different qualities of the heart and mind for centuries. By learning more of this tradition's rich history and its profound insights into the workings of the heart and mind, we Westerners can significantly advance our understanding and application of diverse meditative practices.

In the pages that follow, Lisa Dale Miller takes us on an integrative adventure, exploring the intersection of ancient Buddhist teachings with modern neurobiology and clinical research and practice. While the work of many pioneers has facilitated the integration of mindfulness practices into health care and society by intentionally extracting them from their Buddhist roots, this book offers a different service: it looks unflinchingly at Buddhist understandings of the origins of human suffering and the ways in which various meditative techniques were designed to alleviate this suffering by fostering a radical psychological liberation. The challenge here is that many aspects of Buddhist teaching can be difficult to comprehend without first undertaking extensive meditation practice guided by experienced teachers. So entering these waters requires either such preparation or a humble attitude of open receptivity, since, understood correctly, many of the perspectives of Buddhist traditions directly challenge our conventional understandings of ourselves and our world.

This journey is nonetheless well worth taking. While data continue to pour in that mindfulness practices can help us respond to a remarkable range of human difficulties—including everything from stress-related medical disorders, anxiety and depression to interpersonal conflicts—their greatest potential extends beyond this. Coupled with an understanding of how the human mind works, how it has evolved a strong penchant for suffering, and how it constructs the world we think we live in, these practices have the potential to radically transform our experience of living.

We are fortunate to live at a time when the teachings of great wisdom traditions can be combined with the insights of biological and social science to give us unprecedented opportunities to develop psychological freedom. May we take advantage of this good fortune and use the insights in this book to help ourselves, and those around us, to lead fuller, richer, happier lives.

Ronald D. Siegel, PsyD
Assistant Clinical Professor of Psychology
Harvard Medical School/Cambridge Health Alliance and author of
The Mindfulness Solution: Everyday Practices for Everyday Problems

Acknowledgments

I am humbled by the immense generosity of the following individuals who took time from their unbelievably busy schedules to contribute to this book: Anam Thubten Rinpoche; Ronald D. Siegel, PsyD; Tsoknyi Rinpoche; Phillip Moffitt; Stephen Batchelor; John D. Dunne, PhD; Judson Brewer, MD, PhD; David Vago, PhD; Jose Calderón-Abbo, MD; and Steven Hoskinson, MA. With gratitude I bow deeply to their invaluable expertise, which added authority and richness to this endeavor.

My deepest thanks go to Routledge, most particularly to my editor Anna Moore for her courageous support of this project; to my dear friend Donna Sherman, who patiently heard and critiqued much of this text; and to Esteban and Tressa Hollander for their supportive efforts on my behalf.

Every person I have worked with has been a precious teacher to me. I thank every one of my patients for allowing me to witness their labors, insights, transformations and liberations. Particular gratitude goes to those who offered their experiences for inclusion in this book.

With immense love and appreciation I acknowledge my parents Elinor and Paul Miller, who set aside their fears and lovingly tolerated the strange contemplative proclivities of their child-seeker. I owe everything to you both.

Introduction

This book is a reunification of clinical mindfulness and heartfulness interventions with their source—Buddhist psychology and philosophy of mind. Central to this is an understanding that from a Buddhist psychological perspective genuine mental health is a natural outcome of an undeluded mind. Non-delusion arises from the direct experience of *awakened presence*—an effortlessly embodied, fearlessly accurate reception of and interaction with the way things truly are. Because of its nonconceptual nature, awakened presence requires a natural movement from effortful mindfulness to non-dual or *effortless mindfulness*.

To accomplish that evolution, this book offers a modern Buddhist psychological understanding of mental health disorders through a scholarly, clinically relevant presentation of Theravada, Mahāyāna and Vajrayāna Buddhist teachings and practices. Written specifically for Western psychotherapeutic professionals, it aims to move psychotherapy beyond symptom reduction to the liberative recognition of the empty transparency of self and phenomena.

The Buddha's teachings on *Dependent Origination* and conditioned mind form a primary psychological description of the suffering caused by misapprehending reality. Comprehending emptiness is vital to understanding the root causes of human delusion and resultant mental and emotional suffering.

The book's focus on *awakened presence* and *effortless mindfulness* reflects my personal and professional journey with the Buddhist teachings and practices. Effortless mindfulness or resting in awareness is where most long-term Buddhist practitioners end up, no matter where they start. The utter simplicity of *awakened presence* is its transformative power.

Three weeks prior to receiving the final contract for this book, I fell 10 feet from a ladder. That fall demolished every bone in my left wrist and fractured my left hip. After my hospital stay I remained bedridden at home for a month. During that time effortless mindfulness was my greatest ally and an invaluable part of my healing process. A year and five chapters later, my right retina spontaneously tore, and once again writing was obstructed—this time by surgery and compromised vision. Again, effortless mindfulness and awakened presence were my anchors and greatest source of sanity.

How to Approach and Work With the Material in This Book

While this book was written primarily for clinicians, anyone interested in psychophysical well-being will benefit from this material. The book's historical, contextual and philosophical content is not extraneous or secondary to its clinical information. Buddhist psychological theory is best understood when it is fully explicated in the context of contemporary psycho-neuro-bio-social research. Some of the most highly regarded Buddhist teachers, meditation neuroscience researchers and Buddhist-inspired clinicians have generously shared their knowledge and expertise throughout this book. So take your time digesting this rich and complex material.

Buddhist psychology builds on itself, philosophically and methodologically. The Theravada and Mahāyāna teachings and meditation practices are an indispensable prerequisite for understanding effortless mindfulness. While one could skip around, reading 'only parts of interest,' I don't think that is the best way to receive the richness of Buddhist psychology or gain true understanding of its theoretical orientation.

I have paid great attention to the order in which the meditation practices are presented. Unless you are already a dedicated meditator, I suggest trying the practices in the order they are given. Each meditative/reflective practice is written to give clinicians exact instructions for teaching patients. *However, it is imperative that any clinician teaching meditation be a committed practitioner of the meditation they wish to impart to others.* That does not mean you try it once, or record it and never do it. The information, practices and teachings in this book should not be used frivolously or irresponsibly. Daily meditation and use of informal mindfulness and heartfulness skills are essential for effective delivery of Buddhist-inspired psychotherapy.

Each vignette or exercise is designed to teach clinicians Buddhist psychological inquiry and deconstruction skills. Always use your best clinical judgment. You know your patients best, and only you can determine which skills and practices should and should not be offered. Every clinician is a human being. We miscalculate and make mistakes. So don't be too hard on yourself if you try something and it doesn't work as you would have liked. Make sure to describe an intervention before offering it to a patient, and always use invitational language so she or he can freely refuse or express any reservations.

Above all, please enjoy this book. I have tried my best to describe unbelievably profound, complex and abstract information in easily digestible language, with a bit of humor thrown in for good measure. My greatest aspiration is that reading and implementing this book's content will lead each reader to awaken to his or her true nature. May this book be the cause of liberation for all beings everywhere, and may any accrued merit be offered freely to end suffering in all its manifestations.

Abbreviations

AN	Anguttara Nikāya
DN	Digha Nikāya
MN	Majjhima Nikāya
SN	Samyutta Nikāya
UD	Udāna Nikāya
VM	Visuddhimagga

1

Start From Where You Are

We are in the situation of someone who possesses a beautiful car but doesn't know how to drive.

Bokar Rinpoche[1]

Most mental health professionals find themselves working with people who appear to be hapless, captive passengers in their own untamed minds, with no idea how to drive the vehicle of mind toward its own innate tranquility and clarity. So it makes sense that mindfulness, which cultivates a calm, clear mind, is now widely recognized as an integral part of effective treatment for a variety of mental health maladies. Yet mindfulness is often trivialized or conflated with other interventions.[2]

Coincident with the popularization of clinical mindfulness has been a movement to make mindfulness 'more accessible' to everyone by separating it from 'its Buddhist roots.' There are clinicians (myself included) who consider this effort unnecessary because these 'Buddhist roots' have always been a philosophy/psychology of mind that is, at its core, secular and research oriented. Furthermore, mindfulness is just one of many beneficial tools contained within the profound Buddhist toolbox for awakening. Most of these tools, including mindfulness, have yet to be fully explored.

This book was born from a desire to ignite interest in reuniting clinical mindfulness with its source—Buddhist psychology and philosophy—and, in so doing, to return mindfulness psychotherapy to its primary function as the supreme method for liberating mind from primordial ignorance.

Central to this reunification is a deeper understanding of what occurs when a mind that is lost becomes found in the act of opening to and resting in the flow of experience. This is the innate mind of *awakened presence*, or what Tibetan Buddhist texts refer to as *lhun grub* or *spontaneous presence*. Awakened presence is the simplest state of awareness, yet its effect is profoundly liberating. Even 1 second of awakened presence frees us, in that second, from all manner of self-conceptions, including our incessant negative, self-deprecating, anxious internal narratives—the primary source of mental and emotional suffering.

Spontaneous awakened presence is a direct experience often described as *effortless mindfulness*. Because of its nonconceptual nature, this kind of presence is impossible to achieve if one seeks it from within a conceptual or intellectual frame of reference. It is not a cognitive or behavioral intervention. It is difficult to induce through strained, focused concentration on internal or external phenomena. It cannot be imagined or conjured up through visualization. *Awakened presence is a natural outcome of an embodied mind recognizing what is as it is.*

So in the spirit of embodying this interaction and imbuing it with the presence it deserves, I acknowledge that you, the reader, are meeting me, the writer, for the first time, and we are co-creating the experience of this book. My world includes a mutual resonance with the possibility of your world as it is for you. As I share my experience, you may wish to notice what is arising for you. My sincere wish is to genuinely welcome you with openness and interest.

 Here We Are

Initial encounters are ripe with possibility and fraught with uncertainty. There is a tender, undeniable tentativeness in meeting someone for the first time, particularly when it involves a patient and a mental health professional. A shared meta-sensation of *here we are* can permeate the room and intensify a clinician's natural curiosity about a patient's timing and reasons for seeking out therapy. What threshold has been reached? What symptoms or circumstances have become unmanageable or unmitigatable? What changes is the patient seeking at this time in her or his life? Most clinicians meet their inner curiosity with a minimum of reactivity, focusing instead on cultivating an attitude of attentive caring—the basis of creating a safe, connected therapeutic container. Years ago, the psychological terms used to describe internal observing and deliberate shifting of attention were *monitoring counter transference* and *attending to process*. These days, for better or worse, that entire set of carefully considered choices might now be thought of simply as *mindfulness.*

From the moment I greet a prospective client in the waiting room, I am attending to the reality that along with the experience of meeting each other we are simultaneously co-creating a narrative about each other. Ideally, the clinician's narrative should be attuned to a client's actual experience. Yet there are times when a clinician's narrative of herself/himself as the all-knowing mental health professional meets a patient's narrative of awkwardness about needing help or fearfulness of being judged and diagnosed. This can derail a first meeting and lead to disjointed and forced communication. Buddhist psychology postulates the cause of misattunement as an *attachment to self-identity that obstructs the capacity for clear-seeing and compassionate responsiveness.*

> I'd like to invite you to recall your last experience of meeting someone for the first time. If you are a clinician please reflect on your last intake. If not, it can be an initial meeting that occurred in your personal or professional life. Where was your mind? Were you lost in thoughts about

what you looked like, or worried about the other person's opinion of you, or making sure you were saying and doing everything right? Was your mind busy assessing, critiquing and comparing yourself to the person in front of you? Please take a few moments to reflect on these questions and, if you would like, record your recollections below. (I will join you in this contemplation.)

____

____

____

____

____

The last intake I did was with a clinician seeking therapy. I remember entering the waiting room and making an extra effort to greet her with a lighthearted openness because I immediately sensed her discomfort with the role reversal. In hindsight, attending to ameliorating her discomfort lessened my ability to be fully present. I don't recall seeing the color of her eyes or feeling the force of her handshake. In your inquiry, did you have a full sensory experience of the other person? Or did you realize that most of what you experienced was your own inner landscape of thoughts and emotions about meeting them?

If your experience was the latter, rest assured that this 'not quite being there' or lack of presence is common. And that is the main purpose of this book: to help you reengage with the innately precious human gift of *spontaneous awakened presence.*

 So What Brings You Here, Now?

The inevitable first question has been uttered. Potential answers are as numerous and varied as human experience itself. "I can't stand my work." "Our child is failing in school, taking drugs, and won't listen to us." "I haven't been the same since ____." "My parents don't understand me." "I can't connect with anyone these days." "My life has lost meaning and purpose." "I am isolated and alone." "I live with continual fear and anxiety that keeps me from ______." "My body hurts all over, and the doctors can't find any physical cause." "I have an anger problem." "I feel depressed and anxious most of the time." "I feel out of control." "Nothing satisfies me anymore; I don't remember what happiness is like." "Alcohol helps me relax, but my work and family life is deteriorating because I am always either hungover or drunk."

It all sounds very human to me . . . and difficult. Life is a messy, chaotic mix of joy and sorrow. Unfortunately, the human mind does not readily accept the inevitability of life's joys and sorrows with grace and will employ ingenious mental gymnastics to avoid acknowledging it. Human beings are adept at resisting any insinuation of mortality, impotence and imperfection. We grasp with certainty at an exquisitely constructed neuro-illusion of human primacy, control and pseudo-omniscience. *We want life to be the way we conceive it should be, not the way it actually shows up.*

Buddhist psychology labels this fundamental misperception of the way things are as *delusion* or *ignorance*. I like to think of it as 'Wizard of Oz syndrome.' The façade of an all-powerful homunculus running the show behind the scenes is comforting, maybe even a necessity for some—and utterly false. The self is just like that little man who sheepishly comes out from behind the curtain and announces that *he is the wizard and there is no wizard.*

There is a self, *and* it is not the all-knowing, all-directing, all-powerful self. Ultimately, this mistaken sense of an omniscient self, coupled with our expectation that life must manifest exactly as that self dictates, is the great troublemaker for us all—including psychotherapists.

 A Few Truths to Embrace

During an initial session with a new patient, I often find myself repeating, "That sounds very human," in response to the stream of self-deprecating, harsh commentary used to describe difficulties. At some point in the dialogue the patient will pause, look at me (sometimes with moist eyes) and softly say, "I hadn't thought of it that way. I guess I am human too." That is when I suggest considering the following truths about the human condition.

It Is Human to Resist Pain and Seek Pleasure

All human emotions, impulses and motivations can be divided into two general categories: approach or avoidance. It should not be surprising that human behavior is driven by primal biological imperatives for life regulation.[3] We are human animals wired for survival. Pain induces us to withdraw or freeze in response to an apparent threat. Pleasure inspires us to approach and open to perceived sources of sustenance. Consider how automatically we shrink from the awful, even though our conscience may be compelling us to reach out, or how readily sensual experience entices and overwhelms us, even with the logical mind screaming, "Stop!"

It Is Human to Desire Happiness

Although people have varied opinions about what makes them happy, there is a fundamental difference between what a given person deems an object of happiness and the basic human desire for happiness. Objects of happiness continually change throughout life. The basic human desire for happiness is an aspiration to flourish regardless of the prevailing conditions. Its arising is not dependent on the existence of agreeable circumstances or pleasurable objects. This is the happiness that comes from successful embodiment of virtue, selflessness and skillful responsiveness.

It Is Human to Not Know the Difference Between Pain and Suffering

Although pain is a natural part of life, most people consider pain—be it physical, social or emotional—the most serious impediment to a happy life. Many schools of Western psychology agree that mental distress is stimulated by internal or external pain.

Buddhist psychology offers an alternative perspective. *Pain is a separate and distinct phenomenon from the suffering that can arise in the mind when it is gripped by resistance to the presence of pain.* In other words, resistance-caused responses to pain increase the distress we experience when we are in pain. By masquerading as actual pain, suffering obscures direct knowing of pain. That pain and suffering are separate phenomena must be pointed out. This book is designed to impart skills and established meditative practices for cultivating the awareness needed to distinguish between pain and suffering.[4]

 Recognizing Life's Inherent Unsatisfactoriness

In part because of the unfortunate, persisting mistranslation of the Sanskrit word *dukkha*, Buddhist philosophy has been thought to advocate a rather dour view of life as suffering. An accurate translation of *dukkha* is *a pervasive, blatant or subtle felt-sense of unsatisfactoriness existing inherently in all experience.* No doubt we can agree that life at its most upsetting is definitely unsatisfactory and often unbearable. We might also acknowledge that unsatisfactoriness is a primary cause of incessant wanting. Even when we are satisfied, gnawing thoughts of something better often persist. While it may seem counterintuitive, happiness also leads to unsatisfactoriness.

Dukkha is a part of all experience because, according to Buddhist psychology, human life has three distinguishing marks of existence: *basic pain* (*dukkha-dukkha*), *impermanence* (*anicca*) and *not-self* (*anattā*). The Buddha's own story exemplifies the radical transformation that comes from acknowledging these three characteristics.

THE LIFE OF SIDDHARTHA GAUTAMA

Siddhartha Gautama was a historical figure, a prince who lived in what is now northern India during the fifth and sixth centuries BCE. Siddhartha's father expected his son to succeed him as king. To assure this outcome, he supplied Siddhartha with luxurious palaces and distracted him with a life of entertainments, intoxicants and sensual pleasures. Siddhartha never wanted for anything nor had any occasion to experience the ordinary unpleasantness of day-to-day human existence. He lived unencumbered in the secluded embrace of sensual pleasure.

By his late 20s, a sense of disillusionment grew strong in Siddhartha's mind, and the day came when he announced his intention to venture out into the city accompanied only by a charioteer. The king immediately set about clearing away all unpleasantness from the streets—sick or old people, poverty and decay.

The Four Insights

Although the king did his best to rid the route of ugliness, when Siddhartha rode out into the city, it is said he was visited by four messengers—or, as I view them, *four insights*. The first insight was a feeble, elderly man with dementia; the second, a person disabled with serious illness; and the third, a rotting human corpse. Shocked, Siddhartha questioned his charioteer, "Do all people experience this kind of suffering?" The charioteer replied, "It is the fate of all humans to get sick, grow old and die." With each visitation the prince's heart filled ever more with sadness, confusion and despair. Siddhartha realized he, too, would suffer the same fate.

The final insight came in the form of a wandering monk, something wholly unknown to the prince. The charioteer told Siddhartha that this was a man in search of liberation from suffering. Thereupon, Siddhartha returned to the palace determined to understand the truth of these four insights. He decided that remaining in the comfort of his royal life would surely undermine this effort. So, against his father's wishes, Siddhartha renounced his birthright as king, bid farewell to his wife and child, and set out alone to seek enlightenment.

In Search of Wisdom

For six years Siddhartha wandered in the forests practicing extreme austerities and studying techniques to achieve deep meditative states. It is said he ate only one grain of rice a day, often collapsing from hunger and exhaustion. But when not absorbed in blissful meditative states, he found his mind still suffered. His efforts had not produced the liberation he so desperately sought. Frustrated yet determined, Siddhartha ceased his life of asceticism and began to nourish his body. Regaining his strength, he hatched a plan to attain lasting liberation from suffering. This is the penultimate moment in Siddhartha Gautama's story—the undertaking of an epic battle all too familiar to anyone who has resolved to overcome a distressful mind.

Siddhartha's Inner Battle

Below is a beautiful description from the psychologist and Buddhist teacher Jack Kornfield of the battle between Siddhartha and the demon

Mara. Although Mara was traditionally envisioned as a demon, Buddhist texts acknowledge that Mara is a metaphor for distressful states of mind.

> *As the story is told, on the night of the Buddha's enlightenment, he took a seat under the bodhi tree in northern India. He resolved to sit there, unshakably, and not to rise from his seat until he had achieved complete freedom. After a short time, Mara, the Indian god of delusion and evil, appeared, intent on stopping the Buddha from this goal. To do so, Mara sent his daughters, the most beautiful temptresses imaginable. But the Buddha was unmoved and simply said, "I see you, Mara." When desire failed to work, Mara got angry and sent in his vast armies. There were fierce demons with frightening faces and war cries, hurling cudgels, flaming arrows, and deadly spears. Again the Buddha raised his hand to touch the armies of Mara with compassion and all the spears and arrows fell as flower petals at his feet. Finally Mara attacked the Buddha with doubt: "Who do you think you are? What right do you have to sit here to become enlightened?" At this, the Buddha placed a hand on the ground and said, "The earth is my witness." And with this gesture, the earth goddess arose and bore witness to the lifetimes of patience, dedication, truthfulness, compassion, generosity, and wisdom that had prepared the Buddha for this night. Out of her hair came a flood of water and the armies of Mara were washed away. (2008)*

The story depicts three aspects of Mara: (1) unskillful or unwholesome thoughts, emotions and actions (*klesha-mara*); (2) the intrinsic mortality of the human condition (*mrtyu-mara*); and (3) the basic constituents of perception and human experience (*skandha-mara*). Each one of us contends with 'the Mara' in our own mind: our hatreds, anger, fears, restlessness, doubts and overwhelming wants. Surely anyone who has tried to transform an unhealthy habit, break free of an addiction or adhere to a difficult commitment knows Mara's power to undermine the best of intentions.

Siddhartha's steadiness of mind helped him cut through all deluded mentation. When presented with the promise of intense pleasure, he simply recognized wanting without grasping at it. When challenged by an army of harmful thoughts and emotions, Siddhartha met his destructive mind states with wise, compassionate recognition. When doubt arose in Siddhartha's mind, he firmly touched the earth. This gesture symbolized his interconnectedness with all other phenomena and called all beings to bear witness to his steadfastness. Then from deep within Siddhartha's mind arose the thunderous roar of wakeful awareness. So all-encompassing was this wave of pure awareness that it washed away any vestige of conditioned mentation, leaving only a clear, still, radiant mind.

FULL LIBERATION

For the next 3 days and nights Siddhartha Gautama sat beneath the bodhi tree contemplating three aspects of his awakening. Through the power of his concentration Siddhartha comprehended the essential impermanence and emptiness of all phenomena by directly experiencing the co-arising and passing of all internal and external phenomena, even his sense of self. The second day, he realized human beings are enslaved in endless cycles of suffering, never fully grasping the ramifications of their future actions. The recognition of humanity's unwitting ignorance unleashed an ocean of compassion so deep in Siddhartha's mind-heart it ignited a determination to free all beings from suffering. On the third night, Siddhartha formulated the teachings of the *Four Noble Truths*: the recognition of suffering, the causes of suffering, the cessation of suffering and the path to achieve liberation from all forms of suffering. As daylight appeared and the morning star rose in the sky, Siddhartha Gautama no longer sat beneath the bodhi tree. Instead, on that fourth day, it was a fully illumined Gautama Buddha who greeted the dawn.

The Buddha spent the next 7 weeks contemplating how to shepherd others toward liberation. His first dharma talk was given to five mendicants whom he had known during his years as an ascetic. The Buddha shared the *Four Noble Truths* and spoke of *a Middle Way* to liberation: an eightfold path forgoing the extremes of self-mortification and hedonic indulgence. This marked the beginning of the Buddha's 45 years of teaching the Dharma to all who would listen.

 The Roots of Buddhist Psychology

By directly observing his mind, Gautama Buddha arrived at a remarkable insight: mind itself is the primary instigator of human suffering. The Buddha was an accomplished yogi, brilliant philosopher of mind and probably the first cognitive psychologist.[5] Relying solely on contemplative research (a first-person methodology) into the nature of consciousness, he realized Buddhamind—innate, pristine, luminous awareness—and achieved complete cessation of suffering. But the Buddha did not stop there. Awakened to his true nature, he committed himself to the explication of his realization and the formation of systematic methods for awakening all beings to their Buddhanature.

These vast teachings—referred to as *the Dharma*—are said to possess six virtues:

> It is well taught.
> It is visible here and now and to be seen for oneself.
> It has an immediate effect.

It invites and entails personal verification.
It brings on progress.
It is to be personally realized by the wise.[6]

Buddhist psychology is informed by the Buddha's theory of mind and avails itself of his practical instructions for meditative practice.

> The Dharma is a psychology of cause and effect . . . and of choice. It is a psychology of individual empowerment at the root levels of psychological existence. It is a phenomenologically based psychology for identifying the human condition and the nature of the human mind in regards to suffering. A psychology that points to responsive mind as a means to cultivate choice in one's relationship to all conditions. (Moffitt, 2012)

The foundational Buddhist psychological text is *The Abhidharma*, a scholarly collection of the Buddha's teachings on mind and consciousness, compiled somewhere between 100 and 200 years after the Buddha's death. Buddhist psychology has since expanded to include numerous texts and commentaries written over the last 2,000 years by teachers and adepts from diverse schools of Buddhism.

How Is Buddhist Psychology Relevant to a Western Psychological Sensibility?

Distilling all of Western psychology down to a single theory is impossible. The same is true of Buddhist psychology. But we can point to general areas of agreement between these two disciplines. Both are concerned with mind—its genesis, function and dysfunction; both assert the attainment of valid conclusions from rigorous, empirical introspection.

The roots of Western psychology begin with William Cullen (1710–1790), the most influential Scottish physician and medical writer of his time. Cullen adopted the term *neurosis* to describe all classes of disease for which medicine could find no apparent cause, including psychotic and mood illnesses. Cullen was the first to propose that mental disorders had their origins in the mind/brain and not the body—an idea that was as radical for his time as were the Buddha's realizations about mind and suffering.

The American William James (1842–1910), a Harvard professor, philosopher, psychologist and prolific writer, dramatically accelerated psychological understanding of consciousness, mind, emotion and religious experience. In his master textbook *Principles of Psychology*, James steadfastly adhered to a radical empiricism of introspection, which he defined as "the looking into our own minds and reporting what we there discover" (1890). That is a decidedly Buddhist psychological methodology for understanding the mind. James was the first to proffer the theory that emotions cannot exist apart from bodily experience, insisting that "purely disembodied human emotion is a nonentity"

(1890). This mirrors the *Satipatthāna Sutta*, where the Buddha singles out bodily experience and the feeling tone of experience as the first two objects of mindfulness. Psychiatrist Mark Epstein tells a wonderful story that illustrates William James' favorable opinion of Buddhist psychology: "While lecturing at Harvard in the early 1900s, James suddenly stopped when he recognized a visiting Buddhist monk from Sri Lanka in his audience. 'Take my chair,' he is reported to have said. 'You are better equipped to lecture on psychology than I. This is the psychology everybody will be studying twenty-five years from now'" (1996). If only that prophesy had been true.

The Austrian Sigmund Freud (1856–1939) studied with the French neurologist Jean Martin Charcot (1825–1893) in Paris for one year and incorporated Charcot's method of hypnosis into his early work. By 1896 Freud had completely abandoned hypnosis for *psychoanalysis*, his free association/analysis method. Freud's therapy employed free association to loosen unconscious contents, allowing their emergence into consciousness along with defenses meant to obstruct conscious experience of repressed material.

Freud's other contributions to psychiatry were the theory of the unconscious and the theory of dreams. Both were gleaned primarily through first-person research into his dreams and childhood memories. Much of this deep reflection occurred during a particularly difficult period of Freud's life when, subsequent to the death of his father, he suffered cardiac irregularities and bouts of depression. Connecting loss with the onset of mental and physical distress led Freud to look within his own mind to heal his suffering. That does sound quite like a Buddhist psychological prescription.

Another area of agreement between Freud and Buddhist psychology is the existence of an *unconscious*. Freud's topology of mind posited the unconscious as a storehouse for repressed desires, feelings and instincts, too unacceptable to reside freely in the *preconscious*, where mental activity arises into conscious awareness. Buddhist psychology espouses several competing theories of mind, all of which include some form of unconscious. The Abhidharmic model conceptualizes the unconscious as *bhavanga-citta*—a ground consciousness conditioned by karmically accrued tendencies. Later revisions of that model view the unconscious as *ālaya-vijñāna*—a store consciousness containing the individual's karmic seeds of suffering. Like Freud's unconscious, *bhavanga-citta* and *ālaya-vijñāna* are thought to motivate the mind toward destructive habitual mind states.

Freud had several students who went on to create theoretical models of great import. Carl Jung (1875–1961), the father of *analytical psychology*, accepted Freud's unconscious but regarded it as limited in scope and too focused on destructive libidinous instincts. Jung's theory posited a deeper collective unconscious containing transpersonal archetypes acting on the psyche through images and transcendent impulses. Jung promoted a psychology of liberation based on individuation of the self. His theories were influenced by both Western and Eastern philosophical approaches. Jung's exposition of the *archetypes* was derived from Plato's Forms (primordially existing ideal prototypes) and Friedrich Nietzsche's articulation of a psyche containing inner Dionysian forces.[7] Although Jung admitted that "our way of looking at things is conditioned by what we are," he believed the archetypes were objectively real (1929). This view was contrary to the Kantian philosophy of Jung's era *and* that of Buddhist psychology. Both consider all contents of mind mere representations of sensory data and devoid of any objective reality.

After a traumatic parting with Freud, Jung turned to Vedantic and Buddhist philosophies to help him center and reorient. It is said that Jung found Buddhist meditative practices and mandala paintings resonant with his own contemplative strategies and inner psychic imagery. Jung's later works are replete with references to Vedanta, Taoism, Zen and Vajrayāna Buddhism.[8]

The Austrian Alfred Adler (1870–1937) was the first of Freud's colleagues to leave the psychoanalytic community and form his own school of *individual psychology*. His methods were non-hierarchical and focused on engagement of personal will to effect individual and collective change. This aligns with Buddhist psychology's tenet that one should awaken oneself for the enlightenment of all other sentient beings. Adler championed feminism, wrote extensively on gender role stereotyping and supported the development of many female psychotherapists. Like Adler, the Buddha also held radical views on the caste system and women: he broke with accepted mores that barred women and those of low caste from entering monastic life and opened the *Sangha* to all who wished to join. The Adlerian school also promoted important advancements in early education and child psychology.[9] His emphasis on social equality was far-reaching for his time. Adler influenced some of the greatest psychologists of the 20th century, including Karen Horney, Viktor Frankl, Abraham Maslow and Albert Ellis.

The Austrian Wilhelm Reich (1897–1957) was a controversial psychoanalyst who spent his early medical career treating indigent patients at Freud's psychoanalytic polyclinic, later becoming the clinic's deputy director. During that time Reich was exposed to poverty's impact on mental health and its role in the formation of neurosis. This led to his original work on character structure, which evolved to include the idea of defense mechanisms manifesting in the body. By 1934 Reich used physical touch in his therapy to evoke expression of repressed childhood experiences held in the body. His work spawned noteworthy mind-body psychotherapies such as Body psychotherapy, Gestalt therapy, Bioenergetic therapy and Somatic Experiencing therapy.

The American Carl Rogers (1902–1987), a founding member of the *humanistic* school of psychology, is best known for *client-centered* psychotherapy. Much like Buddhist psychology, Rogers viewed the self as a non-static process and purely phenomenological. Rogerian theories included 19 propositions, some bearing an uncanny likeness to the Buddha's teachings: (1) We perceive ourselves at the center of a world in constant flux, (2) what we perceive becomes our reality, and (3) all beings are deserving of unconditional positive regard. Rogers' definition of what constitutes a fully functional human being was in sync with Buddhist psychology: being open to experience, living each moment fully, developing a greater sense of right and wrong, and acting ethically and constructively for the good of all.[10]

Americans Albert Ellis (1913–2007), the originator of Rational Emotive Behavior therapy (REBT), and Aaron Beck (1921–), father of Cognitive therapy (CT), are credited with creating Cognitive behavioral therapy (CBT), the most researched and widely used treatment for depression, bipolar and anxiety disorders. Ellis began his work as a psychoanalyst but by the mid-1950s declared himself a rational therapist and began disseminating REBT, his new approach to therapy. It seems that the writings of the Greek philosopher Epictetus, who held the view that "Men are disturbed, not by things, but by the principles and notions which they form concerning things" (c. 135), were instrumental in Ellis' formulation of REBT. Epictetus and the Buddha both taught the value of dispassion and rigorous self-discipline as antidotes to life's difficulties. So it is not surprising that by way of Epictetus, Ellis' methodology concurs with Buddhist psychology. Although Ellis did not publicly acknowledge these similarities, he was purportedly writing a book comparing REBT and Buddhism just prior to his death.[11]

Beck, a psychiatrist and professor emeritus at the University of Pennsylvania, developed CT in the 1960s while researching the causes of depression. Beck's research showed that most of his depressed subjects suffered from a stream of negative thoughts about themselves, their world and their future. He deemed this mental activity *automatic thoughts* (affectionately known in Buddhist psychology as *monkey mind*) and set about creating a therapy that would target and lessen them. Thus CT was born.

The parallels of CT/CBT and Buddhist psychology are numerous. On June 13, 2005, Beck and the Dalai Lama met for a public discussion at an international CT conference. In a video interview after the fact, Beck describes his understanding of the similarities between CT and Buddhism:

> I was brought together with the Dalai Lama because people believe that Buddhism and cognitive therapy have many features in common. Both [disciplines] believe in looking at the mind, we both look at negative thoughts, and we both believe that negative thinking can be modified . . . Cognitive therapy does it through looking at automatic thoughts, somewhat similar to Buddhism. Buddhism gets people to look at their negative thoughts and lets them just flow out. Cognitive therapy looks at the negative thoughts and tries to correct them, to test them rationally and scientifically. One of the most important areas is that we both think the biggest problem with people is that they are too self-absorbed. (Beck, 2010)

As for the Dalai Lama, at one point in the conversation with Beck he said, "I saw your book, *Prisoner of Hate*. I think that is almost like Buddhist literature." Toward the end of their discussion, Beck offered an example of working with depression using CT's method of reality testing. The session was with a depressed physicist who been passed over for the Nobel Prize, which he insisted meant everything. Beck inquired about the physicist's wife and children and their level of importance to him. The physicist admitted they were half as important as getting the prize. Beck then pointed out the reality that the Nobel Prize was actually not all-important. This caused the physicist to realize how much time with his children he had sacrificed to finish his research, which was exactly what his father had done to him. The pain of these realizations caused him to weep and rethink his over-allocation of time to work. The physicist left the session wiser and less depressed. To this, a delighted Dalai Lama responded, "Very wise, that is the right method. That, we [Buddhists] call analytical meditation" (in Beck, 2005).

Although we can reasonably conclude that Western and Buddhist psychology have a good deal in common, there are some glaring differences. Phillip Moffitt, a highly respected Western Buddhist teacher, author and expert in Theravada Buddhism, highlights two important dissimilarities:

> To a large degree Western psychologists work with their clients within the story. For instance, a traumatic childhood: You, a person who had a traumatic childhood, do compensatory things to become whole all the while staying in the story. For many people every recycling of it or memory of the story can be retraumatizing. In Buddhist psychology, the story is not ignored, yet its elements are seen as phenomena rather than narrative. Buddhist psychology is interested in the immediacy of experience and one's response to it. It doesn't ignore the timeline of past/present/future narrative, but it is not constrained by it. Another aspect is Buddhist psychology cultivates skills for staying within experience as a participatory observer. It presents a ground in which to experience and relate to experience; a groundless ground if you will. (Moffitt, 2012)

That brings us to the subject that most divides Western and Buddhist psychology: the self. Throughout its history Western psychology has consistently asserted the primacy of the self and healthy development of the self as a necessity for mental health. Buddhist psychology has no quarrel with healthy development of the mind and heart. In fact, it remains a primary objective of this methodology. However, Buddhist psychology, with its rigorous phenomenological approach, reveals this solid, separate self to be nothing more than an interdependently co-arising stream of shifting phenomena lacking any inherent permanence or solidity. Hence, the self is deemed *not-self*.

In Buddhist psychological terms, ignorance of not-self means psychic imprisonment in unrelenting projections of *me and mine*, a pervasive subject/object dualism that, from a Buddhist perspective, is the root source of all forms of *dukkha*, or unsatisfactoriness. Direct realization of not-self—and the resulting dissolution of the illusory self's subject/object dualism—frees mind from delusion, awakening it to innate, subjectless/objectless knowingness or *luminosity*.

This awakened mind defines Buddhist psychology's ultimate vision of genuine mental and emotional health.

 Stepping Onto the Path

Since clear comprehension of Buddhist psychology's path to liberation is the fundamental goal of this book, let's begin by investigating the Buddha's initial teachings. The *Four Noble Truths*, the heart of the Dharma, are concise and direct. Yet fully unpacking their intent and meaning takes time. Phillip Moffitt authored a marvelous book on the Four Noble Truths titled *Dancing With Life*. During a recent conversation he offered the following insights about the Four Noble Truths.

LDM: *In your estimation, what is the most salient aspect of the Four Noble Truths?*

PM: I would point to a two-part salience: (1) it presents an accurate description of the human experience/challenge, and (2) it presents a way of responding to the human situation/challenge, which adds both meaning and a sense of well-being to life regardless of conditions.

LDM: *When you say challenge, I think of the Four Noble Truths as showing us the challenges of life while they challenge us to awaken. What do you mean by challenges?*

PM: That life is challenging is why the First Noble Truth is *dukkha*. This realm has *dukkha* in it. One of the beautiful aspects of the Buddha's teaching is it morphs, so the deeper you get, the deeper it gets. At a certain point of maturity, the meaning is that there is freedom. That one does not have to be confined by conditions. This is what the Buddha means when he says, "The dharma is good at the beginning, good in the middle and good at the end."

Remember the Buddha did not claim to invent this [the *Dharma*]. He claimed to discover it. It existed and presumably others had discovered it before him. Second, the idea of discovery implies that we can discover it also by learning and using tools for awakening. Remember the Buddha said, "Come see for yourself." This is as radical a message today as it was in his time. It is an invitation to know directly, not a demand to believe in something. There are no chosen people in Buddhism, except those who chose themselves. "Oh you Nobly Born" refers to those who have the capacity to bear the truth of life's unsatisfactoriness. This is so empowering to the individual. If you can bear suffering, be conscious and have intention even while in it, already you have achieved a possibility. It is a human possibility here that is to be acknowledged in our suffering, and in some ways it is the suffering that awakens us to that possibility. There would be no motivation to awaken if we were in a realm where we just got everything we wanted.

LDM: *What part of the Four Noble Truths would you say is most difficult for people to understand?*

PM: Without question, the Third Noble Truth—cessation of suffering. There are many dimensions to cessation, and it is understood in so many different ways. It can be hard to even enter into discussion about cessation. We have to have a certain degree of development for it to be real. Otherwise, is it idealistic, even conceptual. It can be hard to align with it unless one aligns with cessation as a practice rather than simply a belief.

The First Noble Truth of Suffering

> *This is dukkha: birth is dukkha, ageing is dukkha, sickness is dukkha, death is dukkha, encountering what is not dear is dukkha, separation from what is dear is dukkha, not getting what one wants is dukkha. This psycho-physical condition is dukkha.* (Batchelor, 2010[12])

The First Noble Truth states that unsatisfactoriness pervades all experience. Notice that the Buddha did not start by elucidating the reasons for unsatisfactoriness. Recognizing the existence of suffering and the ways in which it manifests must precede seeking its causes.

Many years ago when I first heard this teaching, it seemed like a no-brainer to affirm that life contains difficulty, because surely every human being has experienced pain. But I also felt perplexed. It was hard to imagine what could be noble about pain and suffering. Curiosity led me to look up the word 'noble.' The definition struck a chord: *having or showing fine personal qualities or high moral principles and ideals*. It occurred to me that when I was able to get beyond upset, times of difficulty eventually drew me closer to my own sense of inner rightness, my moral compass. This insight helped me understand how pain and suffering can inspire people to meet life's challenges with a strength and focus they did not previously know they possessed.

There is a similarity between this insight and the Rogerian insistence on development of one's inner sense of right and wrong. In my work I often witness suffering's nobility in a patient healing her or his broken-open heart. Poor mental health can bring people to their knees. Sometimes it takes a great deal of suffering to finally realize one's own heart is a source of salvation, a wellspring of wisdom, kindness and compassion.

Bring to mind someone you highly respect who has dealt with difficult life circumstances. It can be a well-known figure, a family member, a friend or a local hero. Picture a specific instance from this person's life story that exemplifies a time when they chose to meet a distressful situation with courage and authenticity. As you envision her or him engaging with difficulty, can you also sense this quality of nobility? Take some time with this. Now imagine yourself facing a similar situation. How might it move you to know yourself better? As you inquire about this, you may notice thoughts, emotions and body sensations arising. Be curious and observe them. If you would like, record your experience below.

____

____

____

____

____

____

____

The Three Kinds of Unsatisfactoriness

The Buddha taught three distinct categories of unsatisfactoriness (*dukkha*): physical, mental and emotional pain (*dukkha-dukkha*); the reality of constant change (*viparinama-dukkha*); and an underlying discomfort that accompanies our perception of experience (*sankhāra-dukkha*).

Dukkha-dukkha

Dukkha-dukkha is the 'ouch' of life. Siddhartha experienced *dukkha-dukkha* when he stepped outside his controlled environment and got a whiff of the myriad forms of ordinary pain humans encounter and struggle with: illness, decay, failure, loss, violence, abuse, hurt, hatred, fear, poverty, misunderstanding, manipulation, loneliness, betrayal. It is important to understand that when we resist or avoid *dukkha-dukkha*, our suffering only increases. *Pain just is, yet few can just be with pain as it is.*

Dukkha-dukkha requires us to show up and be present when we are in pain, which, contrary to what we might expect, is not an act of masochism. It is a magnanimous and courageous act of self-love. In subsequent chapters you will learn how to cultivate this compassionate, mindful presence—the only lasting curative for *dukkha-dukkha*.

Viparinama-dukkha

Viparinama-dukkha is the suffering associated with *impermanence* (P: *anicca* S: *anitya*). Physics and philosophy tell us that all conditioned phenomena (people, bodies, objects, relationships, health, wealth, ideas, beliefs, emotions, thoughts) are subject to constant change. You might be thinking, "What's wrong with change? I would be bored if everything stayed the same. Change implies evolution and progress, becoming something or someone better! Isn't this a good thing?" Yes, there is much that is desirable about change. However, the perpetual demand for *only* upward, forward movement leads to the *viparinama-dukkha* of impermanence precisely because all things eventually fall victim to entropy and decay.

Conversely, you might be the kind of person who needs to feel grounded and secure. Perhaps recognition of uncertainty produces inner distress. Demanding permanence in order to feel stable in a world where all things come and go is a guaranteed recipe for suffering. Continual grasping at *what was* in an effort to hinder the arrival of *what is* (which always comes anyway) contracts us emotionally and restricts self-actualization.

Recognizing craving for surety and constancy exposes *viparinama-dukkha*. Mindfully resting in that experience awakens us to life as it actually is—a constant flow of shifting variables. When we know this truth, harnessing the energy of continual change becomes possible. As tolerance of impermanence and uncertainty grows, the mind naturally begins to experience its innate spaciousness—the blissful radiance of awareness.

> Take some time to imagine your life as an open process. Envision actively engaging with the ebb and flow of events, people and places with genuine interest and curiosity. Visualize receiving experiences rather than guiding, stopping or controlling them. How might your current life be different if you chose to meet it with this attitude? If you would like, record your experience below.
>
> ____
>
> ____
>
> ____
>
> ____
>
> ____
>
> ____
>
> ____

Sankhāra-dukkha

Sankhāra-dukkha has the flavor of existential anxiety. It is a sense of being burdened by existence itself, a 'rubbing up against' feeling that comes with being alive in a human body. Some people truly feel the pain of *sankhāra-dukkha* even though it is a subtle form of suffering. Most of us don't sense it directly because it relates to processes of mind. So we might not be aware of it until we experience it for ourselves. No doubt at some point in your journey with this material, the discomfort of *sankhāra-dukkha* will become apparent to you.

 How Does Suffering Absent Us From Our Lives?

Think back to the last time you conversed with someone and suddenly noticed a far-away look in their eyes. Chances are that person is mentally elsewhere. Distracted mind states absent us from the actual 'here and now' of experience and imprison us in painful internal narratives.

The more *here-but-gone* moments we have, the greater our underlying sense of unsatisfactoriness becomes. This suffering has more to do with conditions *in the mind* than actual difficulties occurring in the here and now of experience. When life becomes little more than an unending stream of distracted mind moments, we live hindered by the constant soundtrack of own distressful thoughts. This is how suffering absents us from our lives.

Modern neuroscience has become very interested in studying two types of distracted mind states: (1) mind wandering and (2) time traveling (remembering past events or formulating future scenarios). Interestingly, research shows when the mind is engaged in either of these two modes, it is more likely to produce ruminative, negative, self-focused thoughts. Buddhist psychology calls this *proliferation mind* (*papañca*). Chapter 3 includes a discussion on the effects of mind wandering, time traveling and proliferating mind.

 Does More Presence Always Equal Less Suffering?

That depends on what kind of presence we are talking about. Hyper-focused, hyper-vigilant states generally lead to distress in the body and mind. For instance, air traffic controllers are very present but very stressed by the intense focus their job requires. By law they must take a 30-minute break after each 90–120-minute work session. Another example of a stressful form of presence is the fearful, hyper-vigilant psychophysical states many trauma survivors continually experience in daily life.

The quality of mind and body determines the type of presence. When we are not with our body, we are not fully here. Calm, grounded and receptive psychophysical states are a result of *embodied awareness*—a restful, clear presence that naturally decreases systemic agitation.[13] I recently heard Thich Nhat Hahn say that if we are mindful enough, our every step can touch the ultimate reality.

Awakened presence is an embodied, yet nonconceptual, spontaneous awareness. Although the experience of awakened presence is spontaneous and nonconceptual, it is actual. That actuality illuminates not only the interdependent nature of phenomena but also the true nature of mind. So as awakened presence reveals the still cognizance of mind, it simultaneously dissolves habitual distressful mind states. Awakened presence is the ultimate medicine to heal all forms of mental and emotional suffering.

 How Does Awakened Presence Change Our Relationship to Life's Ups and Downs?

Applying mindful attention slows us down. Reducing agitation calms the mind and heart and reveals the actuality of internal and external conditions. Clear knowing lessens mental and emotional fixation. Decreasing mental rigidity frees the mind to experience awareness. *Awakened presence* leads to insight. Wisdom stimulates creativity, flexibility and receptivity, empowering and engaging us in life. That arouses relatedness and compassion for self and others. Compassion decreases fearfulness, motivates problem solving and inspires confidence. This dynamic responsiveness is *awakened presence in action*. That is how wakeful presence radically transforms our relationship to life's ups and downs.

Notes

1 Bokar, R. (1992). *Meditation advice to beginners*. San Francisco, CA: ClearPoint Press.
2 Vago, D. R., & Silbersweig, D. A. (2012). Self-awareness, self-regulation, and self-transcendence (S-ART): A framework for understanding the neurobiological mechanisms of mindfulness. *Frontiers in Human Neuroscience*, 6, 296. Published online 2012 October 25. doi: 10.3389/fnhum.2012.00296
3 Damasio, A. (2010). *Self comes to mind: Constructing the conscious brain*. New York, NY: Pantheon Books.
4 Perlman, D. M., Salomons, T. V., Davidson, R. J., & Lutz, A. (2010). Differential effects on pain intensity and unpleasantness of two meditation practices. *Emotion, 10*(1), 65. Zeidan, F., Martucci, K. T., Kraft, R. A., Gordon, N. S., McHaffie, J. G., & Coghill, R. C. (2011). Brain mechanisms supporting the modulation of pain by mindfulness meditation. *Journal of Neuroscience, 31*(14), 5540–5548.
5 Wallace, B. A. (2007). *Contemplative science: Where Buddhism and neuroscience converge*. New York, NY: Columbia University Press.
6 MN 1:37; AN 3:285; VM 7.68–88/213–218.
7 Jung, C. G. (2012). *Nietzsche's "Zarathustra": Notes of the seminar given in 1934–1939*. (Vol. 99.) Princeton, NJ: Princeton University Press.
8 Clarke, J. J. (1994). *Jung and Eastern thought: A dialogue with the Orient*. New York, NY: Routledge.
9 Adler, A. (1927). *Understanding human nature*. New York, NY: Greenberg. pp. 214–215.
10 Rogers, C. R. (1951). *Client-centered therapy: Its current practice, implications and theory*. London: Constable. p. 491.
11 Porter, J. (2009). Albert Ellis, cognitive restructuring and short-circuting stress. *Stress Stop*. Retrieved August 29, 2012 from www.stressstop.com/stress-tips/articles/albert-ellis-cognitive-restructuring-and-short-circuiting-stress.php
12 Stephen Batchelor refers to this translation as "a bare bones translation in progress," personal communication, July 2012.
13 Levine, P. (2010). *In an unspoken voice: How the body releases trauma and restores goodness*. Berkeley, CA: North Atlantic Books.

2

Know the Conditioned Mind

The problem has been named; the patient seeks relief. Conventional mental health treatment will primarily seek out and address symptoms. The *Diagnostic and Statistical Manual of Mental Disorders* (*DSM*) blatantly disregards the neurobiological, somatic, environmental and genetic causes of mental health disorders. Its hyper-focus on categorization does little to help patients (and clinicians!) recognize why distressful mind states manifest. The director of the National Institute of Mental Health recently announced that *DSM* categories will be removed from its research criteria and added that patients with mental disorders deserve better.[1] I concur.

From a Buddhist psychological perspective, relief requires an integrated exploration of causes rather than mere symptom reduction. Genuine mental health arises from compassionate, mindful inquiry into *conditioned mind* (*sankhāra-khandha*) and its *afflictive mind states* (P: *kilesa* S: *kleśa* or *klesha* T: *nyon mongs*), the root cause of mental and emotional suffering.

Klesha is etymologically derived from the root meaning 'to adhere or stick to.'[2] *Kleshic stickiness*—perseveration on disturbing emotions and self-narratives beyond the point where it is cognitively or affectively useful—is what turns the basic pain of life into the unbearable suffering of affliction.[3] Although it may seem reductive to hold afflictive mind states (*kleshas*) responsible for the arising of all psychophysical distress, this view is based on the Buddha's exhaustive contemplative research into the causes and constituents of unwholesome cognitive-affective states (*akusalacitta*).

From a Buddhist psychological perspective, kleshic stickiness is an effect of *conditioned mind*. Were it not for conditioned mind, humans would be born fully liberated from suffering. Full liberation (P: *nibbāna* S: *nirvāna* T: *mya ngan las 'das pa*) is what so many patients refer to as the "real inner peace and happiness I am seeking." This chapter explores the Buddha's teachings on conditioned mind, its topology and processes.

 What Is Conditioned Mind?

Fortunately, that question has some mind-altering answers. Conditioning entered Western psychology through the work of Ivan Pavlov (1849–1936), a

Russian psychologist who identified conditioned biological responses in animals. His work was later applied to humans by various behavioral psychologies. Behavioral psychologists believed that human actions could be modified without referencing or altering internal mental states.[4] Their sense that human minds could be trained into modification challenged popular analytical approaches of the time.

Buddhist psychology affirms that inborn dispositional tendencies and biological, cultural and educational conditioning dramatically influence the human psyche and personality. It also employs repetitive cognitive strategies to modify distressful mind states. However, what is meant by *conditioned mind* in Buddhist psychology is much more than just a set of conditioned responses and corresponding conditioning behavioral interventions.

Buddhist psychology asserts that life's pains do not have to lead to imprisonment in a distressed mind. Understanding *conditioned mind* is key to comprehending how one can have pain without giving rise to the *kleshas* and, through clear seeing (*sati-sampajañña*) into afflictive conditioning, experience the mind's *unconditioned* (*asankhāra*) essential nature, *nibbāna*.

Despite dramatic advances in Western neuroscience and psychology, our species remains mired in suffering and unaware of its fundamental causes. Something profound must be missing from the modern conceptualization of and response to human affliction. Buddhist contemplative science, with its vision of human wisdom and flourishing, seeks to fill that void.

 Early Buddhist Source Materials

A kind alert to the reader: what follows is a humble attempt at distilling an utterly fascinating, impossibly complex body of knowledge from early Buddhist philosophy which is dedicated to a comprehensive, phenomenologically-based description of mind, its etiology and its inner-workings. Entire books have been written on each piece of this intricate puzzle, and this effort will pale in comparison to the exhaustive research and thoughtful scholarship of the authors cited below. To them, I offer gratitude.

The original teachings of the Buddha, *the Dharma*, are contained in the *Tipitaka* (S: *Tripitaka*), *The Three Baskets of the Doctrine*. It must be acknowledged up front that the 300-year gap between the time when the Buddha lived and the actual writing down of these teachings makes it impossible to authenticate this material as the exact words of the Buddha. Even the *suttas* readily admit oral transmission by starting most discourses with "Thus I have heard. . . ."

The first division of the *Tipitaka* is the *Sutta Pitaka*, containing five *Nikāyas* (collections)—*Digha* (long), *Majjhima* (short), *Samyutta* (connected), *Anguttara* (numerical) and *Khuddaka* (minor)—with more than 10,000 teachings. The second division, *Vinaya Pitaka*, outlines rules of conduct for monastic life in the *Sangha* (monastic community) the primary setting for study and practice of the Dharma.

The third division, the *Abhidhamma Pitaka*, is a scholarly compendium of the Buddha's teachings on mind and consciousness. Although the *suttas* reference monks discussing *Abhidhamma* (S: *Abhidharma*) in debate-like settings, no attribution of its origins or authorship exists. Buddhist scholars agree that the Abhidharma was compiled over several centuries in various monastic communities after the split of the Buddha's original *Sangha* into various competing sects, many of which had their own versions of Abhidharma literature. Authorized versions of the *Abhidhamma Pitaka* were available beginning in the third century CE.[5]

I recently asked Buddhist scholar and teacher Stephen Batchelor why the Abhidharma became such a prominent view in early Buddhism. He replied, "The Buddha spoke for 40–45 years. His students memorized a great deal of what he said. Possibly for memorization the Buddha gave lists. I think defining key terms was a way of making sense of a complex body of teachings. That is basically what the Abhidharma did" (Batchelor, 2013). While it is true that the Abhidharma's relentless deconstruction of mental capacities and processes can seem overwhelming, its insights into conditioned mind can be profoundly transformative.

 Early Buddhist Teachings on Conditioned Mind

The Pāli teachings on *conditioned mind* are found in the *Sutta Pitaka*, *Abhidhamma Pitaka* and *Visuddhimagga*, an extensive commentary on the aforementioned texts written around 430 CE by Buddhaghosa, a renowned Indian Theravada scholar.

Our analysis of conditioned mind is best begun with the *Second Noble Truth*, the Buddha's insight into *craving and aversion*—the underlying cause of stress and suffering. *The Second Noble Truth* states: "*This is the arising: it is craving [tanhā], which is repetitive, wallowing in attachment and greed, obsessively indulging in this and that: craving for stimulation, craving for existence, craving for non-existence*" (Batchelor, 2010).

Craving (*tanhā*) obstructs our capacity to know things as they actually are. *The Second Noble Truth* illustrates that supposition by referencing three compulsive mental activities—rumination, grasping and obsessive indulgence—and three psychophysical impulses—wanting, becoming and resisting. These six afflictions are by-products of the three unwholesome roots (P: *akusala-mūla* S: *akuśala-mūla*): greed (*lobha*), hatred (*dosa*) and delusion (*moha*), which manifest as the three principal *kleshas*: craving (*tanhā*), aversion (*dosa*) and ignorance (P: *avijjā* S: *avidyā*). These mind states are mentally unhealthy and morally blameworthy, and they produce suffering.[6]

The Abhidharma suggests that while craving and aversion (*tanhā*) never exist simultaneously, ignorance (*avijjā*) is present in every instance of suffering. But if ignorance underlies all craving, would that not make ignorance the primary cause of unsatisfactoriness? If so, why did the Buddha implicate *tanhā*? The answer is twofold: (1) *tanhā* is a catchall that includes all possible *kleshas* rooted in greed (*lobha*) and hatred (*dosa*), and (2) *avijjā* is pre-wired and primordially present in human beings and for that reason is more difficult to recognize than the potent viscerality of *tanhā*. Knowing craving (*tanhā*) and aversion (*dosa*) is easy. We feel them with an immediacy that overwhelms us. One must inquire mindfully into *tanhā* to recognize its origin in ignorance (*avijjā*).

To accomplish the task of fully understanding *tanhā* we will examine the Buddha's teachings on causality, specifically *Dependent Origination*—a complex, yet subtle, perceptual chain of causation that is *conditioned* (*sankhata*) from its inception and includes *tanhā* as one of its 12 links. Dependent Origination—that all things have both a causational and a resultant nature—is in the Dalai Lama's estimation "the fundamental principle of Buddhism" (Gyatso, 1990). Exploring these 12 links also explicates the *Five Aggregates* (P: *khandā* S: *skandha* T: *phung po lnga*): form/matter (*rūpa*), feeling (*vedanā*), perception (*saññā*), volition (*cetanā*) and consciousness (*citta*), the basic building blocks of all phenomena, including the self.

 Dependent Origination (P: *paticca-samuppāda* S: *pratītyasamutpāda* T: *rten 'brel*)

In the *suttas*, the Buddha succinctly describes Dependent Origination:

> When this exists, that comes to be; with the arising of this, that arises. When this does not exist, that does not come to be; with the cessation of this, that ceases. (MN 115)

Although that version has an elegant pithiness, deconstructing conditioned mind requires a more fleshed-out description. Below is a modern translation[7] of a seminal discourse on Dependent Origination from the *Samyutta Nikāya*. It depicts the causal relationship of mind and action using 12 successive links (*nidāna*), each conditioning the following one. In this *sutta*, the Buddha describes the links bidirectionally.

> And what is dependent co-arising [origination]? **From ignorance as a requisite condition come fabrications** [volitional formations]. From fabrications as a requisite condition comes **consciousness**. From consciousness as a requisite condition comes **name-&-form** [mind and matter]. From name-&-form as a requisite condition come the **six sense media** [bases]. From the six sense media as a requisite condition comes **contact**. From contact as a requisite condition comes **feeling**. From feeling as a requisite condition comes **craving**. From craving as a requisite condition comes **clinging**. From clinging as a requisite condition comes **becoming**. From becoming as a requisite condition comes **birth**. From birth as a requisite condition, then **aging & death, sorrow, lamentation, pain, distress, & despair** come into play. **Such is the origination of this entire mass of stress & suffering.**

> Now **from the remainderless fading & cessation of that very ignorance comes the cessation of fabrications** [volitional formations]. From the cessation of fabrications comes the **cessation of consciousness**. From the cessation of consciousness comes the **cessation of name-&-form** [mind and matter]. From the cessation of name-&-form comes the **cessation of the six sense media** [bases]. From the cessation of the six sense media comes the **cessation of contact**. From the cessation of contact comes the **cessation of feeling**. From the cessation of feeling comes the **cessation of craving**. From the cessation of craving comes the **cessation of clinging**. From the cessation of clinging comes the **cessation of becoming**. From the cessation of becoming comes the **cessation of birth**. From the cessation of birth, then **aging & death, sorrow, lamentation, pain, distress, & despair all cease. Such is the cessation of this entire mass of stress & suffering.** (SN II 12(1); emphasis added)

Ignorance (P: avijjā *S:* avidyā *T:* ma rig pa*)*

> *Not knowing suffering, not knowing the origination of suffering, not knowing the cessation of suffering, not knowing the way leading to the cessation of suffering: This is called ignorance.* (SN II 12:2)

When *avijjā* (*ignorance/delusion*) is the conditioning from which we start the journey of human life, our unawareness condemns us to an existence of unsatisfactoriness. If that sounds bleak, remember that recognizing ignorance can happen in any moment of awareness.

The *Visuddhimagga* distinguishes between the *sutta* method and the Abhidharma method of explaining *avijjā*, or *primordial ignorance*. The prior includes the four instances of suffering shown above. The latter adds four more instances related to ignorance of temporality and conditionality, "Unknowing about the past, unknowing about the past and future, unknowing about specific conditionality and conditionally-arisen states" (Buddhaghosa, 1975). The Abhidharma also emphasizes a temporal division of the 12 links into past, present and future. Ignorance (*avijjā*) is a consequence of preceding ignorance. As the progenitor of itself, *avijjā* is said to be not only recursive but *primordially existent* from the "beginningless beginning"[8] and as such is represented as the progenitive agent of its fruit—the next link, *volitional formations* (*sankhāra*).

In Buddhist psychology, *avijjā* refers to *primordial confusion* with respect to the actuality of experience. It is a fundamental misconstruing of internal and external phenomena (most important, the self) as separate and permanent. Our human perceptual apparatus has evolved to create what feels like an independent, substantial, permanent self, functioning in a world populated by equally solid enduring, autonomous entities. But that view is patently false: actuality is composed of ever-shifting phenomena, or *dhammas*, interdependently arising, existing and ceasing discontinuously from moment to moment.[9]

Brain science offers many examples of how we construct reality. For instance, to make sense of incomplete images, sounds or phrases, the brain routinely fills in all manner of missing information garnered from its own internal 'files'.[10] Even our perception of the continuance of conscious experience is an illusion. "Discontinuity in a series of conscious events is a counterintuitive feature," says neuroscientist Benjamin Libet. "Our experiment showed that people thought they were aware of the sensory stimulus about 500 msec before they could possibly have become aware of the stimulus" (2004). This objective evidence of *automatic subjective referral back in time* to responses in the sensory cortex shows that conscious awareness of percepts or the conscious *now* is, in reality, the unconsciously experienced *past*.[11]

Certainly the question of what is real, non-delusion (*vidyā*), becomes quite interesting when we consider all that exists that we do not actually perceive. Sometimes I like to ask my patients to imagine our eyes could see us, the room and the world from a microscopic or quantum physical level—everything a swirling mass of continually shifting particles of information organizing into vibrating objects that only appear to be solid, permanent and unchanging. Take a moment to engage with that visualization and contemplate how such a dramatic perceptual shift might impact your relationship to life, people and objects, your attachment to beliefs, hurts and self-conceptions. Might it all feel a bit less solid and true? Would our species be moved to harm each other if the wave and the particle were our primary experience?

Here's another example from cosmology. Matter makes up only 4% of our universe. That means 96% of us and everything else is something other than what we perceive. Astrophysical calculations point to the existence of dark matter and dark energy, and although it is everywhere, throughout everything, it remains undetectable and unmeasurable. For Buddhist psychology these and other human perceptual imperfections are problematic at best, and at worst a reflection of *avidyā, primordial ignorance.*

Volitional Formations (P: **sankhāra** *S:* **samskāra** *T:* **'du byed***)*

> *Volitional formations construct the conditioned. They construct conditioned form as form, conditioned feeling as feeling; conditioned perception as perception; conditioned volitional formations as volitional formations; conditioned consciousness as consciousness.* (SN III 22:79)

"*Sankhāra* is derived from the prefix *sam*, 'together' and the verb *karoti*, 'to make.' . . . Thus *sankhāras* are both things which put together, construct, and compound other things, *and* the things that are put together, constructed, and compounded" (Bodhi, 2000). That definition might lead one to conclude that volitional formations and form/matter are equivalent. However, there is no linguistic relationship between *rūpa* (matter) and *sankhāra/samskāra* (volitional formations).[12]

Volitional formations are antecedent to form/matter and, as with ignorance, exist temporally in the past. Formations are their own cause and result. But their volitional aspect also makes them the cause of subsequent conditioned, dependently arising phenomena (*paticca-samuppāda dhammā*). As one of four mental aggregates (*khandha*), *sankhāras* function as volitional impulses occurring from contact with any one of the six sense-bases (five senses and mind). These impulses function as dispositional tendencies that eventually result in wholesome or unwholesome actions.

In daily life, *sankhārakhandha* manifest through body, speech and mind, and their expression is categorized as karmically meritorious or deleterious. Say we are driving on the highway and a car cuts us off. Our automatic physical/emotional reaction will vary depending on the perceived level of danger. When we are not physically threatened, awareness and clarity of mind allow us to choose a response that is wise and calming—like slowing down and maybe wishing that person safety. Without awareness, reactive angry thoughts, words or actions can overtake us. Wise responses are meritorious and in this case reap the benefit of well-being. Agitation and anger are deleterious and can lead to further harm. Although meritorious action is preferable, it is still conditioned by inner and outer causes. The Buddha taught that *nirvāna* is the only unconditioned reality. All other existent phenomena are conditioned by the antecedence of *avidyā* (ignorance) and *samskāra* (volitional formations).

Sankhāra/Samskāra *and Karma in Early Buddhism*

> *Unshakable is my liberation of mind; this is my last birth; now there is no more renewed existence.* (The Buddha in Bodhi, 2000)

Sankhāra is karmically active—hence volitional—and ultimately responsible for rebirth. The Sanskrit words *samskāra* (P: *sankhāra*) and *karma* (P: *kamma*) are both derived from *krnoti* (P: *karoti*), the root form of the Sanskrit verb for 'to make or build.' This etymological relationship shows itself in *samskāra*'s dual nature as both karmically hindering and liberating. When activated, karmic residue distorts the psyche's relationship to the present. But awareness of karmic distortion can actuate volitional responses that free the psyche from habitual, biased and/or destructive predispositions. Hence, deeper inquiry into *karma* is critical to understanding Dependent Origination.

In Theravada Buddhism, the adherence to 'all things impermanent' extends to any 'substance' that might be considered to 'continue' after death and be 'reborn.' The assertion is that there is no continuance of 'sameness,' because any existing mental or physical event-factor disassembles prior to reassembly, and that new form cannot be the same as what arose from it, nor can it be wholly different.[13] Yet the *suttas* insist on rebirth and mention it throughout.

For example, the Buddha was teaching at Kotigāma and said, "Because of not seeing things as they are, the Four Noble Truths, we have wandered through the long course, in the various kinds of births . . ." (SN V 56:21). Here the Buddha makes clear that *avidyā*, or ignorance, is the cause of successive rebirths and refers to 'we' only as an indicator of 'something' that is reborn. What is that 'we'?

Early Buddhism vigorously disputed the Vedic/Hindu belief in an eternal Self (*atman*) that is reborn life after life:

> When [one] is confused about dependently-arisen states, instead of taking the occurrence of formations to be due to ignorance, etc., [one] figures that it is a self that knows or does not know, that acts and causes action, that appears in rebirth-linking, and [one] figures that atoms, an Overlord, etc., shapes its body in the various states of the embryo and endows it with faculties, and that when it has been endowed with faculties it touches, feels, craves, clings, and endeavors, and that it becomes anew in the next becoming. . . . Thus [one] figures, blinded by ignorance. (VM XVII:117)

So if one were not blinded by the illusion of an enduring Self (*atman*), what would one know about what undergoes rebirth? Early Buddhism envisioned rebirth as occurring through a successive grouping of discrete consciousnesses: *life-continuum consciousness* becomes *death consciousness* at death. This becomes *rebirth-linking consciousness* and *dependent adjacent consciousness*.[14] Notice the word 'adjacent,' which implies 'next to' rather than 'of the prior.' The actual linking (*patisandhāna*) occurs across a gap that separates death consciousness from *becoming consciousness*, which is not thought to arise directly from death consciousness but in theory could have a retrocausal[15] relationship with death consciousness via rebirth-linking consciousness. Becoming consciousness is actualized by karmic residue (and its formations) dependently 'pushing' into a conditioned, objective field of *endless rounds* (*samsāra*).

Notice the deliberate effort to avoid any notion of a self, entity, doer or reaper. 'No one' (*Anātman*) gets reborn. For early Buddhists, karmic rebirth is an endless cycle of discrete yet interdependent consciousness/expression/result events occurring within an objective field of causality with no discernible beginning. That exegesis does hint at an almost rational early neural-approach to the vexing problem of explaining rebirth devoid of an eternal Self.

Those who view karma as no more than an archaic cultural relic have called for removing it from Western Buddhism and Buddhist psychology.[16] That would be an unfortunate decision. No matter where Buddhism has traveled, it has managed to retain its prime directive of relieving human suffering through compassionate wise action. Attending to karmic repercussions remains Buddhism's ethical framework for achieving that aim.

Even so, I realize that those of you who accept a doctrine of only one lifetime may still feel unsatisfied. See what happens if you reread the last two paragraphs in the context of this life and its 'endless rounds' of forming, deforming and reforming discrete moments of consciousness. Even brief direct perception of *avijjā* (ignorance) dissolves the unsatisfactoriness associated with resistance to impermanence. This is how we are repeatedly liberated, moment to moment, from this life's 'endless rounds' of habitual suffering.

Phillip Moffitt offered his own perspective on the relevance of karma and rebirth to Western practitioners:

> The mystery of whether or not there are multiple lives is fine, because one does not have to believe one way or other as far as I am concerned. Since it is unknown, why would we negate something we have no definitive knowing of? I teach the immediacy of the effect of karma, of intentionality. You are not just planting a seed, for future result but you are also changing the manifestation of past karma that would have blossomed differently without intervention of wisdom. This has huge impact. You may get angry because of habit anger or you go into crazy anger because of current circumstances, but one might choose to use angry words, or angry thoughts rather than physical violence. This means moment to moment we have choice and are co-creating our lives. (2012)

Another take on karmic legacy is the new science of *intergenerational genetic inheritance*. Animal studies have established that traumatic prenatal environments negatively influence stress hardiness in offspring and result in pathophysiological changes.[17] Analogous human studies looked at children born to women who were pregnant during war, natural disasters or traumatic life events. Growing evidence from comparable animal and human studies show stress-related system changes ('stress imprinting') are not confined just to the first generation.[18] It now appears that *transgenerational memory of fetal experience* can extend the persistence of "fetal nutritional and endocrine insults into subsequent generations" (Matthews, 2010).

Thanks to epigenetics we know that gene expression is altered positively or negatively by mechanisms other than direct changes in the underlying DNA. Epigenetics has explained inconsistencies found in Holocaust survivors with post-traumatic stress disorder and in the presence or absence of psychopathologies coincident with frailty and hardiness in offspring. "From the point of view of epigenetics, any inherited (genetic) dispositions can be either turned on or off, and thus activate either overwhelming anxiety or sufficient coping in the same person at different times, according to certain aggravating and mitigating (environmental) factors" (Kellerman, 2009).

So the trauma of one generation persists genetically in the psychophysical traits of successive generations, and those traits are dependently activated or mitigated in response to internal or external conditions. Therefore, genes are subject to causes and conditions and like all other conditioned phenomena are modifiable. Together, genetic transgenerational memory and epigenetic alteration could provide a modern revisioning of the relationship between karmic residue and dispositional tendencies.

Of interest is research on positive genetic changes achieved through reducing cognitive stress and stress arousal and increasing positive states of mind. It appears that meditation strengthens mitochondrial function, enhances telomere maintenance and diminishes expression of genes linked to inflammatory responses.[19]

Consciousness (P: **viññāna** *S:* **vijñāna** *T:* **rnam shes***)*

> *These six are classes of consciousness: eye-consciousness, ear-consciousness, nose-consciousness, tongue-consciousness, body-consciousness, intellect-consciousness. This is called consciousness.* (SN II 12:2)

In the mid-1990s, the philosopher David Chalmers distinguished the *easy problems* of consciousness (how the brain cognizes, discriminates, attends to, accesses, directs and integrates information) from the *hard problem* of consciousness (why we have subjective conscious experience). Thanks to advances in EEG, fMRI and PET technologies, the easy problems of cognitive-affective brain function are being solved. But the hard problem, "What is consciousness, and where are its neural correlates?" continues to be the single most frustrating unanswerable question in neuroscience and philosophy. More than 2,500 years ago the Buddha was doing his utmost to tackle the easy and hard problems of consciousness.

In Sanskrit *vijñāna* is formed from *vi* = 'separating' and *jñā* = 'to know,' which together connote 'the act of discerning, knowing.' In early Buddhism, consciousness (S: *vijñāna* P: *viññāna*) manifests in two different forms with two separate functions: (1) life-continuum consciousness—a discrete yet retrocausal sentience inhabiting a fetus in utero, remaining throughout its life and departing at death; and (2) cognitive awareness arising from *avidyā* and *sankhāra*, the receiver and processor of information arriving at the six sense-bases (five senses and mind).[20]

The cognitive aspect of *vijñāna* plays a major role in an unfortunate karmic feedback loop. Pre-existing ignorance and volitional formations influence the quality of receiving and processing consciousness. When afflicted by *avidyā*'s lack of discerning wisdom and *samskāra*'s karmic formations, *vijñāna* becomes the medium for conditioned mentation and action:

> The physiological organs and the psychological faculties that condition this 'world of experience'—that is, karmic structures (*samskāra*') that enable us to have any cognitive experience (vijñāna) at all—are themselves largely results of past karma. . . . This is the vicious cycle outlined in the formula of dependent arising. (Waldron, 2003)

Buddhist teachers from various schools view receiving consciousness as 'bare' and, as such, untainted by affliction. Some Theravada Buddhist scholars agree that *viññāna* "represents pure consciousness, or pure sensation without any content" (Stcherbatsky, 1970). In the context of Dependent Origination, the arising of this consciousness prior to full apprehension of an object is always conditioned by the presence of *avidyā* and *samskāra*, rendering it habituated but not afflicted.[21] The wheel of *samsāra* turns endlessly because 'inhabiting sentience' remains unaware of 'its' own luminosity.[22] Therefore, the Buddha considered the conditioned arising of consciousness a link in the chain of suffering. Consciousness is the first of the series of links that exist in the present.

Mind and Matter (P & S: **nāmarūpa** *T:* **ming gzugs***)*

> *Feeling, perception, intention, contact, & attention: This is called name. The four great elements, and the form dependent on the four great elements: This is called form. This name & this form are called mind and matter.* (SN II 12:2)

Mind (*nāma*) *and matter* (*rūpa*) are the constituents and potentiators of all psychophysical experience. The interdependent relationship of mind and matter is reflected in their amalgamation in a single word, *nāmarūpa*. One cannot exist without the other, and neither can be experienced without the six organs of perception. *Nāmarūpa* has two major divisions: (1) material reality as it exists independent of its perception and (2) the myriad forms of material reality apprehended by the senses.[23]

Mind (*nāma*) is 'mentality,' the mental processes that 'bend' (*namana*) toward an object—feeling, perception, intention, contact, attention. In the Abhidharma, *nāma* is comprised of consciousness and the mental factors (*cittacetasikasankhāta*). Labeling and categorizing are 'concepts' (*paññatti*), not mentality. *Nibbāna* is also considered *nāma* primarily because it bends into itself.[24]

Matter (*rūpa*) is composed of the *four elements* (*dhātu*): earth (*pathavīdhātu*), water (*āpodhātu*), fire (*tejodhātu*) and air (*vāyodhātu*). These are primary and inseparable and exist in all forms. From them come the 24 *derived material phenomena* (*upādāya rūpa*). Ten of these 24 are non-concrete characteristics found in concrete matter, including the space element (*ākāsadhātu*), which acts as a limiting force (much in the same way as dark energy/dark matter contains material substance). A good metaphor to describe this relationship is soil and plants. Soil and plants are not the same, but plants owe their existence to and are therefore derived from soil. These 24 material phenomena comprise all of what can be perceived by mentality.

Six Sense-Bases (P: **salāyatana** *S:* **āyatana** *T:* **phyi'i skye mched drug***)*

> *These six are sense-bases: the eye-base, the ear-base, the nose-base, the tongue-base, the body-base, the intellect-bases.* (SN II 12:2)

In Dependent Origination the first five sense-bases are the five sense-organs. The Abhidharma also delimits the sense-bases as 'physical supports.'[25] However, in the wider world of Buddhist philosophy, each base (*vatthu*) is understood to have an internal and external manifestation: the organ and its objects. The six internal sense-bases are the eye, ear, nose, tongue, body and mind. The six external sense-bases are visible forms, sounds, odors, flavors, touch (proprioceptive and interoceptive) and mental objects. Later commentarial writings envisaged anatomical correlates for each sense-base, referred to as 'sensitivity.'[26]

The sense-base of mind or the mental organ of thought (P: *mano* S: *manas*) is referred to as the *heart-base*. It supports mind-element and mind-consciousness, and its function is to observe or carry them.[27] Few anatomical details are offered about the heart-base, though Buddhaghosa located it in a cavity situated within the physical heart.[28]

Distinguishing the mental organ of thought (*mano*) from consciousness (*viññāna*) is important. *Mano*, the faculty of mind, retrieves sense impressions from the five senses and initiates the production of concepts (*paññatti*) about actual sense impressions: meaning-making or labeling. Consciousness (*viññāna*) continues without interruption as the substrate for all sensory information and processing.[29] *Mano* is also distinct from *mano-viññāna*, the mental cognitive awareness of 'I am.'

According to early Buddhism, perception of a stimulus requires three ingredients: an internal sense-base (i.e., the ear), an external sensory object (i.e., a sound) and a sense-specific consciousness (i.e., hearing) arising from the meeting of base and object. The six sense-bases and the four elements make up objective material reality. The subjective quality of material reality is made possible by contact with sensory objects.

Buddhaghosa claims that the first instance of material reality is the "setting up" of the six sense-bases. Repeated instances of this "setting up" lead to the growth of material reality, and its increase fabricates the illusion of continuous material reality.[30] This is why the Buddha insisted that when one sees, hears, smells, tastes, touches and thinks, one must be mindful of these phenomena as they really are.

Contact (P: **phassa** *S:* **sparśa** *T:* **reg pa***)*

> *These six are classes of contact: eye-contact, ear-contact, nose-contact, tongue-contact, body-contact, intellect-contact.* (SN II 12:2)

Because the sense-bases are part of material reality, their presence presumes the inevitability of contact (*phassa*). Imagine a mind so honed and attentive that it can apprehend the subtlest levels of experience, even the birth of an experience. Such is the result of intensive training in the Buddha's contemplative science.

Phassa comes from the verb 'to touch.' Contact is the meeting of consciousness (*viññāna*), a sense-organ and an object. The touching of consciousness and material reality is fundamental to every instance of cognition and apperception. Each contact-event can be likened to a mini big bang, setting off an explosion of rapid-fire mental processes involving consciousness, its mental factors and the interplay of mind and matter.

At the point of contact with phenomenal reality, consciousness emerges in three ways: (1) *viññāna*, which discerns objects; (2) *citta*, distinct conscious states that process objects from the sense-sphere (mundane), the fine-material-sphere (absorptive meditative states), the immaterial-sphere (formless meditative states) and the supramundane sphere (consciousnesses that realize *nibbāna*); and (3) *mano/manas*, the source of mentation about cognition.

The Abhidharma's first chapter explains *citta* in great detail. *Cittas* arise with one of four basic natures: *unwholesome* (*akusalacitta*), *wholesome* (*kusalacitta*), *resultant* (*vipāka*) and *functional* (*kriyā*).[31] *Citta* precedes the 52 mental factors (*cetasikas*) that share the following attributes: they (1) arise with consciousness (*citta*), (2) cease with consciousness, (3) share objects with consciousness, and (4) share bases with consciousness. Like *citta*, the mental factors vary in valence and effect and are transient. The rapidity with which these discrete states arise and cease makes it difficult to discern their impermanent nature.

Of the 52 mental factors, only 14 are defined as unwholesome. The remaining 38 fall into two categories. The Ethically Variables: 7 *universals* found in all types of consciousness (contact is one of them) and 6 *occasionals* found only in certain types of consciousness. The Beautiful Factors: 19 *universal beautifuls*, 3 *abstinences*, 2 *illimitables* (compassion and lovingkindness) and *amoha*, non-delusion, the wisdom faculty that illuminates the actuality of the objective field.[32] The Abhidharma's emphasis on explicating innate states of mind that promote well-being stands in sharp contrast to Western psychology's focus on syndromes and symptomatic states of mind.

Contact (*phassa*) marks the point at which direct involvement with *cittas* and *cetasikas* becomes a possibility. The remaining links in the chain represent powerful forces in the human mind that impede or obscure direct engagement with reality. Once knowledge about these forces and their function is revealed, direct interaction with them and their processes can begin. At first, access can feel like gazing through a window at psychophysical phenomena. Yet with practice and awakened presence, connecting with these hindrances becomes an intimate and vibrant experience of spontaneous liberation.

Feeling (P & S: **vedanā** *T:* **tshor ba***)*

> *These six are classes of feeling: feeling born from eye-contact, feeling born from ear-contact, feeling born from nose-contact, feeling born from tongue-contact, feeling born from body-contact, feeling born from intellect-contact.* (SN: II 12:2)

Vedanā is derived from the root *ved*, meaning 'to experience,' which refers to encountering sensory stimuli. Contact (*phassa*) occurs when sensory phenomena are objectively received by consciousness (*viññāna*) and a sense-base. This meeting activates the body's capacity to quickly process and respond to incoming sensory stimuli. An approach/avoidance response is largely determined by the psychophysical system's *subjective feeling* about a sensory object. *Vedanā* is this subjective determining of valence.[33]

Vedanā is most often said to arise in three distinct feeling tones—pleasant, unpleasant and neutral—but some *suttas* list up to 108 classes of mental and bodily *vedanā*. The verse above lists six classes of *vedanā*—five bodily and one purely mental. The subjective nature of bodily generated *vedanā* presumes co-occurring interpretative mental activity. Purely mentally generated *vedanā* is an outcome of mentation about experience that is subjective and concept-based (*paññatti*). Buddhism calls this mentation the Second Arrow, which will be explored in Chapter 3.

Vedanā is endogenous, multivalent and imperative for our survival. But it is an imperfect receiver of reality. Approach/avoidance was evolutionarily engineered: "what we have come to perceive as feelings of pain or pleasure, or as punishments or rewards, corresponds directly to integrated states of living tissue within an organism, as they succeed one another in the natural business of life management" (Damasio, 2010). The human reptilian brain, with its approach/avoidance response capability, is key to the detection of danger.

Neuroscience once credited good decision-making to rational thought. But affective neuroscience has revealed the critical role emotions play in determining choices.[34] Emotions help us organize priorities and assist with focusing our attention on goals. *We are, in large measure, what we feel.*

Emotions originate in the body, are transmitted to the unconscious, commingled with dispositional tendencies (*samskāras*) and conceptualized, and arrive in conscious awareness long after the body and lower brain areas have already reacted. So how do we appropriately respond to stimuli that affect us long before we are conscious of them? Buddhist psychology suggests that the only way to have more insight into *vedanā* is to fully know the conditioning from which it arises, the manner in which it exists and the impermanence that leads to its ceasing.

Vedanā and *saññā* go hand in hand. *Saññā* (S: *samjñā*) is the cognitive faculty that recognizes percepts and facilitates concept formation.[35] Concepts and images evoked by approach/avoidance reactions commingle with feeling, its object representation and ensuing body states.[36] A good example is seeing a form on a trail that at first glance looks like a snake. The body jumps because the form is perceived and then instantly labeled as snake = danger. Sometimes first impressions are right, and we act accordingly. More often, upon careful inspection the snake turns out to be a rope or stick.

This tendency to pattern-match and label by association is biologically engineered in us (for good reason, as we can see) and happens constantly. The hard work of seeing *dhammas* as they actually are is bypassed when the brain readily pattern-matches and reaches conclusions based on its own imagery and conditioned, repetitive habits. Clouded by conditioned mind and its tendency toward ignorance and volitional formations, *vedanā* and *saññā* readily become the cause for afflictive mind states.

In most interpretations of Dependent Origination, the presence of *vedanā* is said to always result in craving. This has been disputed by several Buddhist scholars based on a lack of any direct reference to it.[37] In the *suttas*, the Buddha appears to imply that without clear comprehension of feelings, one *tends to cling* to approach/avoidance responses. Conversely, when fully knowing *vedanā* one can feel bodily/emotional pain and move away from that pain, or feel bodily/emotional pleasure and appreciate that pleasure, with a present, equanimous mind, free of *mano/manas's* conditioned conceptual mentation.[38] Therefore, craving arises because of *avidyā* (primordial ignorance) and its conditioned responses to *vedanā*, not the presence of *vedanā* itself.

Craving (P: **tanhā** *S:* **trsnā** *T:* **dod sred***)*

> *These six are classes of craving: craving for forms, craving for sounds, craving for smells, craving for tastes, craving for tactile sensations, craving for ideas.* (SN II 12:2)

We've come full circle and have arrived back at *tanhā*, hopefully with a better understanding of the conditions and conditioning that lead to its arising. Now we can more fully investigate craving and aversion. Philosopher Jeremy Bentham once said that "pain and pleasure . . . govern us in all we do, in all we say, in all we think" (1789/1907). The Buddha came to the same conclusion and one-upped Bentham by singling out three forms of *tanhā* that together comprise our biological (sometimes neurotic) impulses to approach or avoid.[39]

The three kinds of craving can best be explained in modern psychological terms: (1) *kama-tanhā*, the drive toward pleasurable experience, which feels good in the short term but is ultimately unsatisfactory because of its unsustainability; (2) *bhava-tanhā*, the drive to become, which implies the existence of subtle or blatant dissatisfaction with current conditions; and (3) *vibhava-tanhā*, the drive for non-existence, which primarily arises from intolerance of distress and ultimately reflects ignorance of the impermanent nature of phenomena. Each of these forms of *tanhā* has the power to enslave us in a perpetual battle with life as it manifests from moment to moment.

Kama-tanhā

Every one of us can relate to wanting more of the good things life has to offer: tasty food, a comfortable home, great sex, pleasing sights and sounds, happy relationships, natural beauty, stimulating conversation, interesting and fulfilling work, enjoyable leisure activities. These are examples of *kama-tanhā*. Hopefully we can agree that in principle there is nothing inherently wrong with desiring pleasurable experience. But suffering arises when we believe contentment depends solely on the presence of pleasurable sense objects. This false definition of happiness impedes temperance and generosity and results in attachment to hedonistic views of what constitutes pleasure. *When we grasp at the continuance of pleasure, we invite the suffering of insatiability to rule our lives.*

Bhava-tanhā

A desire to *become what one is not* certainly furthers our species along a trajectory of growth and evolution. There is much that is positive in the desire to better oneself physically, psychologically, educationally, professionally, socially and economically. The desire to be more helpful, to act more philanthropically, to engage in spiritual practice, the commitment to become healthy—these are virtuous aspirations. When we embrace an intention for betterment without judging or hating the person we are right now, we can make change happen without incurring the suffering of *bhava-tanhā.*

Bhava-tanhā can increase feelings of self-dissatisfaction and anxiety by feeding internal narratives of worthlessness. "I will feel good about myself when I have a better job with a bigger salary, a happier relationship, a grander house, a more beautiful body, or a better mood." These longings can be inculcated through exposure to cultural conditioning from parents, schools, religion, advertising or peer pressure. *Buddhist psychology reminds us that when we forget the magnificence of our own being, we get lost and believe false ideas about who we truly are.*

Vibhava-tanhā

The desire to end pain is another biologically engineered function designed to keep our species safe from harm. For example, a child puts his or her hand on a hot stove for the first time and gets burned. The child quickly learns that a safe stove is a cool stove, but this does not keep the child from screaming and crying for a parent to make the pain of the burn go away NOW! *Humans are like this child, screaming for the pains of life to go away NOW!*

The Need to Fix; the Need for a Fix

Our comfort-driven culture has significantly lowered our threshold for unpleasantness. Generally, aversive experiences trigger automatic rejection-responses like "Get me out of here," or "I can't take this," or "I need to fix this." A minute of pain can seem interminable when we grasp at relief and resist the experience of pain as it is. *Craving a fix is something the mind does automatically when it rejects what it perceives and determines to turn it into something else.* Unfortunately, the actions we take to resist, deny or escape difficulties all too often lead to a greater measure of suffering than any specific instance of pain. People with active substance use problems know this reality all too well, and those in recovery remember how painful their lives used to be.

It is critically important to not confuse staying present when difficulty arises with being a victim or giving in. Once we learn appropriate and effective techniques to cultivate presence, it is actually a relief to observe painful sensations, thoughts or feelings. Recognizing the awfulness of life with clear comprehension of its causes makes us better able to intentionally transform negatives to positives. We cannot do this if turning away is our only response to unpleasantness.

Vibhava-tanhā also refers to affective states of boredom, apathy and ambivalence. People with histories of depression or addiction do well to pay attention to their reactivity to boredom. Studies show that almost half of those queried mention boredom as their number-one trigger for relapse.[40] Underlying boredom and apathy is a basic hatred of 'what is,' a greed for something different. Paying attention to boredom naturally gives rise to excitement and curiosity.

The Neuroscience of Tanhā

The motivation to seek out pleasure occurs in the *mesolimbic dopamine system*, also known as the *reward pathway*, which informs us about what feels good and motivates us to get more of it. The hub of the brain's reward system is the *ventral tegmental area* (VTA), a group of neurons located in the midbrain with projections out to other important brain areas involved with decision-making and emotional responses. When we engage in pleasurable activity, the VTA is activated, sending brief electrical impulses down axons that deliver information to other brain regions. Some of these axons end up in the *nucleus accumbens* (NAc) and stimulate production of the neurotransmitter dopamine, which binds to dopamine receptors. The VTA also has dopamine-releasing axons terminating in brain regions that control emotions (the *amygdala* and *anterior cingulate*), learning (*dorsal striatum*), memory (*hippocampus*) and executive function (*prefrontal cortex*). The feeling of dopamine release is one of pleasure. Dopamine release is vital for positive emotions and the seeking out of experiences that feel good. But as we all know, there are things in life that feel good but end up not being good for us.

Dopamine also interacts with and influences brain regions that control movement and motivation. The subcortical areas of the brain's reward system (VTA and NAc) have a measurable impact on higher cortical functions like decision-making. These subcortical areas of the reward system can be activated by stimuli as short as 30 milliseconds, too short for us to be fully aware of them as they occur. Cravings stimulated by sensory experiences arrive in subcortical brain areas long before conscious knowing of craving occurs in the prefrontal areas. This is precisely why cravings and urges *can seem so uncontrollable* and why addiction researchers view craving as the hardest problem to solve.[41]

The neurons in the VTA also receive information from other brain regions. Of particular interest are the *medial forebrain bundle*, which releases the excitatory neurotransmitter *glutamate* into the VTA, and the (NAc), which stimulates production of *gamma-aminobutyric acid* (GABA) and inhibits neural firing in the VTA. GABA and glutamate are major biochemical players in calming or exciting the psychophysical system. Alcohol's calming and/or euphoric effect results from GABA release. Consumption of too much alcohol floods the body and brain with GABA. This triggers the brain to release more glutamate. When the effects of alcohol wear off, the brain and body suffer from high levels of glutamate, causing irritability, pain, agitation and hangover. That can activate craving for more alcohol to relieve high levels of discomfort.[42] In fact, evidence shows that once one has entered the cycle of addiction, pleasure derived from substance use diminishes, and wanting increases. That want is primarily focused on ameliorating the negative effects of a substance. This use/withdrawal/use cycle is a perfect example of the imprisoning impact of *tanhā*.

Clinging (P & S: **upādāna** *T:* **bdag 'dzin***)*

> *These four are clingings: sensuality clinging, view clinging, rules and vows clinging, and clinging to the doctrine of self.* (SN: II 12:2)

Upādāna, *clinging* or *attachment*, is derived from *ādāna*, meaning 'to catch hold of strongly,' and *upā*, added for emphasis. Clinging occurs when the impulse to approach or avoid triggers the projection of and fixation on solidity, permanence or false identity. Returning to the snake/rope analogy, clinging is akin to seeing a snake while continuing to grasp at the idea that the snake is actually a rope.

Grasping is such a common experience in daily life. Before I removed sugar from my diet, walking by the freezer section in the store would inevitably lead me to Haagen Dazs ice cream. With widened eyes and a watering mouth, I would feel my body edging closer to the freezer case. My mind—gripped by mental images of the taste and pleasure I had derived from coffee Haagen Dazs' rich flavor—would blaze with excitement. Colliding with those images were thoughts of an inevitable runny nose, a horrible sugar headache and unwanted extra pounds. But I held to the hope that this time would be different. There I was, clinging to false identity and lost in an internal world of turmoil. In a moment like that, liberation from suffering looks like waking up in the experience of clinging: really seeing the pint of ice cream as it actually is, devoid of concepts and associations, and reaffirming an intention to eat healthy foods.

A momentary grasping at ice cream pales in comparison to the human habit of clinging to certainty. However misguided, the false view of permanence and continuance persists because of repeated misapprehension that hard-wires the mental habit of chronically attributing solidity to objects, thoughts, emotions and *mano-viññāna* (the feeling or consciousness of a self).[43]

So what are we to do when our inborn perceptual apparatus is flawed? The only cure for grasping is to identify and investigate the *Five Aggregates of Clinging* (P: *khandās* S: *skandhas*): form (*rūpa*), feeling (*vedanā*), perception (*saññā*), volition (*cetanā*) and consciousness (*citta*). Although we have already discussed these five separately, as a collection of noumena, the *skandhas* exemplify the process by which we assume substantiality.

> *Form is like a lump of foam,*
> *Feeling like a water bubble;*
> *Perception is like a mirage,*
> *Volitions like a plantain trunk,*
> *And consciousness like an illusion.*
>
> *However one may ponder it,*
> *And carefully investigate it,*

It appears but hollow and void
When one views it carefully. (SN III 22:95)

Foam looks solid but dissolves on contact. Water bubbles fascinate us but are unstable and easily burst. A mirage appears real but is no more than a perceptual magic trick. Grand trees are merely the outcome of embedded, hidden roots. Illusions are deceptive, unreliable representations of reality. All phenomena (*dhammas*) amount to little more than the continual compounding of discrete momentary appearances. When combined, collected appearances seem solid, attractive or repulsive, real, volitional and oh so personal.

Becoming (P: bhava *S:* bhāva *T:* mi srid*)*

These three are becomings: sensual becoming, form becoming, & formless becoming. (SN II 22:2)

Bhava (becoming) demarcates a threshold of grasping that results in the impulse to be something, take birth in something or identify with something. *Bhava is the psychological commitment to mind states of being—bonded and bound to ascribed thingness—and the cognitional determination to identify or disidentify with imputed internal or external appearances.*

The Buddha listed three spheres of experience in which *bhava* generates activation or reception of karma. Each of Dependent Origination's links are either *kammabhava* (karmically active) or *uppattibhava* (karmically passive).[44] *Avidyā* and *sankhāra* arise from the past as active karmic expressions determining and conditioning the next grouping of resultant *uppattibhava* links: *viññāna*, *nāmarūpa*, *salāyatana*, *phassa* and *vedanā*. Although each of those links functions in the present, they operate from passive automaticity. In the immediacy of decision-making, the next three links—*tanhā*, *upādāna* and *bhava*—determine future karmic dispositions.

When we remain unaware of craving and clinging, *bhava* gives rise to afflictive mind states and unwholesome actions. Awareness increases the likelihood of actualizing wholesome mind states and skillful actions. However, since 'wholesome' does not necessarily imply awakened, we may act wisely and still suffer from subtle misattribution of thingness. Therefore, *bhava* can be karmically profitable, unprofitable or indeterminate.[45]

Birth (P & S: jāti *T:* skye ba*)*

Whatever birth, taking birth, descent, coming-to-be, coming-forth, appearance of aggregates, & acquisition of sense bases. (SN II 22:2)

Traditionally, birth (*jāti*) meant assured rebirth, the natural outcome of *bhava*. For our purposes, *birth* refers to the results of habitual becoming in the current life span caused by primordial ignorance (*avidyā*) and dispositional tendencies (*sankhāra*). *Habitual becoming furthers continuing birth of wrong relationship with one's lived world, a limited world of mentation, governed by an imprisoned mind suffering from unending reactive cycles of feeling, craving, clinging and becoming.* Essentially, birth actualizes mind's identification with ignorance and subject/object dualism, which in turn feed the mind's abject resistance to the inherent entropy of human life.

Aging and Death (P: jaramarana *S:* jāramarana *T:* rga ba 'chi ba*)*

> *Whatever aging, decrepitude, brokenness, graying, wrinkling, decline of life-force, weakening of the faculties of various beings, that is called aging. Whatever deceasing, passing away, breaking up, disappearance, dying, death, completion of time, break up of the aggregates, casting off of the body, interruption in the life faculty of various beings, that is called death.* (SN II 12:22)

Decay and death (*jaramarana*) occur at every level of this living universe—from the microscopic to the macroscopic. Although the Buddha assumed death and rebirth for those caught in the suffering of conditioned mind, there is a passage in which he asserts that "a mind, fortified over a long time by faith, virtue, learning, generosity and wisdom—that goes upwards, goes to distinction [evolving toward *nirvāna*, the deathless, the unconditioned reality]" (SN V:21).

In Buddhist psychology, aging and death are not an endpoint. For all of Dependent Origination's linearity, this formula is circular and sometimes seemingly random. In the web of interdependence all impermanent phenomena (*dhammas*) lead to and from each other.

Dependent Origination deconstructs our penchant for assembling a separate egoic self out of nothing more than compounded concepts, labels and appearances. Donning the armor of a false self, we fight the flow and flux of phenomena, making life an enemy instead of our precious teacher. That unwitting mistake brings about *jaramarana*, aging and death.

Another approach to understanding the 12th link is *The Four Reflections*, a short-form of Dependent Origination. This fundamental practice of Tibetan Buddhism is essentially a meditation on death. It is comprised of four truths meant to turn the mind toward the importance of living this life in full recognition of its utter fragility. I now offer *The Four Reflections* as a contemplative practice.

 Contemplation of the Four Reflections

These reflections may seem simple at first glance, but actively reflecting on them can be difficult for those who find themselves in tough times or for whom life has been quite hard for a long time. For this reason I urge each of you to be gentle with yourselves as you engage with this practice.

Begin by resting in a comfortable seated position. Let your mind be at ease. Let your eyes take in your surroundings. Generate gratitude for this time to contemplate life in its essence.

This Precious Human Life

Bring to mind all the billions of stars, their countless planets. Consider the odds of being born here on this earth in a human body. It is said the Buddha once picked up a little bit of dust with the tip of his fingernail and asked the monks, "What do you think, monks? Which is greater: the little bit of dust on the tip of my fingernail or all the soil on earth?" The monks replied, "All the soil on Earth." The Buddha agreed, "In the same way few beings are born among human beings. Far more take countless other forms. Thus you should train yourselves to live heedfully." How rare it is to attain birth in a human body with its optimal conditions for awakening to one's own true nature. To know that in this very life liberation from suffering is possible inspires urgency and great confidence in one's efforts. Remember this precious human birth and practice even when conditions are difficult. Knowing that human birth is rare cuts through self-doubts like "I am not cut out to be a practitioner," or "This is too hard." Tell yourself: *I will not waste this opportunity to awaken.*

The Recognition of Impermanence

The Buddha taught that even one moment of knowing the impermanent nature of phenomena is more powerful than any other insight. "Impermanent are compounded things, prone to rise and fall. Having risen, they are destroyed; their passing truest bliss." Consider how everything arises out of ever-changing conditions. All things arise and pass away. Nothing is forever; permanence is illusory. It is said that one day some people asked the Theravadan teacher Ajahn Chah, "How can you be so happy in a world of such impermanence, where you cannot protect your loved ones from harm, illness and death?" Ajahn Chah held up a glass, "Someone gave me this glass. It holds my water admirably and glistens in sunlight. One day the wind may blow it off the shelf or my elbow may knock it from the table. I know this glass is already broken, so I enjoy it." True refuge lies in knowing the impermanent nature of all things. Open all your senses; see and hear what passes before you, around you, inside you. Rest in their comings and goings for as long as you wish. *Let go of being the doer and rest as the observer, the experiencer.*

All Our Actions Have Consequences and Results

This is the ultimate reminder of our responsibility to be a source of upliftment and awakening in this world. In one day we take on so many roles and personas. How deliberately are we choosing who we are and how we show up for others and ourselves? Inquire about your motivation for being in this life. See yourself intending to act with a clear mind and open heart as best you are able. Even in a distressful moment we can reflect on what is skillful and unskillful. Know that sometimes inaction can be the most powerful action, and take an intentional pause. Right now . . . rest again in your senses; know sitting, breathing. *Know this practice is the fruit of a wise, loving choice and brings with it the possibility of greater wisdom.*

The Cultivation of Dispassion Toward the Defects of *Samsāra*

Dispassion is the sword that cuts through conditioned mind to reveal reality as it is: devoid of essential thingness, perfect in its expression and lacking nothing. Knowing the Dharma is visible right now, and immediately effective when applied, is a cause for lightening up. See yourself meeting life's challenges with awareness. Know the joy of stepping back and not taking everything so personally. *Dispassion is holding life with the peace that comes from knowing all things arise interdependently and that we are nothing more or less than all that is around and in us.*

Now rest for as long as you like with eyes open or closed.

Notes

1 Insel, T. (2013, April 29). Transforming diagnosis. Blog entry. Retrieved September 1, 2013 from www.nimh.nih.gov/about/director/2013/transforming-diagnosis.shtml

2 From "The Buddha's Victory" by U. Sangharakshita, p. 23. Retrieved August 2012 from www.sangharakshita.org/online_books.html

3 Davidson, R. (2013, February). *Neuroscience and contemplative practice.* Unpublished lecture presented at Upaya Zen Center, Santa Fe, NM.
Schuyler, B.S., Kral, T.R., Jacquart, J., Burghy, C.A., Weng, H.Y., Perlman, D.M., . . . & Davidson, R.J. (2012). Temporal dynamics of emotional responding: Amygdala recovery predicts emotional traits. *Social Cognitive and Affective Neuroscience.* SCAN December 7, 1–6.

4 Skinner, B.F. (1965). *Science and human behavior.* New York, NY: Free Press.
Bandura, A., & Albert, B. (1969). *Principles of behavior modification.* New York, NY: Holt, Rinehart and Winston.

5 For more details see: Nyanaponika, T. (1954). *The heart of Buddhist meditation.* San Francisco, CA: Wieser Books. pp. ix–xv.

6 Bodhi, B. (Ed.). (2003). *A comprehensive manual of Abhidhamma: The Abhidhammattha Sangaha.* Onalaska, WA: Pariyatti Editions.

7 Thanissaro, B. (2010, June). Analysis of dependent co-arising. (T. Bhikkhu, Ed.). *Access to Insight.* Retrieved November 5, 2012 from www.accesstoinsight.org/tipitaka/sn/sn12/sn12.002.than.html

8 I have heard Anam Thubten use this phrase repeatedly when lecturing on the origins of primordial ignorance.

9 Physicist Brian Greene's book *The Fabric of the Cosmos* includes a detailed explanation. Green, B. (2004). *The fabric of the cosmos.* New York, NY: Vintage Books.

10 Eagleman, D. (2011). *Incognito: The secret lives of the brain*. New York, NY: Pantheon Books.
Ramachandran, V.S. (2004). *A brief tour of human consciousness: From impostor poodles to purple numbers*. New York, NY: Pi Press.
11 Seek out Greene's book for more details.
12 In his introduction to the *Samyutta Nikāya*, Bhikkhu Bodhi states that there is no English word sufficient to express the complexity of *sankhāra*.
13 Nyanaponika, 1954, p. 44.
14 Buddhaghosa. (1975). *The Visuddhimagga*. (B. Nanamoli, Trans.) Kandy, Sri Lanka: Buddhist Publication Society. p. 574, note 31.
15 *Retrocausality*, a term from quantum physics, explains how effects can occur prior to their cause.
16 Batchelor, S. (1998). *Buddhism without beliefs*. New York, NY: Tricycle Press.
17 Kapoor, A., Petropoulos, S., & Matthews, S. G. (2008). Fetal programming of hypothalamic–pituitary–adrenal (HPA) axis function and behavior by synthetic glucocorticoids. *Brain Research Reviews, 57*(2), 586–595.
Burdge, G. C., Slater-Jefferies, J., Torrens, C., Phillips, E. S., Hanson, M. A., & Lillycrop, K. A. (2007). Dietary protein restriction of pregnant rats in the F0 generation induces altered methylation of hepatic gene promoters in the adult male offspring in the F1 and F2 generations. *British Journal of Nutrition, 97*(3), 435–439.
18 Matthews, S. G., & Phillips, D. I. (2010). Minireview: Transgenerational inheritance of the stress response: a new frontier in stress research. *Endocrinology, 151*(1), 7–13.
Zucchi, F. C., Yao, Y., & Metz, G. A. (2012). The secret language of destiny: Stress imprinting and transgenerational origins of disease. *Frontiers in Genetics, 3*(96), 1–12.
19 Bhasin, M.K., Dusek, J.A., Chang, B.H., Joseph, M.G., Denninger, J.W., Fricchione, G.L., . . . & Libermann, T.A. (2013). Relaxation response induces temporal transcriptome changes in energy metabolism, insulin secretion and inflammatory pathways. *PLOS ONE, 8*(5), e62817.
Kok, B.E., Waugh, C.E., & Fredrickson, B.L. (2013). Meditation and health: The search for mechanisms of action. *Social and Personality Psychology Compass, 7*(1), 27–39.
20 For a more detailed exposition of *vijñāna*, see Waldron, W. (2003). *The Buddhist unconscious: The alaya-vijnana in the context of Indian Buddhist thought*. London: RoutledgeCurzon. pp. 19–32.
21 The subject of awareness is covered in Chapter 3.
22 See Chapter 3.
23 Boisvert, M. (1995). *The five aggregates: Understanding Theravadan psychology and soteriology*. Delhi, India: India Books Center. p. 48.
24 Bodhi, B. (2000). *The connected discourses of the Buddha: A translation of the Samyutta Nikaya*. Boston, MA: Wisdom Publications. p. 325.
25 Bodhi, B. (1993/1999). *A comprehensive manual of Abhidhamma*. Onalaska, WA: Buddhist Publication Society. p. 144.
26 Visuddhimaggha, XIV:47.
27 Visuddhimaggha, VIII:111.
28 Bodhi, B., 1993/1999, pp. 144–145.
29 Kalupahana, D. (1987). *The principles of Buddhist psychology*. Albany, NY: State University of New York Press. p. 30.
30 Visuddhimaggha, XIV:67.
31 Bodhi, B., 1993/1999, pp. 27–31.
32 Ibid., pp. 78–90.
33 Boisvert, M., 1995, p. 51.

34 Bechara, A. (2004). The role of emotion in decision-making: Evidence from neurological patients with orbitofrontal damage. *Brain and Cognition, 55*, 30–40.
35 Boisvert, M., 1995, p. 78.
36 Damasio, A. (2010). *Self comes to mind: Constructing the conscious brain.* New York, NY: Vintage. p. 119.
37 Stcherbatsky, T. (1968). *The conception of Buddhist Nirvana.* Varanasi, India: Bharatiya Vidya Prakashan.
Kalupahana, D., 1987.
38 SN II 36:3–7.
39 Papies, E. K., Barsalou, L. W., & Custers, R. (2012). Mindful attention prevents mindless impulses. *Social Psychological and Personality Science, 3*(3), 291–299.
40 Oakes, J., Pols, R., Battersby, M., Lawn, S., Pulvirenti, M., & Smith, D. (2012). A focus group study of predictors of relapse in electronic gaming machine problem gambling, part 2: Factors that "pull" the gambler away from relapse. *Journal of Gambling Studies, 28*(3), 465–479.
Lee, T. (2011). A review on "Thirty Days to Hope & Freedom from Sexual Addiction: The Essential Guide to Beginning Recovery and Relapse Prevention." *Sexual Addiction & Compulsivity, 18*(1), 52–55.
Lobera, I. J. (2012). Neurophysiological basis of food craving. In S. Magdeldin (Ed.), *The State of the Art Therapeutic* (p. 29–44). Intechopen.com. http://dx.doi.org/10.5772/2906
41 Volkow, N. D., Fowler, J. S., & Wang, G. J. (2003). The addicted human brain: Insights from imaging studies. *Journal of Clinical Investigation, 111* (10), 1444–1451.
Koob, G. F. (2006). The neurobiology of addiction: A neuroadaptational view relevant for diagnosis. *Addiction, 101*(s1), 23–30.
42 Erickson, C. K. (2007). *The science of addiction: From neurobiology to treatment.* New York, NY: W. W. Norton.
43 Kalupahana, D., 1987, p. 31.
44 Bodhi, B., 1993/1999, p. 298.
45 Visuddhimagga, XVII:51.

3

The Conditioned Mind and Mental Health Disorders

Usually breakthrough happens through breakdown.

Anam Thubten[1]

P had been on medication for irritable bowel syndrome (IBS) for a year with little result. Her gastroenterologist insisted the IBS symptoms were causally related to persistent severe anxiety and suggested psychotherapy. P's first words to me were, "I'll do anything to get rid of this pain and fear." P claimed she never felt relaxed as a child and was relentlessly bullied throughout childhood. Her mother, whom she described as critical, angry and self-absorbed, told her to just ignore the bullying. P managed to do well in college. But IBS presented during her senior year as a result of financial difficulties. Now, at 25, P worked 12-hour days as a junior salesperson in a high-stress corporate environment. IBS had put a stop to her once-active social life, and business travel tied her in knots: "I am always nervous because I can never tell when I am going to be sick and need a bathroom."

 The Way Things Were and the Way We Are

The basic composition of the human brain and body has remained much the same for the last 50,000 years and virtually the same since the time of the Buddha. At that time, 2,600 years ago, humans were dependent on nature and attuned themselves to the rhythms of the natural world. They were part of nomadic tribes of hunter-gatherers, centralized city-states or agrarian societies—very different settings with equally divergent lifestyles. Hunter-gatherers migrated seasonally, sustained by the bounty of plains, forests and oceans. Agrarian societies lived and worked according to planting-harvest-dormancy cycles. Trade among city-states encouraged intermingling of customs and cultures. Even the Buddha's *Sangha* mirrored the close-knit familial-communal structures of the time. A monk or nun's individual practice of ethical conduct (*sīla*) was made possible by communal support for and adherence to dharmic values. Since monks and nuns were barred from owning money or possessions, the *Sangha* relied on the generosity (*dāna*) of lay practitioners. However different, these societies promoted multi-generational, attachment-rich, communal environments, excellent conditions for healthy child brain development.[2]

Of course life was hardly idyllic. Peoples of that time were plagued by hunger, strife and destruction resulting from human and natural causes. The *Three Poisons*—greed (*lobha*), hatred (*dosa*) and delusion (*moha*)—were as active in their minds as in ours. But their level of stress and the kinds of stressors were different and most likely held within an extended familial-communal context.

The last 150 years of worldwide industrialization have wrought dramatic societal and environmental changes—some beneficial and others disastrous. Today many adults live with multiple chronic life stressors, disconnected and isolated from extended family (some from immediate family), community and their natural surroundings. While it is true that mass use of devices has created interactional surrogates like posting on social media sites, tweeting and texting, those activities are often just another source of stimulation or a distraction from the demands of embodied relationship. When was the last time you were at a social gathering where more people were conversing on devices than engaging with others in the room? In Silicon Valley, where I live, it happens quite often.

Humans have developed adaptive strategies to cope with stress. But the human nervous system is ill equipped to handle intense and sustained levels of chronic physical and psychological stress.[3] The human nervous system has two main parts: (1) the *central nervous system* (CNS)—the brain and spinal cord, and (2) the *peripheral nervous system*—the nerves and basal ganglia. The *peripheral nervous system* is divided into two divisions: *afferent*, which detects stimuli from the five senses and internal organs and sends it to the CNS for processing; and *efferent*, which sends motor information from the CNS to the body. The *sensory-motor system* is subject to conscious control, while the *autonomic nervous system* processes stimuli and functions largely unconsciously. The autonomic system regulates organ functioning and respiration and is intimately connected to the psyche through the *vagus system*. It has two main branches: (1) the *sympathetic nervous system*—fight or flight activation response mechanisms, and (2) the *parasympathetic nervous system*—sympathetic arousal deactivation mechanisms.

Stress is a physical or mental challenge to one's psychophysical system and a belief that one has inadequate resources to cope. The body marshals its resources to meet stress by activating the sympathetic nervous system or what is popularly referred to as *the stress response*. Extended periods of exposure to stress require the body to work overtime to maintain equilibrium or *homeostasis*. This process is mediated by the hypothalamic-pituitary-adrenal axis. Stress induces production and release of hormones such as *cortisol*. Over-production of cortisol contributes to cognitive problems, suppressed immune system function, raised blood pressure, increased serum cholesterol, secretion of stomach acids, wasting of muscle tissue and increased fat production.

Chronic psychological stress is associated with the body losing its ability to regulate inflammatory response. "Specifically, immune cells become insensitive to cortisol's regulatory effect. In turn, runaway inflammation is thought to promote the development and progression of many diseases" (CMU, 2012). High levels of cortisol and proinflammatory cytokines and excessive or inadequate basal activity wear down the body and mind, exacerbating the likelihood of developing any of a number of behavioral and somatic stress-related disorders.[4] And now for the really bad news.

Dependent Co-arising: Childhood Trauma and Psychophysical Maladies

In my beginning is my end. (Eliot, 1968)

Natural selection favored long periods of development in our species, requiring years of close infant–parent contact. This capacity for intense parent–child attachment and love was evolutionarily engineered into our species. A secure parent–child attachment during the first 3 years of life is the most positive force for child development.[5] "Attachment organization reflects the quality of the parent–child relationship as that relationship coalesces by the end of the 1st year. The early relationship quality can then substantially moderate . . . children's antisocial outcomes" (Kochanska, 2009).

Currently, the United States has an epidemic of chronically stressed, overworked, sleep-deprived parents. Many parents are expected to work 60–80 hours a week and never turn off their devices. Constant accessibility makes a full day away from work stress a rare occurrence. And, sadly, the embrace of this brutal lifestyle is growing worldwide.

Financially sustaining a family requires two working parents, and many American children spend their critical early years in daycare settings receiving less-than-optimal physical and emotional nurturing. A major multi-year study conducted by the National Institute of Child Health and Human Development concluded that more hours spent in all qualities of daycare negatively affects attunement and mother–infant sensitivity. It also increases aggression among kindergartners and contributes to higher rates of disobedience through grade six.[6]

Over the last 4 years, one in four children in the US were born to single mothers, and around 30% of all households were single-parent. Unfortunately, our highly moralistic, non-communal society does not readily compassionately support these deserving families, ultimately contributing to their high levels of stress and exhaustion.

Childhood abuse, neglect, parental stress, impoverished environments and prenatal exposure to toxic substances negatively impact cognitive-affective-social brain development.[7] Persistent shock or threat in childhood environments leads to developmental trauma and chronic activation of the autonomic nervous system. This thwarts an infant/child's curiosity and empathic-connective impulses. Fifteen percent of babies have inhibited or reactive temperaments—the result of abusive, traumatic environments. In novel situations these babies secrete high levels of cortisol and become almost frozen in withdrawal. They frequently develop into children with shyness, high negative emotions, behavioral issues and high distress.[8] A 2011 study of children with disruptive behavior problems showed that any past exposure to interpersonal violence was related to more severe issues.[9] When infants and children experience chronic threat and trauma (especially from caregivers), it leads to persisting feelings of unsafety in adulthood, regardless of the actual situational or emotional circumstances.

Numerous studies have shown that childhood trauma is a determinant of aggression levels in youth and adults, especially in prison populations.[10] Inmates with substance use problems who report higher levels of childhood trauma show increased rates of psychoticism and neuroticism, impulsivity, poor resilience and suicidal ideation.[11] There is also evidence that early childhood maltreatment results in long-lasting epigenetic alterations. These changes predispose individuals to later risk for post-traumatic stress disorder (PTSD) and contribute to persistence of PTSD symptoms associated with subsequent adult traumatic events.[12]

In 1991 the *American Journal of Psychiatry* published a study exploring the relationship between incidence of childhood trauma, disrupted attachment and later self-harming behavior in adults with bipolar II and personality disorders. A clear link was found in two areas: (1) childhood trauma and initiation of self-destructive behavior, and (2) lack of secure attachment and continued reliance on self-harming in response to current stresses.[13] Successive research has determined a clear relationship between childhood trauma history and emotional dysregulation, most prominently in women.[14]

What about the general population? As discussed earlier, recent studies show a correlation between the prevalence of stress in utero and in childhood environments and adult onset of psychiatric and/or biomedical problems. Kaiser Permanente San Diego conducted an extensive group of studies on adverse childhood environments (ACE) to determine how these may contribute to mental and physical problems in adulthood.[15]

During routine office visits, 17,000 Kaiser patients were asked whether during their first 18 years of life they had experienced any of eight categories of household dysfunction, abuse or neglect. Answers were scored by incidence of each category ("yes" counted as 1), although the numbers of incidents were not calculated. This "solidly middle-class group" (Felleti, 2010) scored unexpectedly high. Only one-third had a score of 0. A score of 1 carried an 87% likelihood of the presence of at least one more category, and one in six participants had a score of 4 or more. Women were 50% more likely to have experienced five or more categories. High rates of adult depression correlated to higher numbers of categories, and suicide attempts were much more likely in those who had experienced four or more categories.

A similar correlation was found between the predominance of ACE categories and somatization disorders and fibromyalgia. ACE correlation was also found with adult biomedical diseases such as liver disease, obstructive pulmonary disease, autoimmune disorders and coronary disease, as well as early mortality rates. That linkage is attributed to chronic stress characterized by high cortisol levels and presence of proinflammatory cytokines.[16] Not surprisingly, a similar study found that ACEs account for one-half to two-thirds of adolescents and adults who had serious problems with drug and cigarette use.[17]

Early trauma is fast becoming the leading indicator of poor mental and biomedical health outcomes. Changing this pattern of rampant trauma and its resulting psychophysical diseases can happen only if the psychological and medical community acknowledges that medicating symptoms and altering cognitive strategies is not enough to free the human mind from the root causes of suffering—greed (*lobha*), hatred (*dosa*) and delusion (*moha*).

 Conditioned Mind and Specific Mental Health Disorders

What follows is a distillation, from a Buddhist psychological perspective, of mental health maladies commonly treated in clinical settings. Because the Buddha recognized the primacy of radical empiricism and body-mind-heart interdependence, somatic theories and neuroscientific evidence will also be presented. Toward the end, simple yet powerful beginning practices will be offered to help you develop greater interoceptive mind-body presence.

Depression and Anxiety

In a given year, depression is thought to affect more than 15 million Americans, and 40 million American adults are said to have anxiety disorders. Those suffering from severe unipolar depression have a 50% chance of recurrence after their first episode, increasing to 70% with two occurrences. In these cases, attaining safety and stabilization should precede the use of any Buddhist psychological intervention.

The terms 'depression' and 'anxiety' have been definitionally and interpretationally diluted by pop psychology. In my experience what most patients call 'depression' does not meet major depressive disorder's criteria: suicidality, inability to get out of bed or feelings of sadness all day long for days on end. When most people say, "I feel depressed," the symptoms they describe are low energy, negativity, ambivalence, dissatisfaction, sadness, lack of motivation, sleep problems, low confidence, self-doubt, self-deprecation, and feelings of isolation and loneliness. Similarly, "I have anxiety" more often means restlessness, agitation, worry and fearfulness rather than severe phobias or panic events. Many people also report fluctuating between anxiety and depression or experiencing them simultaneously. I prefer to use the term *depressive/anxious symptoms* when referring to this varied collection of mind–body states.

I believe it is important to inquire whether the epidemic of depressive/anxious symptoms is a psychophysiological response to unhealthy lifestyles of chronic stress and resulting systemic body-mind inflammation. Studies have found that depressed and high-risk groups have significantly smaller left and right hippocampal volumes,[18] possibly resulting from chronically elevated glucocorticoids (GC) secreted by the adrenal glands as an endocrine response to stress.[19] Research also shows that depression is associated with increased levels of proinflammatory cytokines and other acute-phase proteins.[20]

There is also growing evidence for a microbiota–gut–brain relationship. Bacteria in the gastrointestinal tract appear to activate neural pathways and central nervous system signaling systems. Changes in the functioning of microbiota "may lead to alterations in fat storage and energy balance; general low-grade inflammation (GI and systemic); increased stress reactivity; and increased anxiety and depressive-like behaviors. Each of these mechanisms is implicated in the pathophysiology of mood and anxiety disorders" (Foster, 2013). Additionally, low intake of omega 3 fatty acids, fruits and vegetables and consumption of high amounts of refined sugar and processed foods increase the risk of depression.[21]

I would like to emphasize that antidepressants are no more effective than placebo for this spectrum of mild to moderate depressive symptoms. In 2010 the *Journal of the Medical Association* (*JAMA*) published a meta-analysis of SSRI antidepressant medications that confirmed their inability to outperform placebos for mild to moderate depression.[22] Additionally, a review of Food and Drug Administration data found that "the relationship between initial severity and antidepressant efficacy is attributable to decreased responsiveness to placebo among very severely depressed patients, rather than to increased responsiveness to medication" (Kirsch, 2008).

Buddhist psychology considers all depressive/anxious symptoms varied flavors of aversion (*dosa*) to what is and craving (*tanhā*) for what isn't. Generally this manifests as intense resistance to engagement, often associated with a strong belief that one cannot energetically meet life with willingness, openness and curiosity. There can be many reasons for such resistance, including biomedical disease or dis-ease in the psyche. Integrative treatments using mindfulness and heartfulness practices, exercise and a non-inflammatory diet are recommended to systemically reduce stress and promote prosocial emotions.

The Polyvagal Theory

Current psychophysiological research has expanded work on heart rate variability and its role in predicting psychological states to include the autonomic functioning of the CNS and its effect on behavior. The *vagus nerve* runs from the brainstem through the neck, chest and abdomen. It transmits sensory information from the internal organs to the brain and is the mechanism for lowering heart rate in response to parasympathetic activation. The polyvagal theory[23] proposes that primary emotions are related to autonomic function and distinguishes two vagal motor systems, each with distinctive neurophysiologically mediated affective and adaptive behavioral responses.

In safe environments, *ventral vagal* activity promotes psychophysical growth and restoration by activating the parasympathetic nervous system: slowing the heart rate, dampening the stress response and lowering production of cortisol and proinflammatory cytokines. This 'vagal brake' enables self-soothing behaviors by facilitating rapid engagement and disengagement with objects and people.[24] Vagal influence on the heart also initiates spontaneous social engagement behaviors.[25] High vagal tone (a measure of autonomic flexibility) encourages social and psychological well-being, increased trait positive emotionality, prosocial behaviors and decreased maladaptive coping strategies.[26] *High vagal tone is the ultimate coherence and presence mediator.*

Conversely, during perceived threats, vagal withdrawal occurs: mobilizing fight or flight responses that activate the sympathetic nervous system. This leads to increased levels of cortisol and cytokine inflammation. When a threat is great enough, the immobilizing function of the *dorsal vagal* system activates behavioral shutdown, otherwise known as the *freeze response* or *collapse*. This is how a rabbit feigns death in response to a predator's attack, only to spring back to life once the predator, bored with its lifeless prey, has dropped the bunny and moved on.

Unfortunately, in humans, repeated collapse in response to an ongoing threat or abuse, especially in childhood, leads to dissociation. Psychophysiological collapse states are a primary obstacle to being present in one's here-and-now experience. These are our chronically depressed, dissociated or dysregulated patients who don't seem to derive benefit from talk therapy or have limited success with cognitive-behavioral approaches. When asked, they will likely report adult trauma or childhood maltreatment. What most clinicians miss is how hard their autonomic nervous system is continually working to defend against perceived threats.[27] These patients are caught in a double bind. Systemic activation (positive or negative) triggers a habituated threat response, agitation and fearfulness. Even in the midst of auspicious circumstances, remaining lifeless and depressed can feel safe, contained and known (even if what is known is inaccurate).

Emotional Dysregulation Is Trauma Symptomatology

Emotions are fleeting, with displays lasting only about 10 seconds. Short-lived as they may be, emotions organize priorities, focus attention on goals and facilitate good decision-making. But emotions can become dysregulated through over- or under-arousal, a primary feature of mood and personality disorders. As stated earlier, we have definitive research correlating childhood trauma and emotional dysregulation, especially in women.

During emotional over-arousal brain processing moves from the frontal cortex (responsible for decision-making, attention, morality, empathy) to the posterior cortex (involved in vigilance, fear, anger, survival instincts). Chronic emotional over-arousal can contribute to a range of psychophysical problems: muscle tension, digestive and cardiovascular issues, poor concentration, memory impairment, impaired decision-making, anxiety and depression.

At some point in my internship I realized that each time my supervisor would say, "This one will be hard," it meant I was about to work with a person who would turn out to be very interesting, very wounded, largely misunderstood and challenging. Prior to my psychotherapeutic training I had many years of involvement with yogic and Buddhist meditation. Dialectical Behavior Therapy (DBT)[28] with its conceptual mindfulness module made sense to me from the moment I encountered it in graduate school. But DBT did not help me feel more comfortable with the label borderline personality disorder (BPD). Somehow these 'awful borderlines' would turn out to be ordinary people suffering intensely.

Back then meditation was largely thought to be contra-indicated for 'borderlines.' Yet as an intern I offered 8-week groups combining the DBT skills curriculum with mindfulness meditation practices and chi gong exercises. Most participants found at least one of the featured meditation practices enjoyable, and all enthusiastically embraced chi gong. During the last class participants would evaluate the skills. The majority cited 'mindful pause & breathe' and chi gong as most helpful and DBT skills as useful.

Research shows that Buddhist-derived meditation practices involving slow deep breathing have a beneficial effect on vagal modulation of the heart[29] and stimulate the neural circuitry of emotion regulation.[30] Abundant research suggests that experienced mindfulness meditators are less affected by emotional stimuli. A 2013 study looked at whether this effect is largely due to emotional detachment. Mindfulness was actually associated with increased emotional engagement, more intimate contact with emotions and rapid recovery from distressing emotions.[31] Mindfully being with emotions is not only less sticky but an emotionally intimate experience.

By the time I entered private practice, my training had already expanded to include affective neurobiology, attachment theory and trauma therapy. John Briere's correlation of BPD and trauma symptomatology radically changed my approach.[32] Normalizing a patient's sudden emotional reactivity as a trauma response created the 'in' I needed to offer skills for remaining present and curious in moments of dysregulation. It also heightened patient awareness of how parasuicidal behaviors or substance use are triggered by the need to ameliorate trauma-related dysregulation.[33]

My training in Somatic Experiencing therapy (SE) allows me to offer patients access to somatically stored trauma memories. SE gently unwinds psychophysical systemic trauma in a titrated fashion and, by encouraging systemic coherence, actuates re-embodiment of the psyche. Years ago, after one of his lectures, I asked Peter Levine one-on-one whether mindfulness and SE were related. He replied, "SE is all about mindfulness; theirs [patients] and ours [therapists]."

Bipolar and Schizophrenia

Bipolar disorder affects 2% of population worldwide. Mania is said to progress in three stages: (1) hypomania—the presence of pleasant energetic and creative states; (2) increased self-absorbed, hyper-energetic states resulting in loss of judgment and impulse control and increased substance abuse (often for down-regulating manic states); and (3) onset of psychosis, grandiosity and disorganization. One manic episode predicts a 90% chance of subsequent manic, depressive or mixed-state episodes. Half of these people will attempt suicide if bipolar symptoms go untreated. Resistance to treatment is common among bipolar patients due to the preferability of hypomanic/manic states over normal/depressed states and the unpleasant side effects of mood-stabilizing medications.

Worldwide 1% of the population has schizophrenia—a constellation of hallucinations, delusions, breakdowns in the structure of thinking and agitated behaviors. Onset typically occurs in late adolescence, but only a minority will suffer with lifelong schizophrenic symptoms. Sadly, young children with schizophrenic symptoms have worse long-term outcomes. Schizophrenia has a 60% chance of being inherited genetically.

Much of what has been said about how trauma and inflammation contribute to depression, anxiety and emotional dysregulation seems to be equally true for psychotic disorders. This is not to imply that this is the sole source of psychosis. However, recall research cited above showing that environmental stressors increase the likelihood of switching on trauma-altered genes among those with inherited dispositions for psychosis and neurosis. Here is some of the latest research. Proinflammatory cytokines, including IL-6, play a prominent role in heightening levels of anxiety among bipolar patients.[34] Research suggests that levels of systemic inflammation are higher in manic episodes than during periods of relatively positive, non-depressed moods.[35] Migraine is often co-morbid with mood disorders, particularly in bipolar patients. The main culprit seems to be proinflammatory cytokines.[36]

Over the last 20 years research has targeted cytokine alterations in schizophrenia.[37] Schizophrenics with a history of childhood trauma have a proinflammatory phenotype with current stressors contributing to existing proinflammatory conditions.[38] Proinflammatory cytokines like IL-6 are acutely elevated during psychotic episodes and may actually be 'state markers.' Other cytokines remain elevated even after antipsychotic treatment and might be 'trait markers' for schizophrenia.[39] First-episode psychosis is also characterized by a proinflammatory state.[40]

Substance Use Problems

Substance use problems are often a method of self-medicating symptoms of schizophrenia, bipolar, depression, trauma and anxiety. Hopefully, we can agree that drugs and alcohol are a singularly ineffective method of relief in the long term, but we must acknowledge the short-term gains patients perceive when they turn to substances to fix, avoid or relieve suffering. Offering these patients healthy, effective strategies to alleviate distress and skills to heal underlying mental health issues is a critical part of long-term recovery and maintenance of sobriety or management of moderation.

Co-morbidity makes it a given that similar proinflammatory effects are present in substance use sufferers. I have yet to work with a patient gripped by a substance or food addiction who has not reported a trauma history. As discussed in Chapter 2, addiction has neurobiological antecedents in the reward circuitry of the brain. Persistent, uncontrollable early life stress negatively impacts (at a genetic level) dopamine transmission and neuroimmune signaling in the stress and reward pathways.[41] These epigenetic changes increase susceptibility for emotional distress and alter dopamine transmission, strengthening the propensity to develop substance use problems.[42] The stress associated with cycles of increased drug/alcohol cravings and negative withdrawal symptoms, coupled with tolerance, causes progression from substance use to dependence to addiction.[43] Stress has also been shown to play a central role in relapse following treatment.[44]

Abuse of prescription pain medications has become the number-one addiction problem in the US, and this class of drugs kills more people each year than any other substance. It is estimated that 90% of patients receiving treatment in pain centers are on opioids, which are uniquely addictive. Chronic pain patients are seldom told of the weak evidence for the long-term effectiveness of morphine and transdermal fentanyl in managing chronic pain, or about the lack of evidence for the effectiveness of all other controlled substances, especially oxycodone and hydrocodone, the two most commonly prescribed pain medications.[45] Few such patients know that proinflammatory cytokines promote and maintain inflammatory pain or that proinflammatory mediators are implicated in referred nerve pain.[46] All chronic pain patients should be offered integrative psychoimmunological treatment.

So what does all of this have to do with Buddhist psychology and its interventions? Everything. *The Buddhist toolbox is replete with contemplative tools for lessening inflammatory states and promoting positive brain changes.* Disorders deserve to be broken down into their component parts. Doing so reveals their common thread—afflictive mind states (*kleshas*). Deconstructing and healing harmful conditioned thoughts and emotions is like removing a massive obstruction with sustained intention and highly efficient tools. It may take some time, but a cleared path is assured. When one applies insights from Buddhist psychology and supporting neuroscientific findings, common mental health maladies can seem less intractable.

Studies show that reduced emotional reactivity is critical for those suffering from chronic inflammatory conditions. Mindfulness meditation appears to effectively reduce inflammatory symptoms and promote well-being.[47] In fMRI studies on novice and long-term Buddhist meditators comparing their responses to painful stimuli, the long-term meditators report equal pain intensity but less unpleasantness.[48]

Many years of research studies on Mindfulness-Based Stress Reduction (MBSR) have shown that mindfulness meditation definitively decreases stress. We now have evidence that mindfulness meditation lowers proinflammatory cytokines and increases anti-inflammatory cytokines.[49] Research also shows that mindfulness-based interventions like Mindfulness-Based Stress Reduction, Mindfulness-Based Cognitive Therapy (MBCT) and Mindfulness-Based Relapse Prevention (MBRP) improve mental health by increasing well-being and decreasing depressive/anxious symptoms and craving.[50] Positive outcomes correlate significantly with the number of days one has meditated.[51] Mindfulness-Based Cognitive Therapy for individuals with non-remitting bipolar disorder showed improved mood, greater emotional regulation and better daily functioning.[52] A meta-analysis of mindfulness interventions for serious mental illness shows "promise in reducing symptom-associated distress, increasing feelings of self-efficacy, and reducing psychiatric hospitalizations for individuals with psychotic disorders" (Davis, 2012).

Mental Proliferation: Its Calculations and Miscalculations (*Papañca-saññā-sankhā*)

At the center of what goes wrong cognitively in a mind overcome with depression and anxiety is an allied pair of bad actors: rumination and worry. Amplifying each other, they contribute to the longevity and intensity of symptoms. Worry has been shown to magnify both anxious and depressive symptoms, while rumination exacerbates depression by binding repetitive thoughts to negative beliefs and attitudes.[53] These findings support the Buddhist psychological hypothesis that mental suffering is a by-product of *papañca-saññā-sankhā (notions arising from conceptual proliferation).*

The mind retrieves information from the senses and facilitates concept formation through labeling, naming and meaning-making. These complex neural feedback loops of associative image and language processing are helped along by the willing participation of *mano-viññāna*, self-reflexive cognitive awareness or the feeling of 'I am.' The Buddha called this entire mentative process *conceptual proliferation* (P: *papañca* S: *prapañca* T: *spros bcas*).

Papañca-saññā-sankhā includes all mentative elaborations arising from *papañca* and its concepts (*paññatti*) about the self and the world. Mental proliferation arises from the psyche's conceptual formations (*saññā*) and underlying volitional formations or dispositional tendencies (*sankhāras*), which are rooted in *primordial ignorance* (*avidyā*). Rumination and worry—two aversive forms of *papañca*—arise from hatred and unwholesome conceptual formation. Each is nurtured and sustained by self-directed negativity.

Mindfulness has been shown to reduce chronic worrying and generalized anxiety.[54] Worry is mental time traveling to a dreaded, uncertain future. But when asked about uncertainty, chronic worriers usually speak with certainty of future danger or failure. That ideation of uncertainty runs counter to its total possibility. Uncertainty is "I don't know," not "I know it will be bad."

Rumination is passive, repetitive fixation on meaning, causes and consequences.[55] Rumination and depression have been shown to increase attentional fixation and decrease cognitive flexibility.[56] Imaging studies of depressed subjects show ruminative self-focus is associated with enhanced recruitment of limbic areas (emotion processing), and medial and dorsolateral prefrontal (self-referential processing) regions.[57] Research shows that self-reflection can lead to self-rumination and confirms that self-rumination does not lead to self-reflection.[58]

Papañca *and Stress*

Rumination and worry also diminish stress coping. According to Stress and Coping Theory[59] perceived capacity to cope with stress is largely determined by accurate assessment of control over outcomes, which in turn predicts effective problem solving. Worry and its fallacious scenarios of failure undermine accurate assessment of self-capacity. Rumination's withdrawal into a mind-made world of obsessive thoughts causes disengagement from problem solving, which lowers a person's perception of their ability to cope effectively with stress and increases depressive/anxious symptoms.[60] Negative cognitive content and rumination heighten vulnerability to stressful events and predict continued depressive symptoms.[61] Stress-reactive rumination coupled with negative self-referential thoughts also predicts the potential onset, number and duration of major depressive episodes.[62]

Mind Wandering and Rumination

Another common form of *papañca* occurs when the mind spontaneously wanders away from active engagement in the external environment and becomes passively involved in internal mentation. Mind wandering is the brain's 'default-mode' of functioning: a baseline state to which it returns when focus on the external world is relaxed. We spend about half of our daily lives wandering into passive spontaneous, task-unrelated thoughts about the past or the future.[63] This is accomplished by a grouping of brain regions called the default mode-network (DMN).[64]

Mind wandering is interrupted when we become aware of having shifted away from the external environment. The ability to note shifts in consciousness is called *meta-awareness*. Although mind wandering happens spontaneously, research has shown that in daily life, periods of mind wandering are mostly characterized by unhappy moods and mentation on past-related events. Subjects reported they were happiest when the mind was engaged in activity and not wandering.[65]

Spontaneous mind wandering can devolve into recursive self-focused thinking, especially for those who may be habituated to negative mind states. Major depressive disorder (MDD) is linked to excessive activation of the DMN and Area 25 (implicated in depression and the modulation of emotional behavior). In research studies with MDD sufferers, mind wandering occurs most prominently in rest periods between mental tasks, during which subjects report ruminative, negative self-referential thinking.[66] Other studies found MDD subjects fail to down-regulate default-network regions involved in monitoring of internal emotional states, self-referential processing and rumination.[67] Mind wandering may further strengthen the habit of destructive mental proliferation by exacerbating pre-existing high levels of neuroticism (a stable tendency toward negativity). Studies show experienced mindfulness and compassion meditators exhibit decreased activity in the DMN, consistent with decreased mind wandering.[68]

Normalizing Papañca

Papañca is the result of the conditioned mind's craving and clinging. *Papañca* represents a spectrum of sticky mentation from musing to rumination to obsession. Think of the last time you rehashed a disagreement by imagining better outcomes or smarter comebacks, or craved what no longer was, obsessively remembering something or someone you loved and lost, possessions or status once enjoyed. *Papañca*'s mental proliferations may offer momentary relief from disappointments or may feed anger and vindication, but in the long run it keeps us from the liberation of resting in what is. Recognizing *papañca* helps us work with its cognitive distortions and afflictive mind states.

Narrative Focus: Recognizing the Inner Story

C: I get irritated when I think about how I can't go out and play sports like I used to. Then I feel awful about myself because I am irritated, and that increases my irritation. That can make me angry and kind of mean.

LDM: *Yes . . . feeling bad about ourselves makes everything worse. Let's try that again. See what happens this time when you are noticing thoughts of not being able to play sports, if you just let yourself get curious about what happens next.*

C: That time when I watched the irritation, I didn't have thoughts of being bad. Instead, I felt a little sad about not being able to play sports. But that made me remember back when I was so much sicker and really sad because I was missing everything! And that felt even worse because I was not even thinking about the little bit of sadness anymore, just remembering the huge sadness I used to feel.

LDM: *Isn't that amazing how we can get so caught up in memories of old pain and lose contact with our here-and-now emotions, which may be so much less painful?*

C: Yeah, that sucks . . . so what do I do?

LDM: *This time, if you sense sadness, be kinder toward it. . . . Don't hate it; don't try to make it go away. It's hard to not be able to do something you love. That's a loss. . . . Okay, just rest in observing the experience of sadness with kindness toward sadness and see what happens.*

C: Well, that time I felt sad, but when I told myself it was okay to feel sad, it wasn't so bad. I was just sad. I didn't think about the past either. And then I realized I felt more relaxed. Not happy, but sort of at ease.

This vignette illustrates two powerful internal hindrances to well-being that arise in response to distressful sensations, thoughts and emotions: (1) negative self-narrative and (2) associative neural-linking to past distress. These mental activities give rise to secondary afflictive mind states (*kleshas*) that obstruct one's capacity to remain present with actual phenomena.

The Second Arrow

> *When an uninstructed person is touched by a painful (bodily) feeling, one worries and grieves, weeps and is distraught. One thus experiences two kinds of feelings, a bodily and a mental feeling. It is as if one were pierced by an arrow and, following the first piercing, is hit by a second arrow. So that person will experience feelings caused by two arrows. . . . Having been touched by that painful feeling, one resists (and resents) it. Then one who so resists (and resents) that painful feeling [is overtaken by] an underlying tendency toward [mental] aversion.* (The Buddha in Bodhi, 2000)

The Buddha describes two forms of cognitive processing: experiential and narrative. The first arrow is the direct experience of actual pain. The second arrow is the conditioned-arising of derivative narratives about actual pain. *For Buddhist psychology the first piercing is pain; the second piercing is suffering.* This is not a semantic distinction. It is an attempt at accurately depicting the automaticity of the conditioned mind with its proliferation of secondary distressful thoughts and emotions about painful experience.

To be as clear as possible: *feeling painful sensation is not an afflictive mind state.* The *suttas* show the Buddha years after his enlightenment mentioning feelings of exhaustion or back pain. He had a human body that was subject to physical laws. Freedom from suffering does not mean the end of bodily pain. It signifies the mind's freedom from mental fixation on distressful narratives about pain.

The same could be said of painful emotions. They arise and we feel them. Aversion to painful emotions causes fixation on similar past hurts, negative self-narratives of doubt and brokenness, or withdrawal behaviors. Emotions come and go of their own accord. Their permanence is an illusion created by inner resistance to experiencing their impermanent nature.

Narrative focus reduces attention to temporally present incoming sensory objects. This is due to the recruitment of midline prefrontal cortices (ventral and dorsal medial prefrontal cortex [mPFC], implicated in conceptual self-representation), left hemisphere language areas (left inferior frontal gyrus, middle temporal gyrus) and the hippocampus (consolidation of memory).[69] These brain areas link subjective experiences over time, supporting a form of self-awareness that feels like an enduring autobiographical experiencer.

For many people that is an ongoing inner self-story of ineptitude and failure. Imaging studies of depressed patients show self-referential processing of negative stimuli activates the mPFC, the posterior cingulate cortex (PCC) and the anterior cingulate cortex (ACC), with levels of activation correlating to depressive symptom severity.[70] Other research highlights the PCC as the source of the awful feeling of clenching that accompanies negative self-narratives. "We just did a replication of our study with double the numbers of subjects and again the PCC was implicated more than the mPFC. When the PCC gets out of the way, the mPFC can do its job of conducting the orchestra" (Brewer, 2013).

The Inner Narration That Is Untrue and Self-Destructive

Genuine mental health depends on one's ability to mindfully recognize habitual, inaccurate internal representations. Distorted mentation is composed of compounded, conditioned, negative, fearful or doubt-filled appraisals about the self and the world. Many of us are ruled by these false appraisals, which dictate actions, responses to life and relationships, and most especially self-ideation. Negative self-narratives—personifying as the one who most hates us—interject false self-narratives into every experience and turn them into more proof of innate vileness. Call it rumination, fixation, negative cognition or negative appraisal: at their core these conditioned, habitual, afflictive mind states (*kleshas*) arise from *primordial ignorance* (*avidyā*).

Vileness and brokenness are not our true nature. Every human being is innately good, kind and eminently worthy of compassion and respect. When we awaken to the truth of non-delusion, *primordial wisdom* (*vidyā*) is known. Buddhist psychology asserts an innate human impulse to see beyond the imperfections of conditioned suffering. That impulse is *awakened presence.* Available in any moment of turning away from the inner narration of experience, it is an allowing of phenomena to present themselves in their actuality.

 Experiential Focus: Being With The Actuality of Experience

Nothing is set in stone. You have the power to transform your own suffering through purposeful neural plasticity.

> I woke up about 3:00 am with a fast heart rate and thoughts of impending doom. As I became aware of my breath and the bodily feeling of anxiety, I realized I wasn't clinging to the experience of anxiety, trying to end it or diagnose the source of my pounding heart. I was just relaxing into the experience of anxiety. My mind was with the reality of my bed, the warmth and comfort of being in the dark. No threat, no danger, just seeing mind for what it was—a channel of flowing information. Reality was in my body. I felt a distance from the anxiety that was so compelling and clear. The thoughts of sudden death, impending doom, things I had done wrong, cycled through. But I stayed with them, and they felt like just racing thoughts. Then I returned awareness to my body, my refuge. The last thought I had before I fell asleep was . . . "this must have been what Lisa meant. . . . I get it!" I still get chills thinking about the experience. It now seems it takes less energy and focus to explore anxiety. It isn't about burying anxiety, trying to forget in order to function. But rather seeing it for what it is. (Patient experience, 2012)

Experiential focus (EF) is a deliberate opening to the natural flow of sensory stimuli, body sensations, thoughts and emotions, during which self-referencing is momentary and contextually integrated within an ever-shifting continuum of experience. EF promotes a reflexive awareness that naturally shifts mentation away from sticky self-narratives about experience. This happens through deactivation of the PCC[71] and the dorsal and ventral mPFCs. EF defuses emotional reactivity (decreased activity in the left dorsal amygdala)[72] while increasing cognitive control (dorsal and ventrolateral PFCs), visceral responses (posterior insular cortex, somatosensory cortex) and attention (inferior parietal lobule).[73]

Experiential attending to internal phenomena like thoughts or emotions gives rise to a metacognitive awareness that causes *decentering*—described as "the capacity to take a present-focused, nonjudgmental stance in regard to thoughts and feelings" (Teasdale, 2002). Decentering leads to *reperceiving* emotions and thoughts as 'object' rather than 'subject'; that is, "happiness feels like this," instead of "I am happy."[74] EF opens us to the immediacy of phenomena from the perspective of an embodied mind, vividly present in subjectless experience. This fundamental shift is the ultimate goal of all Buddhist meditation practices.

Benefits for the Body

Feeling physical pain is as much about our conceptions and emotional responses to pain as it is about the presence of painful sensation. People who suffer with chronic pain, nerve pain, fibromyalgia and inflammatory diseases often conclude that embodiment is a prison rather than a gift. A recent meta-analysis of 16 trials studying the use of mindfulness-based interventions for chronic pain found significant reduction in pain intensity compared to control groups.[75] Anam Thubten Rinpoche teaches that harsh, negative, fearful thoughts are like knots constricting the psyche. These cognitive-affective knots contribute to physical and energetic contraction in the body, causing the musculature to freeze with fear and aversion.

EF is the first step in learning how to cultivate an awakened, embodied mind that rests easily in what is. EF helps us discriminate the *first arrow* (physical and emotional pain) from the *second arrow* (mental and emotional suffering). Mindfulness-Based Cognitive Therapy has been shown to substantially reduce symptoms of fibromyalgia and depression, even though the actual decrease in pain intensity was slight.[76] Reflexively attending to painful stimuli helps us remain present with physical and emotional pain because inner narration is always more catastrophic than actuality.

 Practices to Develop Presence in the Here and Now

The goal of the following set of practices is to retrain an inner-obsessed, experientially absent mind to participate in the body's experience of the world. Some may appeal more to you than others. Some may be more useful for your particular situation. I suggest you try them all at least once, because each has its own specific value and effect. Together, this set of practices will introduce you to the basic skills needed to move on to more demanding Buddhist meditation practices.

Orienting

Orienting naturally and effortlessly embodies the mind in somatic experience. Because the body knows no apparent separation between it and its world, the mind rejoices when it is grounded in the body's here-and-now experience. Try this practice in your daily life whenever you remember to do so. You don't need to change your body position. As a skill, Orienting is particularly helpful when we feel stressed, emotionally overwhelmed, anxious, panicky, depressed, agitated, lost in rumination or bored. This is an instantly gratifying, "I need help right now!" skill for reducing body-mind inflammation.

Put the book down and let your eyes roam freely around the environment in which you find yourself. Don't try to force your eyes to move, and don't hold them anywhere either. Let them move at their own pace and allow yourself to see the objects before you. Don't strain with seeing; just hold an intention to notice what the eyes see. This should feel natural and easy. You are letting your mind be where the body already is. If the eyes land on something interesting or beautiful, let that happen. Enjoy the wholesome feelings that beauty and interest evoke in your body and mind. But don't let the eyes fixate on objects. That only serves to shift attention inward to concepts about objects. That is not Orienting. If this occurs, let the eyes resume roaming and seeing. At some point open awareness to your mind/body state. Chances are your body will be more relaxed, and your mind will be clearer and less agitated. The practice of Orienting is simple, easy and doable any moment you feel lost in distressful states of mind or body.

Just Hearing

Believe it or not, your senses are doorways to peace and calm. The richness and complexity of sensory experience go largely unnoticed and underappreciated. The wonder of truly hearing a bird call or a car going by cannot be underestimated. Just Hearing is the best way to reengage with phenomena without the mind's habitual labeling of experience. This practice is a bit more meditative than Orienting, but it is informal enough to be done wherever you are, especially while waiting or feeling bored.

If you feel comfortable closing your eyes, let that happen. Otherwise, let the eyes rest easily in a downward direction, not looking at anything in particular. Now let your awareness open to sound. Be like an antenna opening to whatever sounds occur, not rejecting nor holding to any sound in particular. You may notice the mind labeling sounds: 'car,' 'heating system,' 'voices.' If you notice labeling, just let the mind be drawn once again to sound—the actual visceral experience of sounds. Become interested in all elements of sound: pitch, movement, intensity and complexity. Notice how sounds come and go. Notice the silence between sounds. Let your awareness rest in sound and the way sounds happen on their own. Your mind needn't do anything but open and receive sounds as they arise, exist and pass away.

Resting in Physical Sensations

This skill can be a bit more challenging, but it has great value for lessening physical suffering. Be gentle with yourself as you engage with this practice.

Forcing is not helpful for the mind or the body. Being a martyr or hero/heroine is not the objective. Recognizing, softening, opening and resting are the intentions I invite you to bring to this practice. Benefits will arise naturally from wise, kind attending to physical sensations. Your mind has a built-in capacity to feel the body from within the body. This is called interoception. However, most of us don't intentionally cultivate this ability. Many of my patients are fearful of feeling the body, because they think it will increase their pain. Instead, exactly the opposite occurs. You will also get to directly experience your narratives about pain by doing this practice. As the Buddha often said, don't take my word for it, but try and see for yourself. This practice is a must for long meditation retreats where we sit in meditation for many days, many hours each day, sometimes with very sore knees, neck or shoulders.

Find a comfortable position, whether sitting or lying down, and make sure you are warm. The goal is to care for yourself. Let your eyes close or rest them easily in a downward direction, softening your gaze, not looking at anything in particular. Open your awareness to the body; note any tension or strain in the muscles, chest or back. Don't try to fix any tension you might find; just notice it. Now let your attention be drawn to a neutral body part, any area that feels as though it is just there. This might take a minute of scanning the body. Once you have found a neutral body part, allow awareness to become interested in what neutral feels like. Gently draw attention into the experience of the body part from the inside. If your eyes are open, don't gaze at the body part. That detracts from feeling the body from within the body. Really take some time and let your mind become intimate with neutral sensation—not wonderful, not awful, just there. If you realize your mind has wandered to thoughts, just return your attention to the neutral body part. Now open your awareness to the whole body, and notice whether any areas that were previously tense have loosened a bit. Note that and the feeling tone of that recognition.

Now let your attention be drawn to a mildly difficult body sensation. Do not choose your most painful body part. This might take a minute of scanning the body to find a sensation that is mildly distressful. Once you have found it, become interested in the sensation itself. You may notice the narrative about the sensation, thoughts like "I don't like pain," "why is this pain happening?" or "how can I make it go away?" That is the suffering we bring to physically distressing experience. It is important to let yourself become aware of its arising. However, when you notice the narrative, gently bring your attention back into the experience of that body part. Get interested in the sensations that make up what you probably label 'pain,' but do not use the label of pain or hurting. Notice movement, intensity and fluctuation. Note how mildly distressful sensations are comprised of interesting physical phenomena like heat, pulsation or tingling, none of which are pain. Let awareness rest in whatever sensations you experience. Don't resist or accept them. Let them be as they are, noticing how recognizing and letting be shifts the actual sensation and your perception of sensation. Any time you need to, you can return awareness to the neutral body part and rest there for a while.

When you feel ready, open your awareness to the whole body and the quality of mind. Notice any lessening of distress or greater mental and emotional ease. Eventually you can use this process with body sensations that are increasingly more difficult. End this practice by lying down for 5–10 minutes.

Noting the Feeling Tone of Experience: Pleasant, Unpleasant and Neutral

The first Mindfulness-Based Relapse Prevention class features the infamous raisin exercise. Although mindfully eating a raisin can be revelatory, few participants ask for more raisins. So I immediately repeat the exercise using chocolate, because the pleasure of eating chocolate is quickly replaced by a craving for more and aversion to the lack of more.

Noting the feeling tone of experience clarifies the difference between craving and *mentation about craving*. It also helps us discern how emotions positively or negatively affect perception and action. This exercise can be done in the midst of an enjoyable, difficult or neutral experience. If you become overwhelmed during the exercise, practice Orienting to ease your distress.

You are in the midst of an enjoyable experience: listening to a favorite piece of music, walking in beautiful natural surroundings or spending time with a person you enjoy. Notice the feeling in your body. Is it relaxed, excited or joyful? Do you notice wanting more? Turn your attention to the quality of mind. Is it at ease or dreading the end of pleasure? Note what the feeling tone of these experiences is and whether they lead to clinging to the continuance of enjoyable experience.

You are in the midst of a difficult experience: taking a test, struggling to finish a project, having a difficult conversation, grieving a loss, enduring distressful physical sensations, feeling anxious about the future or ruminating about the past. Notice the feeling in your body. Is it tense, tight, collapsed, withdrawn or tired? Do you notice aversive sensations? Turn your attention to the quality of mind. Is it exhausted, tight, dissociated, foggy, overwrought, fearful or angry? Note what the feeling tone of these experiences is and whether they lead to clinging to the ending of difficult experience.

You are in the midst of a neutral experience: hanging out, doing a daily task, walking or driving somewhere. Notice the feeling in your body. Is it at ease or tight, energetic or listless? Turn your attention to the quality of mind. Is it even-toned, uninvolved, impatient or bored? Note what the feeling tone of these experiences is and whether you feel the need to change or fix neutral experience.

Notes

1 Thubten, A. (2011, August 7). Unpublished lecture presented at the Dharmata Foundation, Richmond Point, CA.

2 McEwen, B. S. (2011). Effects of stress on the developing brain. *Cerebrum*. September–October 2011 (14), 1–8.

3 Lazarus, R., & Folkman, S. (1984). *Stress, appraisal, and coping*. New York, NY: Springer.

4 Chrousos, G. P. (2009). Stress and disorders of the stress system. *Nature Reviews Endocrinology, 5*(7), 374–381.
McEwen, B. S. (2009). The brain is the central organ of stress and adaptation. *Neuroimage, 47*(3), 911.
Kyrou, I., Chrousos, G. P., & Tsigos, C. (2006). Stress, visceral obesity, and metabolic complications. *Annals of the New York Academy of Sciences, 1083*(1), 77–110.
Cohen, S., Janicki-Deverts, D., Doyle, W. J., Miller, G. E., Frank, E., Rabin, B. S., & Turner, R. B. (2012). Chronic stress, glucocorticoid receptor resistance, inflammation, and disease risk. *Proceedings of the National Academy of Sciences, 109*(16), 5995–5999.

5 Sullivan, R. M., & Holman, P. J. (2010). Transitions in sensitive period attachment learning in infancy: The role of corticosterone. *Neuroscience & Biobehavioral Reviews, 34*(6), 835–844.

6 Belsky, J. (2006). Early child care and early child development: Major findings of the NICHD study of early child care. *European Journal of Developmental Psychology, 3*(1), 95–110.

7 Tomalski, P., & Johnson, M. H. (2010). The effects of early adversity on the adult and developing brain. *Current Opinion in Psychiatry, 23*(3), 233.
Stith, S. M., Liu, T., Davies, L. C., Boykin, E. L., Alder, M. C., Harris, J. M., . . . & Dees, J. (2009). Risk factors in child maltreatment: A meta-analytic review of the literature. *Aggression and Violent Behavior, 14*(1), 13–29.

8 Hinshaw, S. (2010). *Origins of the human mind*. Chantilly, VA: The Teaching Company. p. 53.

9 Ford, J. D., Gagnon, K., Connor, D. F., & Pearson, G. (2011). History of interpersonal violence, abuse, and nonvictimization trauma and severity of psychiatric symptoms among children in outpatient psychiatric treatment. *Journal of Interpersonal Violence, 26*(16), 3316–3337.

10 Lewis, D. O., Shanok, S. S., Pincus, J. H., & Glaser, G. H. (1979). Violent juvenile delinquents: Psychiatric, neurological, psychological, and abuse factors. *Journal of the American Academy of Child Psychiatry, 18*(2), 307–319.
Belsky, J. (1993). Etiology of child maltreatment: A developmental ecological analysis. *Psychological Bulletin, 114*(3), 413.

11 Sarchiapone, M., Carli, V., Cuomo, C., Marchetti, M., & Roy, A. (2009). Association between childhood trauma and aggression in male prisoners. *Psychiatry Research, 165*(1), 187–192.

Cuomo, C., Sarchiapone, M., Di Giannantonio, M., Mancini, M., & Roy, A. (2008). Aggression, impulsivity, personality traits, and childhood trauma of prisoners with substance abuse and addiction. *The American Journal of Drug and Alcohol Abuse, 34*(3), 339–345.

12 Sweatt, J. D. (2009). Experience-dependent epigenetic modifications in the central nervous system. *Biological Psychiatry, 65*, 191–197.

Zovkic, I. B., & Sweatt, J. D. (2012). Epigenetic mechanisms in learned fear: Implications for PTSD. *Neuropsychopharmacology. 38*(1), 77–93.

13 Van der Kolk, B. A., Perry, J. C., & Herman, J. L. (1991). Childhood origins of self-destructive behavior. *American Journal of Psychiatry, 148*(12), 1665–1671.

14 Briere, J., & Jordan, C. E. (2009). Childhood maltreatment, intervening variables, and adult psychological difficulties in women: An overview. *Trauma, Violence, & Abuse, 10*(4), 375–388.

Burns, E. E., Jackson, J. L., & Harding, H. G. (2010). Child maltreatment, emotion regulation, and posttraumatic stress: The impact of emotional abuse. *Journal of Aggression, Maltreatment & Trauma, 19*(8), 801–819.

15 Felitti, V. J., & Anda, R. F. (2010). The relationship of adverse childhood experiences to adult medical disease, psychiatric disorders and sexual behavior: Implications for healthcare. In Lanius, R. A. ,Vermetten, E., Pain, C. (Eds.), *The hidden epidemic: The impact of early life trauma on health and disease*, 77–87.

16 Anda, R. F., Brown, D. W., Dube, S. R., Bremner, J. D., Felitti, V. J., & Giles, W. H. (2008). Adverse childhood experiences and chronic obstructive pulmonary disease in adults. *American Journal of Preventive Medicine. 34*(5), 396–403.

Brown, D. W., Anda, R. F., Tiemeier, H., Felitti, V. J., Edwards, V. J., Croft, J. B., & Giles, W. H. (2009). Adverse childhood experiences and the risk of premature mortality. *American Journal of Preventive Medicine, 37*(5), 389.

Miller, A. H., Maletic, V., & Raison, C. L. (2009). Inflammation and its discontents: The role of cytokines in the pathophysiology of major depression. *Biological Psychiatry, 65*(9), 732–741.

17 Anda, R. F., Croft, J. B., Felitti, V. J., Nordenberg, D., Giles, W. H., Williamson, D. F., & Giovino, G. A. (1999). Adverse childhood experiences and smoking during adolescence and adulthood. *JAMA: The Journal of the American Medical Association, 282*(17), 1652–1658.

Dube, S. R., Felitti, V. J., Dong, M., Chapman, D. P., Giles, W. H., & Anda, R. F. (2003). Childhood abuse, neglect, and household dysfunction and the risk of illicit drug use: The adverse childhood experiences study. *Pediatrics, 111*(3), 564–572.

18 Rao, U., Chen, L. A., Bidesi, A. S., Shad, M. U., Thomas, M. A., & Hammen, C. L. (2010). Hippocampal changes associated with early-life adversity and vulnerability to depression. *Biological Psychiatry, 67*(4), 357–364.

19 Tata, D. A., & Anderson, B. J. (2010). The effects of chronic glucocorticoid exposure on dendritic length, synapse numbers and glial volume in animal models: Implications for hippocampal volume reductions in depression. *Physiology & Behavior, 99*(2), 186–193.

20 Milaneschi, Y., Bandinelli, S., Penninx, B. W., Vogelzangs, N., Corsi, A. M., Lauretani, F., . . . & Ferrucci, L. (2010). Depressive symptoms and inflammation increase in a prospective study of older adults: A protective effect of a healthy (Mediterranean-style) diet. *Molecular Psychiatry, 16*(6), 589–590.

Simon, N. M., McNamara, K., Chow, C. W., Maser, R. S., Papakostas, G. I., Pollack, M. H., . . . & Wong, K. K. (2008). A detailed examination of cytokine abnormalities in major depressive disorder. *European Neuropsychopharmacology, 18*(3), 230–233.

21 Laudano, M., & Bhakta, D. (2010). Vitamin D status and its association with depression in US women; results from the National Health and Nutrition Examination Survey (NHANES) 2005–6. *Proceedings of the Nutrition Society, 69*(OCE6) E460.

22 Fournier, J. C., DeRubeis, R. J., Hollon, S. D., Dimidjian, S., Amsterdam, J. D., Shelton, R. C., & Fawcett, J. (2010). Antidepressant drug effects and depression severity. *JAMA: The Journal of the American Medical Association, 303*(1), 47–53.

23 Porges, S. W. (2011). *The polyvagal theory: Neurophysiological foundations of emotions, attachment, communication, and self-regulation*. New York, NY: Norton.

24 Porges, S. W. (2007). The polyvagal perspective. *Biological Psychology, 74*(2), 116–143.

25 Porges, S. W. (2003). The polyvagal theory: Phylogenetic contributions to social behavior. *Physiology & Behavior, 79*(3), 503–513.

26 Kok, B. E., & Fredrickson, B. L. (2010). Upward spirals of the heart: Autonomic flexibility, as indexed by vagal tone, reciprocally and prospectively predicts positive emotions and social connectedness. *Biological Psychology, 85*(3), 432–436.

Oveis, C., Cohen, A. B., Gruber, J., Shiota, M. N., Haidt, J., & Keltner, D. (2009). Resting respiratory sinus arrhythmia is associated with tonic positive emotionality. *Emotion, 9*(2), 265–270.

El-Sheikh, M., Harger, J. A., & Whitson, S. M. (2001). Exposure to interparental conflict and children's adjustment and physical health: The moderating role of vagal tone. *Child Development, 72*(6), 1617–1636.

27 Austin, M. A., Riniolo, T. C., & Porges, S. W. (2007). Borderline personality disorder and emotion regulation: Insights from the polyvagal theory. *Brain and Cognition, 65*(1), 69.

28 Linehan, M. M. (1993). *Cognitive-behavioral treatment of borderline personality disorder*. New York, NY: Guilford Press.

29 Appelhans, B. M., & Luecken, L. J. (2006). Heart rate variability as an index of regulated emotional responding. *Review of General Psychology, 10*(3), 229.

30 Ditto, B., Eclache, M., & Goldman, N. (2006). Short-term autonomic and cardiovascular effects of mindfulness body scan meditation. *Annals of Behavioral Medicine 32*(3), 227–234.

Gillespie, S. M., Mitchell, I. J., Fisher, D., & Beech, A. R. (2012). Treating disturbed emotional regulation in sexual offenders: The potential applications of mindful self-regulation and controlled breathing techniques. *Aggression and Violent Behavior, 17*(4), 333–343.

31 Greenberg, J., & Meiran, N. (2013). Is mindfulness meditation associated with "feeling less?" *Mindfulness, 4*(1), 1–6.

32 Briere, J., & Scott, C. (2006). *Principles of trauma therapy: A guide to symptoms, evaluation, and treatment*. Thousand Oaks, CA: Sage Publications.

Briere, J., Kaltman, S., & Green, B. L. (2008). Accumulated childhood trauma and symptom complexity. *Journal of Traumatic Stress, 21*, 223–226.

33 Briere, J. (2000a). *Inventory of Altered Self Capacities (IASC)*. Odessa, FL: Psychological Assessment Resources.

Van der Kolk, B. A., Pelcovitz, D., Roth, S., & Mandel, F. S. (1996). Dissociation, somatization, and affect dysregulation: The complexity of adaption to trauma. *American Journal of Psychiatry, 153*(Supplement), 83–93.

Sansone, R. A., Songer, D. A., & Miller, K. A. (2005). Childhood abuse, mental healthcare utilization, self-harm behavior, and multiple psychiatric diagnoses among inpatients with and without a borderline diagnosis. *Comprehensive Psychiatry, 46*, 117–120.

34 Fang, S., Soczynska, J., Woldeyohannes, H., & McIntyre, R. (2012). The association between comorbid anxiety disorders and pro-inflammatory cytokine levels in individuals with bipolar disorder. *University of Toronto Journal of Undergraduate Life Sciences, 6*(1). Retrieved January 5, 2013 from http://juls.library.utoronto.ca/index.php/juls/article/view/15773

35 Brietzke, E., Stertz, L., Fernandes, B.S., Kauer-Sant'Anna, M., Mascarenhas, M., Escosteguy Vargas, A., . . . & Kapczinski, F. (2009). Comparison of cytokine levels in depressed, manic and euthymic patients with bipolar disorder. *Journal of Affective Disorders, 116*(3), 214–217.
36 Brietzke, E., Mansur, R.B., Grassi-Oliveira, R., Soczynska, J.K., & McIntyre, R.S. (2012). Inflammatory cytokines as an underlying mechanism of the comorbidity between bipolar disorder and migraine. *Medical Hypotheses. 78*(5), 601–605.
37 Erbagci, A.B., Herken, H., Koyluoglu, O., Yilmaz, N., & Tarakcioglu, M. (2001). Serum IL-1beta, sIL-2R, IL-6, IL-8 and TNF-alpha in schizophrenic patients, relation with symptomatology and responsiveness to risperidone treatment. *Mediators of Inflammation, 10*, 109–115.
Zhang, X.Y., Zhou, D.F., Zhang, P.Y., Wu, G.Y., Cao, L.Y., & Shen, Y.C. (2002). Elevated interleukin-2, interleukin-6 and interleukin-8 serum levels in neuroleptic-free schizophrenia: Association with psychopathology. *Schizophrenia Research, 57*, 247–258.
38 Dennison, U., McKernan, D., Cryan, J., & Dinan, T. (2012). Schizophrenia patients with a history of childhood trauma have a proinflammatory phenotype. *Psychological Medicine, 42*(9), 1865.
39 Miller, B.J., Buckley, P., Seabolt, W., Mellor, A., & Kirkpatrick, B. (2011). Meta-analysis of cytokine alterations in schizophrenia: Clinical status and antipsychotic effects. *Biological Psychiatry, 70*, 663–671.
40 Crespo-Facorro, B., Carrasco-Marin, E., Perez-Iglesias, R., Pelayo-Teran, J.M., Fernandez-Prieto, L., Leyva-Cobian, F., & Vazquez-Barquero, J.L. (2008). Interleukin-12 plasma levels in drug-naive patients with a first episode of psychosis: Effects of antipsychotic drugs. *Psychiatry Research, 158*, 206–216.
41 Olsen, C.M., Huang, Y., Goodwin, S., Ciobanu, D.C., Lu, L., Sutter, T.R., & Winder, D.G. (2008). Microarray analysis reveals distinctive signaling between the bed nucleus of the stria terminalis, nucleus accumbens, and dorsal striatum. *Physiological Genomics, 32*(3), 283–298.
Liu, D., Diorio, J., Tannenbaum, B., Caldji, C., Francis, D., Freedman, A., . . . & Meaney, M.J. (1997). Maternal care, hippocampal glucocorticoid receptors, and hypothalamic-pituitary-adrenal responses to stress. *Science, 277*(5332), 1659–1662.
Crews, F.T. (2011). Immune function genes, genetics, and the neurobiology of addiction. *Alcohol Research-Current Reviews, 34*(3), 355.
42 Sinha, R. (2009). Stress and addiction: A dynamic interplay of genes, environment and drug intake. *Biological Psychiatry, 66*(2), 100.
43 Sinha, R., Talih, M., Malison, R., Cooney, N., Anderson, G., & Kreek, M. (2003). Hypothalamic-pituitary-adrenal axis and sympatho-adreno-medullary responses during stress-induced and drug cue-induced cocaine craving states. *Psychopharmacology, 170*(1), 62–72.
44 Schwabe, L., Dickinson, A., & Wolf, O.T. (2011). Stress, habits, and drug addiction: A psychoneuroendocrinological perspective. *Experimental and Clinical Psychopharmacology, 19*(1), 53.
Noone, M., Jagdish, D., Markham, R. (1999). Stress, cognitive factors, and coping resources as predictors of relapse in alcoholics. *Addiction Behavior, 24*(5), 687–693.
45 Center, M.P. (2008). Effectiveness of opioids in the treatment of chronic non-cancer pain. *Pain Physician, 11*, S181–S200.
46 Schaible, H.G., von Banchet, G.S., Boettger, M.K., Bräuer, R., Gajda, M., Richter, F., . . . & Natura, G. (2010). The role of proinflammatory cytokines in the generation and maintenance of joint pain. *Annals of the New York Academy of Sciences, 1193*(1), 60–69.

O'Callaghan, J. P., & Miller, D. B. (2010). Spinal glia and chronic pain. *Metabolism, 59*, S21–S26.
Milligan, E. D., & Watkins, L. R. (2009). Pathological and protective roles of glia in chronic pain. *Nature Reviews Neuroscience, 10*(1), 23–36.

47 Rosenkranz, M. A., Davidson, R. J., MacCoon, D. G., Sheridan, J. F., Kalin, N. H., & Lutz, A. (2012). A comparison of mindfulness-based stress reduction and an active control in modulation of neurogenic inflammation. *Brain, Behavior, and Immunity, 27*, 174–184.

48 Lutz, A., McFarlin, D. R., Perlman, D. M., Salomons, T. V., & Davidson, R. J. (2012). Altered anterior insula activation during anticipation and experience of painful stimuli in expert meditators. *NeuroImage, 64*, 538–546.

49 Koh, K. B., Lee, Y. J., Beyn, K. M., Chu, S. H., Kim, D. M., & Seo, W. Y. (2012). Effects of high and low stress on proinflammatory and antiinflammatory cytokines. *Psychophysiology, 49*(9), 1290–1297.

50 Fjorback, L. O., Arendt, M., Ørnbøl, E., Fink, P., & Walach, H. (2011). Mindfulness-based stress reduction and mindfulness-based cognitive therapy—a systematic review of randomized controlled trials. *Acta Psychiatrica Scandinavica, 124*(2), 102–119.
Piet, J., & Hougaard, E. (2011). The effect of mindfulness-based cognitive therapy for prevention of relapse in recurrent major depressive disorder: A systematic review and meta-analysis. *Clinical Psychology Review, 31*(6), 1032–1040.
Witkiewitz, K., & Bowen, S. (2010). Depression, craving and substance use following a randomized trial of mindfulness-based relapse prevention. *Journal of Consulting and Clinical Psychology, 78*(3), 362.
Brewer, J. A., Bowen, S., Smith, J. T., Marlatt, G. A., & Potenza, M. N. (2010). Mindfulness-based treatments for co-occurring depression and substance use disorders: What can we learn from the brain? *Addiction, 105*(10), 1698–1706.

51 Perich, T., Manicavasagar, V., Mitchell, P. B., & Ball, J. R. (2013). The association between meditation practice and treatment outcome in mindfulness-based cognitive therapy for bipolar disorder. *Behaviour Research and Therapy, 51*(7), 338–343.

52 Deckersbach, T., Hölzel, B. K., Eisner, L. R., Stange, J. P., Peckham, A. D., Dougherty, D. D., . . . & Nierenberg, A. A. (2012). Mindfulness-based cognitive therapy for non-remitted patients with bipolar disorder. *CNS Neuroscience & Therapeutics, 18*(2), 133–141.

53 Ciesla, J. A., & Roberts, J. E. (2007). Rumination, negative cognition, and their interactive effects on depressed mood. *Emotion, 7*(3), 555.

54 Delgado, L. C., Guerra, P., Perakakis, P., Vera, M. N., Reyes del Paso, G., & Vila, J. (2010). Treating chronic worry: Psychological and physiological effects of a training programme based on mindfulness. *Behaviour Research and Therapy, 48*(9), 873–882.

55 Nolen-Hoeksema, S. (1991). Responses to depression and their effects on the duration of depressive episodes. *Journal of Abnormal Psychology, 100*, 569–582.

56 Joormann, J., Levens, S. M., & Gotlib, I. H. (2011). Sticky thoughts: Depression and rumination are associated with difficulties manipulating emotional material in working memory. *Psychological Science, 22*(8), 979–983.

57 Cooney, R. E., Joormann, J., Eugène, F., Dennis, E. L., & Gotlib, I. H. (2010). Neural correlates of rumination in depression. *Cognitive, Affective, & Behavioral Neuroscience, 10*(4), 470–478.

58 Takano, K., & Tanno, Y. (2009). Self-rumination, self-reflection, and depression: Self-rumination counteracts the adaptive effect of self-reflection. *Behaviour Research and Therapy, 47*(3), 260–264.

59 Lazarus, R. S., & Folkman, S., 1984.

60 Hong, R.Y. (2007). Worry and rumination: Differential associations with anxious and depressive symptoms and coping behavior. *Behaviour Research and Therapy, 45*(2), 277–290.

61 Ciesla, J.A., J.W. Felton, and J.E. Roberts. (2011). Testing the cognitive catalyst model of depression: Does rumination amplify the impact of cognitive diatheses in response to stress? *Cognition & Emotion, 25*(8), 1349–1357.

62 Robinson, M.S., & Alloy, L.B. (2003). Negative cognitive styles and stress-reactive rumination interact to predict depression: A prospective study. *Cognitive Therapy and Research, 27*(3), 275–291.

63 Andrews-Hanna, J.R., Reidler, J.S., Huang, C., & Buckner, R.L. (2010). Evidence for the default network's role in spontaneous cognition. *Journal of Neurophysiology, 104*(1), 322–335.
Levinson, D.B., Smallwood, J., & Davidson, R.J. (2012). The persistence of thought: Evidence for a role of working memory in the maintenance of task-unrelated thinking. *Psychological Science, 23*(4), 375–380.

64 Christoff, K., Gordon, A.M., Smallwood, J., Smith, R., & Schooler, J.W. (2009). Experience sampling during fMRI reveals default network and executive system contributions to mind wandering. *Proceedings of the National Academy of Sciences, 106*(21), 8719–8724.
Andrews-Hanna, J.R., Reidler, J.S., Sepulcre, J., Poulin, R., & Buckner, R.L. (2010). Functional-anatomic fractionation of the brain's default network. *Neuron, 65*(4), 550–562.

65 Killingsworth, M.A., & Gilbert, D.T. (2010). A wandering mind is an unhappy mind. *Science, 330*(6006), 932.
Smallwood, J., & O'Connor, R.C. (2011). Imprisoned by the past: Unhappy moods lead to a retrospective bias to mind wandering. *Cognition & Emotion, 25*(8), 1481–1490.

66 Berman, M.G., Peltier, S., Nee, D.E., Kross, E., Deldin, P.J., & Jonides, J. (2011). Depression, rumination and the default network. *Social Cognitive and Affective Neuroscience, 6*(5), 548–555.

67 Burg, J.M., & Michalak, J. (2011). The healthy quality of mindful breathing: Associations with rumination and depression. *Cognitive Therapy and Research, 35*(2), 179–185.

68 Brewer, J.A., Worhunsky, P.D., Gray, J.R., Tang, Y.Y., Weber, J., & Kober, H. (2011). Meditation experience is associated with differences in default mode network activity and connectivity. *Proceedings of the National Academy of Sciences, 108*(50), 20254–20259.

69 Farb, N.A., Segal, Z.V., & Anderson, A.K. (2012). Attentional modulation of primary interoceptive and exteroceptive cortices. *Cerebral Cortex. 23*(1), 114–126.

70 Yoshimura, S., Okamoto, Y., Onoda, K., Matsunaga, M., Ueda, K., & Suzuki, S. I. (2010). Rostral anterior cingulate cortex activity mediates the relationship between the depressive symptoms and the medial prefrontal cortex activity. *Journal of Affective Disorders, 122*(1), 76–85.

71 Brewer, J.A., Davis, J.H., & Goldstein, J. (2012). Why is it so hard to pay attention, or is it? Mindfulness, the factors of awakening and reward-based learning. *Mindfulness, 4*(1), 75–80.

72 Farb, N.A., Segal, Z.V., & Anderson, A.K., 2012.

73 Goldin, P., Ramel, W., & Gross, J. (2009). Mindfulness meditation training and self-referential processing in social anxiety disorder: Behavioral and neural effects. *Journal of Cognitive Psychotherapy, 23*(3), 242–257.

74 Fresco, D.M., Segal, Z.V., Buis, T., & Kennedy, S. (2007). Relationship of posttreatment decentering and cognitive reactivity to relapse in major depression. *Journal of Consulting and Clinical Psychology, 75*(3), 447.

75 Reiner, K., Tibi, L., & Lipsitz, J.D. (2012). Do mindfulness-based interventions reduce pain intensity? A critical review of the literature. *Pain Medicine, 14*(2), 230–242.
Salomons, T. V., & Kucyi, A. (2011). Does meditation reduce pain through a unique neural mechanism? *Journal of Neuroscience, 31*(36), 12705–12707.
Grossman, P., Tiefenthaler-Gilmer, U., Raysz, A., & Kesper, U. (2007). Mindfulness training as an intervention for fibromyalgia: Evidence of postintervention and 3-year follow-up benefits in well-being. *Psychotherapy and Psychosomatics, 76*(4), 226–233.

76 Parra-Delgado, M., & Latorre-Postigo, J.M. (2013). Effectiveness of mindfulness-based cognitive therapy in the treatment of fibromyalgia: A randomised trial. *Cognitive Therapy and Research, 37*(5), 1–12.

4

Know the Unconditioned Mind

For years S had endured a stinging internal narrative of self-loathing and self-doubt. Most occurrences were accompanied by intense gripping in the chest, which he called 'anxiety.' After we had worked together for a few months, its intensity and incidence had lessened. During a recent session, S expressed impatience with the negative narrative's ongoing presence and asked if I could help him face it head on. We decided to try three 60-second periods of opening to the field of mind and observing it directly, much the way one might watch a movie. After the first 60-second period, S reported observing distressing thoughts of self-doubt coming and going. But he also felt a slight release of tension in his chest. The second time, I asked him to observe mind and see if he could find any internal phenomena that lasted for the entire 60 seconds. S reported fewer negative thoughts, each coming and going pretty quickly. "*But there was an 'it,' a 'something' that was there, but more like nothing, in that it wasn't a thing like the tissue box.*" That time his body felt more relaxed, with no gripping in the chest. During the final 60-second session he experienced just a few thoughts way in the background with no negativity. "*The 'it' was an awareness that required no effort to maintain and was easy to rest in.*" After this experience S was excited to spend the week practicing this exercise.

Unconditioned mind is not an entity or a non-entity. Pure awareness, the groundless ground of being, is merely what remains when the obscurations of the conditioned mind are removed.

 Revisiting Consciousness and Awareness

Consciousness is the fact of anything showing up at all. (Thompson, 2013)

During a conversation about consciousness with a group of scientists, Jeff Hawkins, author of *On Intelligence*, proposed that "consciousness is simply what it feels like to have a cortex" (2004). While that may seem simplistic, there may be something to it. The cerebral cortex is the primary receiver and processor of sensory information. Its six layers and various lobes facilitate memory, perception, thought, language, conscious processes and most definitions of self.

But we are more than a cortex. Much of human functioning seems to be powered by vast networks of unconscious 'zombie' subroutines, all of which bypass conscious awareness. We don't have to think about how to breathe, digest, see, taste, smell, feel or hear. Once mastered, the mechanics of walking and speech become opaque to conscious processing.

Some neuroscientists envision higher-order consciousness emerging from a system of automated subroutines that have reached a level of complexity sufficient to necessitate a high-level manager to control and direct neural processes, enable neurnal communication and allocate brain–body resources.[1] This conscious overseer functions primarily on autopilot until something goes awry or, as neuroscientist David Eagleman puts it, "violates your expectations" (2012). It needn't matter whether the violation is biological and systemic or self-referential; higher-order, self-aware consciousness will take notice of stimuli and manage responses as needed. This occurs in the presence of *salience*—a state, object, sensation or event that stands out from the multitude of simultaneous mental events.

I had a visceral experience of subconscious processing during a recent visit with my mother. Upon my arrival, I entered her bedroom, where she was reading in her favorite chair. I took a seat on the bed opposite her, and we began to have a conversation. As we talked I noticed a feeling of agitation. Something in my peripheral vision was nagging at me. My eyes were drawn to an old painting my grandmother had made, which was hanging just to the left of Mom's chair. The painting looked wrong. It now featured a solid white shape in the bottom left-hand corner. Not only did the painting I was seeing not match previously stored images in my brain, but the white rectangle was impossibly located in a river! I watched my mind try to make sense of it, to no avail. Finally, I stood up and moved close enough to see that a photograph of my uncle's gravestone had been placed in the bottom left corner of the frame to honor his recent passing. Long before I became consciously aware of any actual discrepancy, my psychophysical system was struggling with the incongruities of reality and its internally stored images. I marveled at how simple clashes like this end up creating unnecessary feelings of distress.

Although unconscious and subconscious processes may include certain types of awareness, they are generally not thought to be consciousness, because neuroscientists define consciousness as *what it feels like to be something*.[2] This is *qualia*—the feeling of individual subjective experience.[3] If you and I were walking outside and a red sports car passed by, we would both know it is red (assuming neither of us is colorblind). But neither of us could know whether we are seeing the same 'red.' Neuroscience is far from solving the mystery of how mere brain function gives rise to subjective experiences like 'red.'

Another debatable question is whether subjectivity is a requirement for conscious experience. One can be conscious of blue but not have the thought, "I am seeing blue." Or one can attend to an object but not be consciously aware of its presence. Furthermore, consciousness does not require emotions—brain-injured patients can be conscious but unable to emote, and consciousness is independent of long-term episodic or autobiographical memory. Mostly, consciousness refers to *when one has access to awareness and the ability to report on experience.*

 Unconditioned Mind

Early Buddhist psychology does not mention unconscious processing; however, it becomes a topic of great interest in later Indian Buddhism. The Buddha taught that the six sense consciousnesses (five senses and mind) arise in concert with contact (*phassa*) of sense-bases and objects, all of which are conditioned by pre-existing ignorance (*avidyā*) and volitional dispositions (*sankhāra*). The Abhidharmic position is that "consciousness itself essentially consists in the activity of cognizing an object" (Bodhi, 2000).

The Abhidharma uses two terms for *object*: (1) *ārammana*, 'to delight in,' and (2) *ālambana*, 'to hang onto.'[4] The assertion is that objects arise from ignorance and that all perceptions (*saññā*) resulting from contact (*phassa*) with objects are conditioned by the mental suffering of craving (*tanhā*) and clinging (*upādāna*). Hence, they are *samsāric.*

Yet the Buddha made a clear distinction between *samsāra* (conditioned existence) and *nibbāna*, the cessation of the suffering of *samsāric* existence. Cessation (*nirodha*) is the subject of the Buddha's Third Noble Truth: "*This is the ceasing: the traceless fading away and cessation of that craving, the letting go and abandoning of it, freedom and independence from it*" (Batchelor, 2010).

Two phrases stand out in that translation: 'traceless fading away' and 'letting go and abandoning.' Traceless fading away does not refer to the cessation of wanting or aversion, both of which fall under the general meaning of *tanhā*. The arising of *tanhā* is part of daily existence. Conceptual efforts to let go or extreme asceticism will not end *tanhā* nor bring about liberation from adventitious suffering. What fades away without trace is clinging (*upādāna*) to the notion that desirous and aversive thoughts or feelings are solid, true and of the self. This wise knowing (*prajñā*) is the proximate cause of *nibbāna*.

Liberation is accomplished by an unconditioned (*asankhata*) mind freed from its own mental afflictions (*kilesa-parinibbāna*) and devoid of greed (*lobha*), hatred (*dosa*) and delusion (*moha*). Unconditioned mind is *empty* (*suññatā*)—it knows its interdependent nature; *signless* (*animitta*)—it has gone beyond the permanency of concepts and labels; and *desireless* (*apanihita*)—it is released from delusional, conditioned wanting. Remember these three qualities, for they constitute an excellent working definition of *awakened presence.*

Unconditioned mind is also defined by what it is not. A quick scan of the Pāli Canon yields the following descriptors: unborn, unformed, unaging, deathless, sorrowless, undiversified, uncreated, unoriginated. The un-ness of these terms leads one to inquire, when the mind has 'gone beyond' concepts, wanting and delusion, where does it arrive, and what, if anything, does it perceive?

After his enlightenment, the Buddha acknowledged the difficulty of conveying his realization of unconditioned mind: "This Dhamma I have realized is profound, hard to see and hard to understand, peaceful and sublime, unattainable by mere reason, subtle, to be experienced only by the wise" (SN, 6:1). Yet he managed to pull together an effective methodology for realizing unconditioned mind through wise contemplation, renunciation of false identification, and ethical/skillful means.

Wise contemplation affords visibility into the essential constituents of all phenomena. It shows us who we really are. Insight (*vipassanā*) requires a quiescent mind. If you toss a stone into a still lake, the ripples will be clearly visible. When the lake is turbulent, a single stone's effect is barely noticeable. The same is true of mind.

The Buddha employed two types of contemplative practice to develop stability of mind and discerning wisdom: *concentration* (P: *samatha* S: *shamatha* T: *zhi gnas*) and *insight* (P: *vipassanā* S: *vipashyana* T: *lhag mthong*). In the scientific literature, these forms of meditation are known as *Focused Attention* and *Open Monitoring.*

Concentration meditation (*samatha*) fosters *samādhi*—a tranquil, pliable mind. The Buddha chose Mindfulness of Breath (P: *ānāpānasati* S: *ānāpānasmrti*) meditation to develop *samādhi.* Detailed instructions for this practice are contained in the *Mindfulness of Breathing Sutta.* The Buddha's rich set of *vipassanā* instructions are featured in the *Four Foundations of Mindfulness Sutta* (P: *Satipatthāna Sutta* S: *Smrtyupasthāna Sutra*). These introspective practices develop clear comprehension (P: *sati-sampajañña* S: *smrti-samprajanya*) through careful attending—with mindfulness and discrimination (*sati-nepakka*)—to four fields of experience: body (*kāyā*), feelings (*vedanā*), mind/consciousness (*citta*) and mental contents (*dhammas*). Most clinical mindfulness meditations are derived from instructions contained in these two *suttas.*

Attention and Attending (P & S: *manasikāra* T: *yid la byed pa*)

William James thought that experience is that which we attend to. Wilhelm Maximilian Wundt (1832–1920), the first physician to call himself a psychologist, commenced Western psychology's study of attention by inventing a method to measure the time it takes to voluntarily shift attention from one stimulus to another. Since then, cognitive psychology and neuroscience have identified key types of attention and tracked their neural correlates.

Attention has three main functions—*alerting, orienting* and *executive functioning*—each with its own network of brain areas.[5] *Alerting* facilitates response readiness. Its felt sense is arousal, interest, or even vigilance, and it is sometimes characterized by clarity or brightness. The alerting network includes the dorsolateral prefrontal cortex and thalamus. *Orienting* facilitates stimulus-driven or goal-driven attentional shifts from or between internal and external phenomena. The orienting network includes the superior colliculus, frontal eye fields, temporoparietal junction, the insula and pulvinar. *Executive control* assists the making of deliberative choices with respect to the placement of attention. The executive control network includes the prefrontal cortex, anterior cingulate gyrus and supplementary motor area. *Executive control* enables *selective* or *top-down* attention to stimuli and voluntary sustained attention. Conversely, *bottom-up* attention occurs when we are involuntarily drawn away from chosen objects of attention. *Divided* attention is attending to more than one object at a time.

Psychotherapeutic Attention

All psychotherapeutic change is made possible by a therapist's attention to creating a regulated relational container of attunement to the patient's psychophysical presentation. A patient's words are just the tip of the iceberg. We must attend with purpose, curiosity and depth to all forms of human communication: body positioning, facial expression, voice tone, heart rate, eye movements, languaging, emotional states, cognitive material, attentional focus, schemas, schisms, opinions, needs, desires, fears.

Without attentional balance a clinician cannot effectively meet and co-regulate a patient's cognitive-affective-somatic dysregulation. Co-regulation emerges when dysregulation is met by an attentive, willing regulated mind and nervous system. As the patient continually taps into this flexible yet contained relational field, she or he will naturally strengthen and integrate their own psychophysical system's capacity for *coherence and containment.*[6]

Recollecting and Attentional Balance

Attention and memory go hand in hand. The word *smrti/sati* is most accurately translated as *recollecting*, not 'mindfulness.' To sustain attention to an object, one must remember that one is intending to remain with that object. When the mind inevitably wanders, recollecting reinvigorates the intention to return attention to a chosen object.

According to the Buddhist scholar Rupert Gethin, T. W. Rhys Davids seems to have been the first to translate *smrti/sati* as 'mindfulness' because he thought 'recollecting' did not fully describe the practical application of *smrti/sati.*[7]

> *Sati* has two characteristics (*lakkhana*): 'calling to mind' (*apilāpana*) and 'taking possession' (*upaganhana*). Thus *sati* is explained as calling to mind wholesome and unwholesome qualities such that the meditator is in a position to know which qualities are the ones he should pursue and which are the ones he should not. (Gethin, 2011)

Roshi Joan Halifax describes wise attention thus:

> To perceive in an unfiltered way the nature of suffering and also one's own responses to suffering requires attentional balance. This process of attention is characterized as sustaining, vivid, stable, and effortless; it is as well nonjudgmental, nonreactive, not contracting in relation to adversity, and nongrasping in terms of the desire for a particular outcome. (2012)

Mindfulness: Defining Our Terms

In 2010 psychologist and neuroscientist Richard J. Davidson wrote a commentary on the status of empirical measurement tools for mindfulness. The clarity and honesty he brought to the questions *what do researchers mean when they use the term 'mindfulness,' and how can it be accurately measured* are worth sharing.[8]

Mindfulness is measured as a trait, a state or an intervention. *Trait* mindfulness refers to one's disposition toward mindful attending. Mindful *states* vary in intensity and duration and can be strengthened using *interventions* such as mindfulness meditation practices or mindful movement. Measurements are accomplished with brain imaging tools (fMRI, PET or EKG) or self-report questionnaires, and are generally acquired before and after the application of an intervention. The efficacy of mindfulness meditation has been studied using novice (with hours or up to 8 weeks of meditation training) and long-term meditation practitioners (approximately 2,000 to 45,000 lifetime hours of practice) to accurately assess the impact of cumulative practice.

Dr. Davidson and Dr. Antoine Lutz have been at the forefront of fMRI research on cognitive-affective neural plastic changes found in long-term Tibetan Buddhist and *vipassanā* meditators. During meditation, very long-term practitioners show a remarkable ability to accurately report their mind states. However, the accuracy of first-person self-reports in novices and non-meditators remains an important unresolved issue in mindfulness research, particularly when research studies rely solely on self-report questionnaires and have no correlative third-person measures. Another important issue is how to accurately assess non-classtime practice (quality and sometimes quantity) in 8-week mindfulness-based groups. Additionally, there is the control group problem. What control practice is best to test against meditation, and how much of the positive effect is due to group interaction itself? Researchers are working diligently to resolve these questions and provide more reliable measures of mindfulness.

Focused Attention Meditation

Expertise in meditation requires *manasikāra*—harnessing and mastering attention. In Focused Attention meditation, the mind orients toward and sustains attention on an object. Recognizing that attention has wandered from the object stimulates recollecting (*smrti/sati*) and reinvigorates intention to refocus on the object. *Vitakka* is the impulse to aim the mind toward an object. *Vicāra* is the effort to sustain attention on an object. Applied with diligence, *vitakka* and *vicāra* bring about one-pointed attention (*ekaggatā*), the gateway to *samādhi*.

The more one meditates, the less time is spent generating negative, ruminative, worried mentation. Research shows that when the mind wanders during focused meditation, the self-narrative default mode network is activated. Realizing the mind has wandered and returning attention to the object of meditation recruits brain areas involved in salience and conflict monitoring. Periods of sustained attention primarily engage the dorsolateral prefrontal cortex.[9]

Studies reveal a strong relationship between long-term meditation practice and increased connectivity within and between attentional regions and medial prefrontal areas. This appears to be related to reduced mind wandering and greater sustained attention, a trait that 'spills over' into non-meditative rest periods.[10] Long-term meditators show greater functional connectivity and functional changes in regions related to internalized attention even when meditation is not being practiced.[11] Baseline and meditation-induced high frequency gamma wave brain activity is greatest in practitioners with more years of daily meditation practice. These practitioners showed greater limbic area receptivity to stimuli as well as enhanced global brain processing activity that seems to give rise to calm, yet alert, states of mind.[12]

David Vago, PhD, a psychology instructor and researcher at Harvard Medical School, focuses on delineating the neural mechanisms of *Focused Attention*, *Open Monitoring* and *Open Presence* meditation. He and David Silbersweig, MD, have created the *S-ART framework*: a theoretical and neurobiological model for how mindfulness meditation reduces self-bias and augments healthy mind states through increased *self-awareness, self-regulation and self-transcendence.*[13]

Of particular interest is how Focused Attention meditation modulates limbic reactivity.

> The right frontal polar cortex is a highly evolved area we don't know a lot about except that it is involved in stable forms of attention and awareness. This brain area lights up very brightly during the attentional practices in all meditators. But even more strongly with greater hours of practice (1000–10,000 hours). In psychopathologic disorders we see a relationship between the prefrontal cortex (PFC) and the limbic system. The PFC is a cool, cognitive control area. The limbic system quickly processes and affectively reacts to activating environmental stimuli. It forwards that information to the PFC, which cognitively evaluates and determines appropriate responses. The ventral-medial PFC (vmPFC) determines which affective responses need to be moderated. This relationship of evaluation and suppression is an area of difference in those suffering with depression, anxiety and PTSD. Their vmPFC has less capacity to regulate limbic affective responses. *Meditators are showing modulation in the limbic system*

> *without the need for evaluative suppression.* This is due to activation of the frontal polar cortex (dorsal anterior right) during the practice of concentration meditation. These are preliminary findings and we continue to look more deeply at how deep levels of concentration modulate limbic response. (Vago, 2013)

Another important benefit of Focused Attention breath meditation is its positive effect on vagal tone and heart rate variability, both of which are linked to increased emotional regulation and physical and psychosocial well-being. High vagal tone predicts greater feelings of connectedness and positive emotions.[14] A 4-week smoking cessation program featuring mindfulness meditation practices showed increases in high-frequency heart rate variability correlated with enhanced self-regulation and a decrease in cigarette use.[15]

 *Samatha*: The Gift of Stillness

I hope to inspire clinicians to develop a committed, positive relationship with daily meditation practice by offering *samatha* meditation in an undiluted form. It is misguided for a clinician to teach meditation to patients without being firmly established in the practice. Teach the practice properly, and the rest takes care of itself.

> *Are you quiet?*
> *Quieten your body.*
> *Quieten your mind.*
> *You want nothing.*
> *Your words are still.*
> *You are still.* (Byrom, 1976)

Development of tranquility (*samatha-bhāvanā*) is a gift like none other, one I offer patients with reverence for the psychophysical system's innate capacity to harness its own healing potential. *Samatha/shamatha* is the joy of a still body and calm mind. Take a moment to imagine your body still, your mind tranquil, and the beautiful possibilities this might engender. Now bring to mind a struggling patient or someone in your personal life who is suffering. Imagine that person filled with the joy of a calm body and mind, and the transformations that might result from such peacefulness. As I write this, streaming through my mind are memories of strained, hardened faces melting and relaxing into the joy of just being with the sweet sensation of breath.

Samatha begins with an aspiration for calm, remembering to slow down, relax and enjoy each breath. Aiming the mind at the breath and remaining with the breath maintains alertness in meditation. Effort is applied by remembering (*sati*) that breath (the *prāna*-body) is our aim. Once the actual physical sensation of breath is obtained, surrendering effortlessly into the breath stills the body and mind. The practice continues by balancing these steps as needed.

 *Ānāpānasati*: Cultivation of *Samatha* and *Vipassanā*

The *Ānāpānasati Sutta* contains a dual-purpose set of instructions for achieving quiescence (*samādhi*) and insight (*vipassanā*). It features 16 steps separated into four groups of four. Each group corresponds respectively to the four fields of experience featured in the *Satipatthāna Sutta*—body (*kāyā*), feelings (*vedanā*), mind/consciousness (*citta*) and mental contents (*dhammas*).

Years ago I received instruction in the *Ānāpānasati Sutta* from Santikaro, a monk and primary translator for Ajahn Buddhadasa, a revered Thai Buddhist teacher who wrote a definitive book on this *sutta*.[16] At the beginning of the retreat, Santikaro shared, "The word *vipassanā* appears rarely in the *suttas* and when it does it is most often paired with *samatha*. In these passages, the Buddha is speaking of a very high level of meditation that leads to knowing" (2008).

Mindfulness of Breath meditation is also a superior method to develop the Seven Factors of Awakening: mindfulness (*sati*), investigation (*dhamma vicaya*), energy (*viriyā*), rapture (*pīti*), serenity (*passaddhi*), concentration (*samādhi*) and equanimity (*upekkhā*). These qualities stimulate our motivation to practice and add juiciness to meditative experience. A recent inquiry with a patient illustrates how often people conflate assumptive ideas about breath with the actual physical experience of breath.

B: I kind of taught myself to meditate from books, and I've listened to a couple of CDs. I get so bored with the breath. My thoughts are just so much more fascinating that I end up giving in to them instead.

LDM: (smiling) *Yes, the mind can be very attracting! All those fascinating scenarios, ideas, narratives and images. Who would want to be with ordinary breath?*

B: Exactly! Breath is so ordinary and boring.

LDM: *Well, the ordinary is pretty extraordinary if we are willing to experience it devoid of our mental constructions about it.*

B: What do you mean? I experience breath when I think on breath?

LDM: *Yeah, that's the thing . . . Most people think about breath when they 'meditate on breath' instead of experiencing the physical activity of breathing.*

B: I don't see the difference. Thinking about something is the same as experiencing it.

LDM: *Pick an object in this room. Any object.* (We are not in my office.)

B: Okay . . . that notebook on the shelf.

LDM: *Which one?*

B: The one that says, "Codes and Stipulations."

LDM: *Can you describe what you see?*

B: It is a green notebook, and when I see "Codes and Stipulations" I get really angry because it reminds me of all the years I spent going though pages and pages of regulations for my job. I am sure that notebook is full of pages of grief!

LDM: *Did you notice how your mind constructed a story about that notebook based on your past history of dealing with regulations? And how it colored your experience of that object? How convinced you are that you know exactly what it is and that it is filled with pages and pages of grief?*

B: Well, what else could it be? That's the way they always are.

LDM: *Shall we look and see what is inside?*

B: Why not, I know what is going to be in there.

LDM: (I reach for the notebook. When I open it, there is one page with about six sentences.)

B: Wow . . . I wonder how much I do this with everything else in my life?

LDM: *Well if you are like most of us, probably a lot. We live in our assumptive narratives about experience, not in the actuality of experience. Are you now ready to be with the extraordinary ordinariness of your breath?*

B: Absolutely.

 Mindfulness of Breath Meditation (*Ānāpānasati*)

The first four steps of the *Ānāpānasati Sutta* constitute complete training in the basics of Mindfulness of Breath meditation. These steps foster nervous system and vagal system healing and offer valuable insights into cognitive-affective-behavioral functioning. Most important, the interrelationship of body and mind will become apparent to you. So welcome to the joy of an embodied mind! Stay with these initial four steps until you feel confident in the practice and then progress to subsequent groups.

Ānāpānasati *Group One: Knowing the* Prāna-*Body and Flesh-Body*

PRELIMINARY STEPS FOR SITTING MEDITATION

Good posture is very important. If you are sitting in a chair (preferably one with a straight back), place both feet flat on the floor. Whether you are sitting cross-legged on a zafu or in a chair, let your spine be long and upright but not stiff. Roll your shoulders up, back and down. Relax your arms slightly back and down. Feel as though you are a queen or king sitting regally on a throne. If you are on a zafu, make sure to soften your sitz bones and feel the spine rise up naturally from there. Rest your hands either folded in your lap or flat on your thighs or knees. Tuck your chin in slightly to ease any strain in the back of the neck. Let your eyes gaze diagonally down in front of you, and then soften your gaze, not looking at anything in particular. If your eyes feel the need to close, that is fine as well.

- Begin by setting an aspiration for a period of calm, joyful meditation.
- Generate a determination to meditate regardless of what arises during the practice.
- Wish *"May I be at ease and free from suffering."*
- Now let your awareness be drawn to the felt sense of sitting. Feel the weight of your torso resting on the hips and the actual physical sensation of that weight sinking into the cushion or chair. Let your awareness receive these sensations freely. They are happening without you making them happen. Let mind open to sensation as it is with curiosity and interest. Rest in this experience for a few moments.

Now turn your awareness to receive the actual physical sensation of your body breathing, *not what you think breath is like, but what is actually occurring in your body.* Notice the natural rhythm of your breath. There is no need to change the breath or make it anything other than what it is. Breathing happens all over the body; the *prāna-body* feeds every cell in the *flesh-body.*

For some it is easiest to experience the physical sensations of breath by resting awareness on the rising and falling of the chest—the chest rising on the in-breath and falling on the out-breath. For others the belly and abdomen are an easy place to experience breath—the belly filling on the in-breath and emptying on the out-breath. See which of these two body areas is easiest for you to directly experience the physical activity of breathing in. Investigate this for a few moments.

You may find mind drifting to thoughts, body sensations or feelings. When you notice this has occurred, remind yourself that breath is your aim and gently turn your attention back to the actual physical sensation of breathing. Finding attention away from breath and returning attention to breath can happen many times in a meditation period. This is how we mentally train in mindfulness. Over time, with more practice, your mind will gain stability and eventually one-pointedness. Try not to be frustrated or impatient with the wandering mind.

Step 1: Contemplation of Long Breathing

> *Breathing in long, one discerns, "I am breathing in long"; or breathing out long, one discerns, "I am breathing out long."*

After a few minutes of resting with the breath, the breath may have lengthened on its own. If so, continue to allow this lengthening to occur. If the breath has not lengthened naturally, experiment with inhaling and exhaling a bit more slowly, deeply yet easily. Let your chest and diaphragm relax and open with each inhale and exhale. Don't force anything to happen; in fact, long breaths are less about doing something and more about resting and receiving the naturalness of breathing. You may even notice a pause between the breaths. Just note that for now, but don't focus on it. As your breath lengthens, notice how long breaths affect the body. Is the body relaxing and calming down? Are long breaths pleasurable, or do they feel more refined? Also notice any resistance to being with longer breaths. Let yourself relax into whatever experience arises without generating self-doubt or self-blame. Take note of how long breathing influences the condition of the flesh-body. Investigate long breathing for some time.

Step 2: Contemplation of Short Breathing

> *Or breathing in short, one discerns, "I am breathing in short"; or breathing out short, one discerns, "I am breathing out short."*

Now experiment with short breathing. Any breath that feels short to you is short, so there is no need to strain yourself in short breathing. We are not trying to hyperventilate. Also, breathing high in the chest generally creates shorter shallower breaths than breathing in the lower abdomen. Be relaxed about this distinction between long and short. The difference will be apparent in the flesh-body's response to the *prāna*-body's shortness of breath. Let your awareness take in the physical effects of short breathing. Does the body become agitated or uncomfortable? Is the mind uneasy and less able to rest in short breaths than long breaths? Does short breath have a roughness or staccato-like feeling? Recognize the effect of short breaths on the body and mind. Experience short breathing for a few minutes.

Step 3: Experiencing the Whole Body

> *One trains, "I will breathe in sensitive to the entire body." One trains, "I will breathe out sensitive to the entire body."*

In this step, the aim of our mindfulness is to know the myriad manifestations of the *prāna*-body and the ways in which each of its forms conditions the flesh-body. Now let go of short breathing and allow the breath to find its own rhythm. If you let awareness be receptive the *prāna*-body will naturally regulate itself. In this step, we investigate with greater depth the myriad ways that breath manifests: long or short, even or choppy, refined or gross, soft and shallow or prominent and deep. Become interested in the physical body's response to each form of breath you experience, how the muscles move differently. Pay attention to tenseness, relaxation and openness. Notice what effect breath has on thoughts and emotions. Is mind calmer when breath is long, slow and at ease? Knowing the interrelatedness of breath and body increases our sensitivity to our organism, to what helps it function with greater ease, to conditions that create systemic upset and to the ways our breath can restore physical ease.

Step 4: Calming the Whole Body

> *One trains, "I will breathe in calming bodily fabrication." One trains, "I will breathe out calming bodily fabrication."*

This last step trains our capacity to calm the body with breathing. When we calm the breath, the body responds in kind; it relaxes, softens and opens. Here are two methods to calm the flow of *prāna* through the body. (1) Continue following the flow of breath by diligently aiming the mind at the actual physical sensation of breath. Once some stability of attention on the breath has been obtained, surrender into the experience of breathing. Vigilance and relaxed attention refine the breath and calm the body. (2) Let your attention be drawn to the actual physical sensation of the air flowing in and out of your nostrils. Aim the attention at the soft, cool feeling of air entering the nostrils and the slightly warmer air exiting the nostrils. As you do this, breath will naturally refine and slow. The body drops more deeply into relaxation. The key is to maintain awareness of the flow of air at the tip of the nostrils. As you practice this step, the distinction between breath, body and awareness will lessen, and your experience of the body may become very subtle.

Along with the calming of breath, body and mind, you may notice physical or emotional feelings of joy and bliss. Let these feelings come. Enjoy them, but do not dwell on them or get lost in holding onto them. Their arising is a sign that your attention is naturally stabilizing.

As the breath becomes the prominent feature of awareness, attention will naturally begin to collect and unify with the breath. This will eventually lead to a spontaneously occurring one-pointed concentration on breath to the exclusion of all other objects. This is known as *ekaggatā*. Whenever there is some quality of one-pointedness (*ekaggatā*) there is some form of quiescence (*samādhi*). Continue with this fourth step for at least 10 minutes or as long as you wish.

The Five Hindrances (*Pañca Nīvaranāni*)

Turning attention inward and becoming familiar with our inner world introduces us to many interesting and wonderful experiences as well as a host of obstacles, some of which will feel like old friends or foes and others which may surprise you. The Buddha singled out *Five Hindrances* that can thwart progress in contemplative practice. Meditation is the perfect laboratory to learn how to deal with and dissolve these common obstacles that often plague us in meditation *and* in daily life.

The first hindrance is the *longing* (*kāmachanda*) that accompanies feelings of pleasure and displeasure. During meditation we can experience all kinds of physical, mental and emotional phenomena—some pleasurable and some displeasurable. The human mind is conditioned to lose itself in enjoying/continuing pleasurable experience and ending/avoiding displeasurable experience. *The level of longing and agitation we bring to pleasure and displeasure determines whether these phenomena become hindrances.* The antidote for longing is to get curious about the phenomenology of pleasure or displeasure. Paying attention to the actual nature of wanting dissolves its power over us, because we directly perceive its effect on the mind and body. This is especially helpful when distressful memories intrude and hijack our meditation. Bringing kindness and curiosity to distressing thoughts and emotions lessens their grip.

The second hindrance is *anger* (*vyāpāda*), which includes irritation, frustration and impatience. Everyone who has tried meditation has at some point grappled with one or all of these emotions. What most hinders us is fixation on angry narratives directed toward others or ourselves. Sometimes meditation is filled with replaying distressful interactions from the past. *The antidote for anger is kindness: not rejecting anger as bad and not accepting anger as true.* When we embrace anger with warm-heartedness, it generally dissolves, revealing underlying feelings that may be more vulnerable. If this doesn't work we can remind ourselves of the destructive nature of anger and wish ourselves freedom from its suffering.

The third hindrance is *sloth and torpor* (*thīna-middha*). This hindrance is targeted at the arising of *dullness*, *laziness*, *ambivalence*, *malaise* and *boredom*. All of these feelings impede our efforts to cultivate the clarity and alertness necessary for establishing stability and one-pointed attention. Dullness is not serenity. The antidotes for this hindrance are interest and wakefulness. When we get curious about boredom, it is actually quite interesting. Practice with your eyes open or in a standing position, or become even more interested in the physical movement of breath. A note: In this age of sleep deficits, exhaustion can show up when we first start a meditation practice, especially with the Mindfulness of Breath meditation, which is so relaxing for the body. Sometimes, during the first few months of regular practice, falling asleep in meditation is exactly what the body needs to recover from years of sleep deficit. We don't want to encourage sleepiness, but we also don't need to struggle against it.

The fourth hindrance is *restlessness* (*uddhacca-kukkucca*), usually arising along with mental, emotional or physical agitation. A busy, scattered mind or nervous, agitated body is an obstacle to attending to breath. There is a difference between the energetic feeling of interest and the activation of psychophysical or systemic agitation. Interest collects the mind, and agitation scatters the mind. The antidotes for restlessness range from closing the eyes and letting the attention be a bit more vigilant in its aiming to settling into sensations of the body breathing. Or if you really feel agitated in your body, you can get up and attend to your breath while taking 10–15 steps in one direction, turning around and walking back to your starting point. Continuing in this fashion is a particular style of walking meditation done while maintaining attention on the breath.

The fifth hindrance, *doubt* (*vicikicchā*), is probably the most self-destructive and insidious. So much suffering is fueled by self-doubt. In meditation, doubt shows up as lack of confidence in the practice: doubting our ability to do the practice correctly (even if we are) or dismissing actual signs of progress. Our need for instant gratification and demand for perfection in all things cause much of the doubt that plagues beginning and experienced meditators alike. Doubt can become a slippery slope to not practicing at all. The antidote for doubt is generating faith in your commitment to practice and recognizing it as suffering. This clear knowing will avert its influence. Appreciating the fact that you are willing to engage in your own healing helps to avert doubt about your efforts. Put doubt in its place, and don't let it rule your meditation or your life.

Ānāpānasati *Group Two: Working With* Vedanā: Pīti *and* Sukha

I specifically chose Mindfulness of Breath meditation because it naturally arouses positive tranquil states without relying on cognitive restructuring or reevaluation strategies. Attending to breath naturally stimulates interest, tranquility and joy. One needn't believe that meditation will bring contentment; it just happens because innate bliss is the inherent nature of mind and body.

Direct experience of this truth can radically transform people who have spent years gripped in pain, fearfulness and unhappiness.

Breath meditation (particularly if you are attending to breath at the nostrils) also stimulates movement of the *prāna*-body's subtle energy. This energy is *pīti* (S: *kundalini* T: *gtummo*), and it manifests in waves of mild to intense feelings of bliss felt throughout the psychophysical system. When *pīti*'s waves diminish, as all excitational states invariably do, what lingers is a sweet, soft residue called *sukha* (T: *bde ba*), which feels blissful in a distinctly different way. Unlike *pīti*, *sukha*'s serene joyfulness has a quieting influence on the breath, body and mind. It is a happiness that does not come from stimulation.

Knowing Pleasure and Displeasure From the Inside

Pleasure is a double-edged sword. Clinging to good feelings leads to as much suffering as does trying to avert distressful feelings. These next four steps are all about gaining intimacy with the ways body and mind respond to wanting and pleasure. Steps 5 and 6 use *pīti* and *sukha* as objects for insight into *vedanā—the feeling tone of experience*. At first, one is invited to let go in *pīti*'s excitatory states and *sukha*'s joyful serenity. The pleasurable nature of *pīti* makes it a prime candidate for working with *tanhā* and *upādāna*, the mind's tendency to crave and cling to pleasure. Attending to *sukha*'s subtler feelings of contentment and peacefulness demonstrates the benefits of applying restraint. In steps 7 and 8 we are invited to contemplate the types of mind states incited by *pīti* and *sukha*. The attentional balance of *samatha* gives us insight into how to work skillfully with *vedanā*.

These skills are equally useful for cultivating equanimity and tranquility when the mind and body are suffering from deeply distressing states.

> If a painful experience can be held without reactivity—without judgment, censorship, condemnation—with clarity, openness and compassion—the pain will not produce avoidance or aversion. . . . Pain will simply remain pain, pleasure simply remain pleasure, without the reactive approach-avoidance response. (Engler, 2003)

Knowing craving and aversion helps us regulate our responses to pleasurable and displeasurable experience. And this wisdom is transferable to daily life. Dr. Judson Brewer, a prominent researcher on the neurobiology of addiction and the creator of a successful smoking cessation program called *Mindfulness Training*, offered this wonderful description of how his patients use these skills with patients:

> We use an analogy of a hot coal. For instance, you smoke a cigarette when you are stressed out, but you don't realize that smoking a cigarette doesn't cure your stress, it just gives you cancer. You don't see clearly that smoking is like holding a hot coal that will burn you up. If you don't look closely you

> don't see that you are burning yourself. So mindfulness doesn't teach us to cognitively do something . . . it says, 'pay attention.' And when you see your hand is burning do you think about what to do? No. You just drop the hot coal. It's completely effortless. All you have to do is just pay attention. What we see when we really get our smokers to pay attention when they are smoking is they become disenchanted. They see it is a hot coal burning them and then all they have to do is pay attention, there is no effort beyond that. It's beautiful! (Brewer, 2013)

Clear seeing (*sati-sampajañña*) is the ultimate path to liberation from addictions. When patients directly engage with presence to the actual experience of wanting, whatever perceived benefit they cling to naturally falls away. Presence is clarity; clarity is undeluded; wisdom is healing; healing liberates us from the delusion that real pleasure can ever be derived from anything that causes harm.

Make sure to always begin by practicing steps 1–4, to achieve a mind that is calm, stable and unified with the breath.

Step 5: Ecstasy Is Not Peace

> *One trains, "I will breathe in sensitive to rapture." One trains, "I will breathe out sensitive to rapture."*

Allow the body and mind to calm and become collected by practicing the initial four steps of the Mindfulness of Breath meditation. During the fourth step you may notice the arising of joyful sensations in your body or blissful emotions. This is *pīti*. When *pīti* first arises it is important to not block its expression. Let it expand as you breathe in and out. Fully receive its pleasurable sensations and emotions, enjoying the flow of blissful energy filling the heart and moving throughout the body. Don't force it to come or increase. Just ride the waves of pleasurable sensation. Notice how *pīti* affects the *prāna*-body. Does breathing speed up or become rough? How does *pīti* condition the flesh-body? When *pīti* is rising, is the body agitated, excited or tight? Does it feel tired when the sensations decrease? Get to know how pleasurable sensations nourish or impair the body.

Step 6: Soothing Joy

> *One trains, "I will breathe in sensitive to pleasure." One trains, "I will breathe out sensitive to pleasure."*

Now become interested in the sensations and emotions that exist when the intensity of *pīti* naturally decreases. Notice how the flesh-body softens and relaxes. You may find the *prāna*-body quieting down as the awareness begins to rest in *sukha*, a gentler form of joy. Once you are aware of *sukha*, let it become the main object of your attention. See if you can remain present with the flow of breath while resting awareness in subtle joy. Mindfully investigate *sukha*'s conditioning influence on the breath and body.

Step 7: Knowing Mental Elaboration

> *One trains, "I will breathe in sensitive to mental fabrication." One trains, "I will breathe out sensitive to mental fabrication."*

Now that you have investigated the effects of *pīti* and *sukha* on the breath and body, mindfully examine their impact on mind. What types of thoughts does *pīti* incite? Does mind become fixated on wanting more pleasure? Do you notice feelings of disappointment as it diminishes? Is *pīti* exciting or agitating for the mind? What mind states arise in the presence of *sukha*? Does *sukha* have a refining influence on thoughts and emotions? Seeing the interdependence of feelings, energy and clarity of mind helps us meet *vedanā* on our own terms. Knowing *vedanā* empowers us to cultivate wholesome feelings and abate unwholesome feelings.

Step 8: Calming Elaboration With Vigilant Mindfulness

> *One trains, "I will breathe in, thereby calming mental fabrication." One trains, "I will breathe out, thereby calming mental fabrication."*

However enjoyable, *pīti* distracts us from achieving *samādhi*. Although the joy of *sukha* is certainly peaceful, it is not the unconditioned peace of *nibbāna*. Both are impermanent, conditioned phenomena that ultimately disquiet the mind.

This final step refocuses our intention on developing quiescence and insight through mindfulness of breath. Pleasure is an impediment to *samādhi*. One can accomplish this step by vigilantly attending to the breath rather than giving oneself over to feelings of rapture and joy. Or one can rely on insights gained while investigating *vedanā*—its impermanent nature and impairing effects—and let go of wanting. These techniques are equally useful when one is gripped by negative feelings like doubt, hate, fear, anger and impatience. Knowing the impermanent nature of distressful feelings lessens their potency and helps us return to the object of our meditation.

Ānāpānasati *Group Three: Working With Mind* (Citta*)*

This is the point where the *Ānāpānasati Sutta* invites contemplation of *citta* (mind/consciousness; T: *tsi ta*). One might assume that psychotherapeutic professionals would be particularly skilled at knowing mind, its states and its traits. Yet many clinicians are not interested in learning about mental processes. Some avoid tending to their own internal suffering. It is difficult for me to imagine how one can offer insight into healing a suffering mind if one refuses to know one's own mental and emotional suffering . . . and do the hard *and* beautiful work of relieving that suffering.

These next four steps are designed to show us that mind is not the enemy; mind is merely mired in suffering. "There are many characteristics of mind to contemplate.... We observe their characteristics as they actually exist, in the very moment of their existence" (Buddhadasa, 1988). We can make friends with any mind state—all our dispositions, habits of mind, every thought and feeling state, especially those we blindly follow or purposely avoid. Aligning intention with interest, awareness, kindness and insight, and paying close attention to the field of mind and its contents expose the three roots (*greed, hatred and delusion*) and their afflictions.

The Buddhist teacher Phillip Moffitt envisions an awakened mind as one that is "free of greed, hatred, and delusion in this moment and also with no possibility of it arising—this mind is free of [psychological] tension about causes and conditions which may arouse any of those three" (Moffitt, 2012). The mind's unconditioned nature spontaneously reveals itself in any moment when mind is free of greed, hatred and delusion.

Step 9 is practical and concrete but profoundly insightful and liberating. I recommend practicing this step regularly and even including it toward the end of any meditation session. Steps 10–12 may appear more abstract, but as you engage with them, the vivid pliability of a concentrated mind will excite your interest in its usefulness for recognizing the true nature of reality. Make sure to always begin by practicing steps 1–4, to achieve a mind that is calm, stable and unified with the breath. If you have time, I recommend practicing all 12 steps in succession at least a few times a week.

Step 9: Obstructed or Unobstructed Mind?

> *One trains, "I will breathe in sensitive to the mind." One trains, "I will breathe out sensitive to the mind.*

Anytime during this step you can anchor your attention to the breath when needed. Now let your attention be drawn to the field of mind. Notice how the continually shifting landscape of thoughts and emotions colors the mind. Do not let yourself become fixated on thoughts and their co-emergent feelings. Instead, use attention to shine a spotlight on thoughts and emotions. Observe their influence on the quality of mind. Noticing content helps us recognize how *greed, hatred and delusion* afflict the mind. For instance, "This is boring. I'd rather be working, exercising or watching TV." That thought is rooted in greed and hatred: craving to fix or end the experience and aversion to what is occurring. Or, "This scares me. What am I going to find out about myself?" That fearful thought is rooted in delusion about the true nature of self and its narratives. How is mind when it is obstructed by greed, hatred and delusion? Do certain thoughts contract, agitate or distract mind? Attending to mind states with interest cultivates insight (*vipassanā*) into which of the three roots reside at the source of any afflictive mind state. Recognizing the root source of thoughts loosens the fixation on content. Should you notice moments when mind is absent of thought, observe the unobstructed mind. Know the momentary freedom from greed, hatred and delusion as *nibbāna here and now*. Engage with this step as long as you wish.

Step 10: Goodness of Mind

> *One trains, "I will breathe in satisfying the mind." One trains, "I will breathe out satisfying the mind."*

Return awareness to the breath with relaxed attentiveness. Let mind re-collect and unify on the physical flow of breath. As you rest in the breath, notice any increasing clarity of mind: any clarity that is visibly sharper, brighter or more satisfying than usual. When you experience vivid clarity, note its influence on mind. Is there a sense of mind becoming more exalted (*mahaggatatā*)? Contemplate while breathing in and out whether increased clarity constitutes a superior mind.

Step 11: The Stable, Pure, Able Mind

> *One trains, "I will breathe in steadying the mind." One trains, "I will breathe out steadying the mind."*

Is the presence of vividness increasing concentration in the mind? Let yourself enjoy mind's impulse toward greater levels of concentration. As concentration naturally increases, contemplate whether this calm, stable mind is ready to be used for greater insight. Is this the mind of *samādhi*? Contemplate while breathing in and out whether this stable, pure, able mind is unsurpassable.

Step 12: Liberated Mind

> *One trains, "I will breathe in releasing the mind." One trains, "I will breathe out releasing the mind."*

Now contemplate whether this vivid, concentrated mind is free of grasping or whether it still clings to anything. Contemplate while breathing in and out the mind's lingering impulses and fixations. Notice and release them as they arise. Allow impulses and fixations to liberate in the natural rhythm of dissolution.

Not-Self (P: *anattā* S: *anātman*), Part 1: The Phenomenological Self

Western psychology has championed and elevated the self with an unbending commitment to the belief that ego strengthening is *the* remedy for psychic distress. While this view has not been detrimental, the bias toward individual exceptionalism has undermined psychology's usefulness in ending societal discord.

Another problem with the self-psychological approach is that it pathologizes a person's awareness of profound philosophical truths like emptiness, a knowing that not only runs counter to ego clinging but more accurately reflects the neurobiological view of self. Existential psychology realized this conundrum and abandoned the project of becoming a 'substantive self' by envisioning psychological healing as a process of ego/self-transcendence, a bold shift in a psychological culture with an unflinching attention to self-regard and self-esteem.

The Genesis of an 'I'

Modern neuroscience tells us that self is more process than entity and has no fixed location. No matter how much it feels as though there is a little 'you' that lives behind your eyes and directs this show you call 'your' life, it simply is not true. For the self is merely a collection of interdependent co-arisen phenomena that together create an illusion of permanent self-existence. Exactly how does this happen?

Neuroscientist Antonio Damasio speculates that all life forms—from the simplest organism to the most complex psychophysical system—have a primitive *proto-self.* Its purpose is to generate enough primordial feelings to enable a life form to seek out and fulfill its basic biological needs. In humans this proto-self autonomically directs basic life functions and the sensory perceptual apparatus.

If we revisit the theory of *Dependent Origination*, the first two links, *ignorance* and *dispositional formations*, would certainly inform the proto-self's operational frame. Imagine the first two links as (1) the human psychophysical system and (2) the specific genetic legacy of any particular human. The proto-self's cognitional functions would approximately correlate to the following group of *Dependent Origination* links: consciousness → mind/matter → sense-bases → contact → feeling → wanting.

Damasio then posits emergence of an intermediary *core self* to process the proto-self's affective and somatic responses. The core self consolidates this information into a primitive mental narrative about the proto-self's response-relationship to objects. "The core self is created by linking the modified proto-self to the object that caused the modification, an object that has now been hallmarked by feeling and enhanced by attention" (Damasio, 2010).

It seems to me that Damasio's core self may constitute the earliest impulse of 'I' and 'mine,' making it analogous to Buddhist psychology's *manas*, the source of the basic narrative of a solid 'I.'

> mind includes images regarding a simple and very common sequence of events: an object engaged the body when that object was looked at, touched, or heard, from a specific perspective; the engagement caused the body to change; the presence of the object was felt, the object was made salient. The nonverbal narrative of such perpetually occurring events spontaneously portrays in the mind the fact that there is a protagonist to whom certain events are happening, that protagonist being the material me. . . . [That] connects the actions being produced by the organism to that same protagonist, and, along with the feeling generated by engaging with the object, engenders a sense of ownership. (Damasio, 2010)

Therefore, at any given moment, the core self, or *manas*, is little more than a biologically engineered sense of ownership emerging from a series of mental images (*saññã*) representing an organism and its responses to objects.

The Illusion of an Enduring Self

But we still have to account for our conscious experience of an existent self continuing uninterruptedly in the midst of impermanent phenomena. From an evolutionary perspective, our species has a fundamental need to feel ownership and continuance in order to ensure the survival of our offspring, to whom we must attach. We are tribal animals. Our concept of belonging requires distinguishing between in and out groups, a basic form of social subject/object dualism. So while there appear to be good evolutionary reasons for developing false egoic concepts of permanence, they also have a downside.

Neurobiologically, our felt sense of continuance comes from the *autobiographical self* repeatedly reconstructing and replaying the *core self*'s lived experience through unconscious processing or conscious reflection. "*The self comes to mind in the form of images, relentlessly telling a story of such engagements*" (Damasio, 2010).

Returning once again to *Dependent Origination*, we have now arrived at *becoming*: conscious identification with the autobiographical self's narrative of experience. Each replay is another instance of *taking birth* by rearranging and modifying 'memorized facts' that create new emotional saliences. These consolidate higher-order conscious experience of a permanent, solid self with a full-blown personality.

Interestingly, the coordination of perceived and recalled images is assisted by the brain's default network, strongly implicated in narrative self-focus processes of mind wandering, rumination and worry.[17] So, in a way, the Buddha was right to insist that mentally generated resistance to the realities of *samsāric* existence (*old age, sickness and death*) is the downside of grasping at the delusion of a permanent, unchanging self.

We can now conjecture that self arises from a primitive collection of deductions leading to false conceptions of ownership and continuance, designed to facilitate cognitive-affective stabilization and organization, in an apparent, impermanent, self-aware organism. I speculate that the egoic self may have evolved to shield us from direct contact with uncertainty and impermanence.

 Recognizing the Knower and the Known

Although the self dictates a dualistic reality that appears to separate the knower from the known, from the first instance of contact our perceptual apparatus simultaneously joins with sensory phenomena and receives them through pre-conditioned filters. So it is interesting to contemplate what it might be like to join with and experience sensory phenomena through an unconditioned perceptual apparatus.

In the *Udana Sutta*, the Buddha taught Bahia the Wanderer how to use mindfulness to directly receive the phenomenal actuality of experience: "*You should train yourself thus: In reference to the seen, there will be only the seen. In reference to the heard, only the heard. In reference to the sensed, only the sensed. In reference to the cognized, only the cognized*" (1:10).

Let's use Mindfulness of Breath meditation (*ānāpānasati*) as an example. The breath is experienced both internally and externally. In the sound of breath, there is only the whoosh of air. In the rising of the chest, there is only the movement of muscles, tissue and ribs. The true task of mindfulness of breath is to receive these phenomena as directly as possible devoid of mental imagery, thoughts, autobiographical associations and affective colorings.

Similarly, thoughts and emotions arise in response to received perceptual information. But thoughts and emotions are both generated by and a part of a complex process we call 'mind,' which includes a 'self' that is deluded about its own nature and highly prone to misperceiving reality. This 'self' experiences thoughts and emotions as its own creations and maintains an unshakable belief in their solidity and truthfulness (I am angry, I am sad, I am happy, I am smart, I am confused). This is precisely why destructive mentation creates so much personal and collective suffering.

On the other hand, when we practice mindfulness, the mind can observe the arising, existing and passing away of thoughts and emotions and even contemplate their form and nature. Mindfully observing thoughts and emotions exposes their temporal, transparent nature.

The Buddha continued his teaching to Bahia the Wanderer:

> *When for you there will be only the seen in reference to the seen, only the heard in reference to the heard, only the sensed in reference to the sensed, only the cognized in reference to the cognized, then, Bāhiya, there is no you in connection with that. When there is no you in connection with that, there is no you there. When there is no you there, you are neither here nor yonder nor between the two. This, just this, is the end of suffering.* (UD 1:10)

This kind of direct knowing is another working definition of *awakened presence*. Not only does awakened presence liberate phenomena from self-concepts, but it also uncouples awareness and constructed self-conception. Uncoupled awareness of the phenomenological 'self' is *not-self* (*anattā*). This self-less *awakened presence*, just this, is the end of *samsāric* suffering.

Ānāpānasati *Group Four: Knowing Truth (*Dhamma*)*

These final four steps of the Mindfulness of Breath meditation open us to *dhammic* truth. Throughout the prior 12 steps *ānāpānasati* has required varying degrees of effortful attention to increase the clarity and stability of mind. By this point in the practice it should be evident that the more unified mind is with breath, the less effort it takes to maintain stable attention on breath. In these last four steps mindfulness will naturally expand to include the entire landscape of internal and external phenomena. This form of meditation is known as *Open Monitoring* or *shamatha without support*. This meditation promotes inquiry about impermanence and non-clinging.

Steps 13–15 promote the acquisition of meta-awareness (*bare awareness*) as a vehicle for ascertaining impermanence and its consequent insights of non-clinging and cessation. Step 16 is a contemplation of *not-self* (*anattā/anātman*), the final fruition of the practice.

Make sure to precede this group by practicing steps 1–4 until your mind is calm, stable and unified with the breath. When you get to this stage in the practice, I highly recommend executing all 16 steps, at least a few times a week, to experience the full blossoming of *ānāpānasati* as the Buddha intended.

Step 13: The Truth of Impermanence

One trains oneself, "I will breathe in focusing on impermanence." One trains oneself, "I will breathe out focusing on impermanence."

With a concentrated and vivid mind, practice bare awareness of phenomena: their actual arising, existing and passing away. Breath is a marvelous object for inquiry on impermanence. Every breath has a beginning, middle and end. The clarity and stability of *samādhi* facilitate reception of breath devoid of assumptions, mentation or clinging to any aspect of the experience. Practice bare awareness of the breath beginning in the body: the upwelling impulse to breathe, the satisfaction of taking air in and its effortless movement throughout the body. Rest with bare awareness in the pause between inhale and exhale. Continue with bare awareness of the impulse to expel breath. Note the body's release as air moves out of the lungs and nose. Maintain bare awareness during the pause between breaths. There is nothing to hold on to and nothing to create. Breath comes and goes on its own. It is ever-changing like all internal and external phenomena—sounds, sights, objects, beings, thoughts, emotions, opinions, cravings and aversions—which effortlessly arise and cease of their own accord. Rest wakefully with bare awareness in the shifting sea of impermanent phenomena.

Step 14: The Truth of Non-clinging

One trains oneself, "I will breathe in focusing on dispassion [literally, fading]." One trains oneself, "I will breathe out focusing on dispassion."

When we know the impermanence of all things, clinging fades away. True insight into impermanence stimulates the end of grasping. The old reality of wanting and aversion, needing and fearing, fades away. The truth of transparency and uncertainty inspires us to set aside false dependencies. Recall people, objects or events that once held you with an unstoppable passion and have since lost their appeal. Contemplate that fading of importance, the dispassion you now experience. This will reveal the truth of non-clinging.

Step 15: The Truth of Quenching

One trains oneself, "I will breathe in focusing on cessation." One trains oneself, "I will breathe out focusing on cessation."

In the absence of clinging to permanence, knowing manifests as inner stillness. This is *quenching*: a total lack of the agitation accompanying wantings and aversions. With bare awareness, rest in the end of the fixation to do or become. Or bring to mind something that no longer causes suffering: a distressful way of being, a difficult habit or an unhealthy relationship. With bare awareness, attend to how it is to be free of that suffering, released from its grip, unperturbed by the fixation of wanting or avoiding.

Step 16: The Truth of Non-self

> *One trains oneself, "I will breathe in focusing on relinquishment." One trains oneself, "I will breathe out focusing on relinquishment." This is how mindfulness of in and out breathing is developed & pursued so as to be of great fruit, of great benefit.*

With the cessation of fixation on doing or becoming, one is free to contemplate the relinquishment of clinging to the false frame of 'I' and 'mine.' Just as bare awareness of the breath reveals its impermanent nature, bare awareness of self reveals *not-self* (*anattā*/*anātman*): the ever-shifting construction of forms, perceptions, feelings, volitions and conclusions. As you observe this truth, relinquishment of the self's false frame of ownership and continuance will spontaneously arise. Rest in this supreme letting go. Know the luminosity of unconditioned mind, the fruit of *awakened presence.*

 The *Mahāyāna* Project

Historical Overview

Two centuries after the Buddha's death, on the heels of a war that wrought over 100,000 deaths, King Aśoka (304–232 BCE) ushered in a period of great flourishing for Indian Buddhism. Aśoka applied the Buddha's ethical teachings of wise action, wise speech and wise livelihood to advance political unity and spread these values throughout the Mauryan Empire.[18] He famously oversaw the completion of many sacred Buddhist sites and successfully sent missions northwest to present-day Pakistan and Afghanistan, an area that later became a center of Buddhist learning. From there, Indian Buddhism spread to Central Asia, China and Tibet.

As Buddhism moved north and south, Buddhist schools continued to experience philosophical splits and disagreements regarding textual authenticity and doctrinal interpretations. Even the form of Buddhist practice was in flux in some *Sanghas*. Some monks became interested in offering the laity a path to *nirvāna*. Other monks left monasteries to do intensive meditation alone in the forest. Although its exact origins are unknown, the *Mahāyāna*, or Great Vehicle, emerged as a reform movement around the first century CE. Initially, monks and nuns who aligned with early Mahāyānist ideals lived primarily in Theravada monasteries.

Present-day Buddhist scholars agree that early Mahāyāna texts were most likely authored by monastics in traditional settings, who may have been influenced by forest-dwelling hermit monks.[19] These initial texts emphasized the supremacy of the Buddha's enlightened perception and promoted practices that followed the path of the *Bodhisattva*, a 'Buddha-to-be.' Their Mahāyāna was an arduous emulation of the Buddha's journey from a Bodhisattva to Buddhahood.[20] The small groups of monastics who accepted this new literature may not have had much contact with each other. It took centuries for Mahāyāna followers to establish their own monasteries and openly declare their teachings to be the superior way.[21]

The Bodhisattvic Ideal

Theravada Buddhism teaches that the Buddha endured innumerable lifetimes as a *bodhisatta* (Pāli) single-mindedly focused on the attainment of Buddhahood. According to the Pāli Canon, after his enlightenment, the Buddha did not teach the path of the *bodhisatta* to his followers. He chose to teach the nature of suffering and the end of suffering, teachings designed to awaken an individual to the perfect wisdom of an *arhat* and release them from further rebirth. The Theravada Buddhist path to arhatship required monasticism. This consigned householders to practicing the Buddha's teachings by living ethically (*sīla*) and generously supporting (*dana*) monastics.

Mahāyāna Buddhism offered lay practitioners a path to attain enlightenment based on the traditional teachings of the Buddha with an emphasis on training in the way of the *Bodhisattva*, one endowed with boundless *wisdom* (P & S: *prajñā* T: *shes rab*) and *compassion* (P & S: *karunā* T: *snying rje*), working tirelessly to awaken for the benefit of all other sentient beings. "My own self I will place in Suchness [things as they are], and, so that all the world might be helped, I will place all beings into Suchness" (Conze, 1973).

Although a *bodhisattva* sounds like a non-ordinary being, they are humans dedicated to living selflessly and lovingly in the ordinary world.

> Bodhisattvas earn an honest living or receive the gift of sustenance in some way that serves and elevates beings, rather than in any way which would exploit or corrupt them. These diamond beings interrelate with people in ways which are harmonious rather than argumentative, serving rather than demanding. (Hixon, 1993)

The Bodhisattvic devotion to awakening oneself for the benefit of others is both an aspiration and an accomplishment, made possible through the cultivation of *bodhicitta, the awakened mind/heart*. Upcoming chapters focus on *bodhicitta* and the Theravada and Mahāyāna practices for cultivating boundless love and compassion. For now, let us continue to unpack the wisdom of *emptiness* (P: *suññatā* S: *śūnyatā* T: *stong pa nyid*), this time from the Mahāyāna perspective.

 The *Prajñāpāramitā Sūtras*

Just as little is known about the origins of the Mahāyāna, we also have limited information on its early literature. Scholars agree the *Prajñāpāramitā Sūtras* were probably authored between 100 BCE and 100 CE. The first of these texts, the *Perfection of Wisdom in 8,000 Lines* (*Astasāhasrikā Prajñāpāramitā Sūtra*) delivered Mahāyānist philosophy and metaphysics through an account of profound dialogues between three prominent disciples of the historical Buddha: Sāriputra and Ananda (representing the Abhidharmic teachings) and Subhūti, renowned for his compassion practice and ability to dwell in sustained peacefulness. These dialogues took place while the historical Buddha was dwelling in Rajagriha, where he and 1,250 realized monks and nuns (*arhants*) were gathered at Vulture's Peak.

The Mahāyānists put forth the idea of the historical Buddha teaching different versions of the Dharma to fit each audience's level of understanding. His public teachings (featured in the original *suttas* and Abhidharma) were said to be suited to those with 'inferior understanding,' while other 'higher-level' teachings were delivered to those with greater realization and allegedly kept secret until an appropriate time for their dissemination. While it remains difficult for Theravada Buddhists to accept these assertions, Mahāyāna Buddhists consider the *Prajñāpāramitā Sūtras* to be the direct word of the Buddha. I choose to hold all of these teachings in equal regard because of their equivalent profundity and usefulness for the alleviation of human suffering.

Seeing Through Subject/Object Duality

The Buddha begins the dialogue by requesting that Subhūti clarify for the gathered 'Bodhisattvas' how a Bodhisattva goes forth into perfect wisdom (*prajñāpāramitā*). (Subhūti's words are understood to be the direct transmission of the Buddha's mind.) Subhūti answers in very a surprising way:

> Since I neither find, nor apprehend, nor see a dharma "Bodhisattva," nor a "perfect wisdom," what Bodhisattva shall I instruct in what perfect wisdom? And yet, if, when this is pointed out, a Bodhisattva . . . does not despair or despond, if he does not turn away . . . is not terrified or frightened, it is just this Bodhisattva, this great being who should be instructed in perfect wisdom. It is precisely this that should be recognized as the perfect wisdom. . . . When he thus stands firm . . . he should so train himself that he

> does not pride himself on that thought of enlightenment. That thought is no thought, since in its essential transparent nature, that thought is transparently luminous. (1973)

Subhūti acknowledges that the radical recognition of empty transparency would be horrifying to most beings because it annihilates the solidity of subject/object duality. But the Bodhisattva's capacity to stand firmly without fear in the truthlessness of that truth is the perfect wisdom of which the Buddha speaks.

Subhūti's response represents quite a departure from the Abhidharma's painstaking method of deconstructing mind states to arrive at emptiness/not-self. 'Seeing things as they are' is now defined exclusively by elaboration; all labels, all concepts, are recognized as nothing more than elaborative mental gestures designed to obscure the empty transparency of phenomena. Although both approaches arrive at the emptiness of phenomena and self, the goal of this *sutra* is to fully differentiate its methodology from the traditional Abhidharmic model.

In addition, the context for this dialogue is of great import. This is a gathering of *arhats*, monastics who have realized the deathless and are no longer captivated by greed, hatred and delusion. Emptiness is a given for them. Yet, the Buddha, by way of Subhūti, is ostensibly offering further instruction in cutting through pervasive subject/object dualism to which, it is implied, they still cling.

With this we have arrived at the point of greatest contention between the Abhidharmic and Mahāyānic views of emptiness (*śūnyatā*). Abhidharmic emptiness/not-self is the reduction of the self to its fundamental components, the *Five Aggregates*: form, feeling, perception, volition and consciousness. Although these Five Aggregates are understood to be impermanent, their seeming irreducibility imputes their intrinsic existence. Subhūti's role is to explicate the Mahāyānist's adamant refusal to posit intrinsic existence for the Five Aggregates or anything else—no matter how fundamental or transcendent.

Form Is Emptiness; Emptiness Is Form

The *Prajñāpāramitā Sūtras* reiterate a position the Buddha stated repeatedly in the Pāli texts—emptiness does not imply nothingness, nor does it impute somethingness. *The Heart Sutra* (*Prajñāpāramitā Hrdaya*), the most beloved text in the *Prajñāpāramitā* literature, points this out in its most famous declaration: *form is emptiness; emptiness is form*. All succeeding Mahāyāna and Vajrayāna literature rests on this non-imputation of intrinsic existence to any unmanifested or manifested phenomena. "If the doctrine of emptiness denied the reality of these phenomena, it would be pointless to enumerate them. This suggests that things exist, but not intrinsically so; existence can only be understood in terms of dependent origination" (Gyatso, 2002).

This stance even applies to the roots of human suffering: greed (*rāga*), hatred (*dvesha*), and delusion (*moha*). Does this mean that Mahāyāna and Vajrayāna Buddhism do not proscribe cultivating wholesome mind states to reduce human suffering? Absolutely not. Because of ignorance, the mind can both cause and receive suffering. But it can also recognize interdependence and the lack of intrinsic separateness. Engagement with vigilant practice of mindfulness and compassion is necessary for the realization of this truth.

Thus, the Bodhisattva courageously lives among suffering beings, tirelessly toiling to awaken, so that all beings may awaken out of their suffering. The Bodhisattva stands in the empty transparency of all conventionally constituted self-existence knowing it is none other than the clear-light empty nature of mind: the Buddhamind, the unconditioned mind, *awakened presence.*

Notes

1 Eagleman, D. (2011). *Incognito: The secret lives of the brain.* New York, NY: Vintage.

2 Koch, C. (2013, January). *Mind and life: XXVI consciousness and the brain.* Unpublished lecture presented at Karnataka, India: Drepung Monastery. YouTube. Retrieved from www.youtube.com/watch?v=LFbVn58ETEA&list=PLOafJ4rP1PHwafTGL23zXK29knJsXMbMg

3 Nagel, T. (1974). What is it like to be a bat? *The Philosophical Review, 83*(4), 435–450.

4 Bodhi, B. (1993/1999). *A comprehensive manual of Abhidhamma.* Onalaska, WA: Buddhist Publication Society. p. 135.

5 Posner, M. I., and M. K. Rothbart. (2007). Research on attention networks as a model for the integration of psychological science. *Annual Review of Psychology, 58,* 1–23.

6 Kain, K. (2013, September). *Somatic experiencing training.* Unpublished lecture presented at Mercy Center, Burlingame, CA.

7 Gethin, R. (2011). On some definitions of mindfulness. *Contemporary Buddhism, 12*(1), 263–279.

8 Davidson, R. J. (2010). Empirical explorations of mindfulness: Conceptual and methodological conundrums. *Emotions, 10*(1), 8–11.

9 Hasenkamp, W., Wilson-Mendenhall, C. D., Duncan, E., & Barsalou, L. W. (2012). Mind wandering and attention during focused meditation: A fine-grained temporal analysis of fluctuating cognitive states. *NeuroImage, 59*(1), 750–760.

10 Hasenkamp W., Barsalou L. W. (2012). Effects of meditation experience on functional connectivity of distributed brain networks. *Frontiers in Human Neuroscience.* doi: 10.3389/fnhum.2012.00038
Brefczynski-Lewis, J. A., Lutz, A., Schaefer, H. S., Levinson, D. B., & Davidson, R. J. (2007). Neural correlates of attentional expertise in long-term meditation practitioners. *Proceedings of the National Academy of Sciences, 104*(27), 11483–11488.
Jang, J. H., Jung, W. H., Kang, D. H., Byun, M. S., Kwon, S. J., Choi, C. H., & Kwon, J. S. (2011). Increased default mode network connectivity associated with meditation. *Neuroscience Letters, 487*(3), 358–362.

11 Cahn, B. R., Delorme, A., & Polich, J. (2013). Event-related delta, theta, alpha and gamma correlates to auditory oddball processing during Vipassana meditation. *Social Cognitive and Affective Neuroscience, 8*(1), 100–111.

12 Vago D. R., Silbersweig D. A. (2012). Self-awareness, self-regulation, and self-transcendence (S-ART): A framework for understanding the neurobiological mechanisms of mindfulness. *Frontiers in Human Neuroscience.* doi: 10.3389/fnhum.2012.00296

13 Kok, B. E., & Fredrickson, B. L. (2010). Upward spirals of the heart: Autonomic flexibility, as indexed by vagal tone, reciprocally and prospectively predicts positive emotions and social connectedness. *Biological Psychology, 85*(3), 432–436.

14 Libby, D. J., Worhunsky, P. D., Pilver, C. E., & Brewer J. A. (2012). Meditation-induced changes in high-frequency heart rate variability predict smoking outcomes. *Frontiers in Human Neuroscience*. 6(54), 1–8.
15 Buddhadasa, A. (1988). *Mindfulness with breathing: A manual for serious beginners*. Boston, MA: Wisdom Publications.
16 Damasio, A. (2010). *Self comes to mind: Constructing the conscious brain*. New York, NY: Vintage Books.
17 Bentley, J. (1993). *Old World encounters: Cross-cultural contacts and exchanges in pre-modern times*. New York, NY: Oxford University Press. p. 45.
18 Williams, P. (2008). *Mahayana Buddhism: The doctrinal foundations*. New York, NY: Routledge.
19 Nattier, J. (2003). *A few good men: The Bodhisattva path according to the Inquiry of Ugra*. Honolulu, HI: University of Hawaii Press. pp. 193–194.
20 Williams, P., 2008, p. 44.
21 Conze, E. (1973). *The perfection of wisdom in eight thousand Lines and its verse and summary*. Bolinas, CA: Four Seasons Foundation.

5

Know the Fully Awakened Heart

Up to now our investigations have centered on the wisdom (*prajñā*) aspect of Buddhist psychology, specifically, (1) the apprehension of insight (*vipashyana*) into the truth of conditioned suffering and (2) liberation from suffering through clear seeing (P: *sampajañña* S: *samprajanya* T: *lhag mthong*) of the unconditioned, empty nature (*śūnyatā*) of self and objects.

Buddhism teaches that the bird of enlightenment requires two wings to fly: the wing of wisdom (*prajñā*) and the wing of compassion (*karunā*). This is not a mere tip of the hat to the stirrings of the human heart. It is a practical reality of the path to awakening. Without compassion, wisdom is dry and lifeless. Without wisdom, compassion is codependent and unhelpful.

Buddhist philosophy is unique in its insistence on the unity of mind and heart, a compound entity that co-generates wisdom *and* compassion in a continuous interrelational dance. An awakened heart integrates the insights of mind, and an awakened mind offers solace to a heart open and extended to suffering. The fully awakened heart-mind spontaneously meets experience from within the innate interconnectedness of emptiness.

 Embracing Humanness

Let's review our three propositions about humanness: it is human to resist pain and seek pleasure, to desire happiness and to *not* know the difference between pain and suffering. This chapter focuses on embracing our humanness with kindness and compassion.

We Are Imperfect Beings

> *The rejection of the humanness in each of us is the greatest mistake one can make on the path.* (Thubten, 2011)

Human imperfection is a useful companion on the path of awakening. Yes, it is inconvenient and causes inner and outer harm. Yes, it feels vulnerable and causes misunderstandings and mistakes. *And* . . . . the unsatisfactoriness of human imperfection is the very reason to understand suffering and mitigate its arising as best we are able. Intellectual understanding of imperfection is not enough. We must attitudinally soften toward imperfection and its consequences.

Unfortunately, when faced with imperfection most of us automatically respond with rejection and fear. For some this is a basic defense against feeling shame. For others it is a necessary shield against the self-loathing triggered by the slightest hint of imperfection. Psychotherapists often notice this painful response-reactivity in those with early narcissistic wounding.

A popular intervention for handling imperfection is "Accept yourself just as you are" or "Accept things as they are." I am not a big fan of broad-stroke acceptance because people often conflate it with agreement, inaction or weakness. Sometimes when patients are encouraged to practice acceptance, they end up feeling that acceptance obliges them to allow unacceptable circumstances to continue. Since these common misunderstandings happen too often, in lieu of acceptance I teach *kind recognition.*

Kind Recognition

> *We must remember that the most powerful medicine we can offer for suffering of any kind is simply kindness. It says, "You're not alone. I see you; I hear you; I'm with you."* (Ponlop, 2010)

I am always amazed at how much trouble people have being kind to themselves when they are struggling. Try right now to simply recognize that the difficulties of life don't feel very good and can be very hard to accept. Take some time to see how your mind-heart responds to that statement.

Like many people, you may have tried to logically convince yourself otherwise. Or maybe you called on a spiritual belief to mitigate the reality that life can be hard. Possibly you saw yourself circumventing distressful feelings by blaming others or even life itself. Some of you may have thought about using a substance to fix your distress. None of these common responses changes the fact of suffering. More important, they are neither wise nor compassionate.

To receive life's difficulties Buddhist psychology offers the skill of *kindly recognizing what is.* Adding kindness to recognition helps us soften into and receive 'this is hard.' When life is truly distressing, relying solely on mindfulness may feel harsh or sterile or may activate existing habits of disassociating or disconnecting from experience.

Kind recognition begins by *recognizing what has arisen*, for the fact of its arising cannot be altered. What comes next is the '*ow!*' of it. The key is to *let ourselves open to and directly receive the 'ow!' with kindness and then remain open to recognizing the distressful thoughts and feelings that follow.* Kind recognition builds our capacity to meet distressful feelings and difficult circumstances with less blame, shame and avoidance. It also promotes the cognitive-affective responsiveness needed to remain engaged, empowered and able to make skillful choices.

The kindness implied here is comprised of a potent collection of intentional positive emotions including empathy, warm-heartedness, generosity, compassion, altruism and equanimity. Positive emotions are evolved adaptations that enable humans to forge lasting relationships and accumulate resources.[1] These positive emotions are rooted in an essential love, one with the power to open and heal even the most wounded heart. When we engage in the intentional cultivation and active offering of these emotions—known in Buddhism as *The Four Immeasurables* (P & S: *Brahmavihāras* T: *tshad med bzhi*)—the human heart becomes a vehicle for boundless compassion and wisdom.

 Empathy: Feeling Into the Experience of the Other

In recent decades empathy has been the subject of much study. A basic definition of empathy is "(1) an affective response to another person, which may (but not always) entail sharing that person's emotional state; and (2) a cognitive capacity to take the other person's perspective" (Decety, 2009). This definition separates empathy into two functions: *cognitive empathy* (perspective-taking to predict another's mental states) and *affective empathy* (detecting another's feeling states).

Empathy makes the remarkable task of *intersubjectivity*, or knowing other minds, possible. Intersubjectivity has three attributes: agreement, commonly understood shared meaning and divergent meaning. When we see a person smile, we share a common understanding that the smile signals some form of enjoyment. But discerning the reason for another's smile is less assured.

Humans empathize to varying degrees. Empathic response depends on the intensity of another's pain or emotional reaction, one's capacity for empathy and the target of that response.[2] The ability to accurately internally depict and empathically resonate with another person's feelings, thoughts and experiences is crucial for healthy psychosocial bonding.

Empathy is facilitated by *neural mirroring*,[3] a process of internally constructing representations of others' actions and verbal/non-verbal communication. When we witness someone stub his or her toe, *mirror neurons* in our brain assist in the formation of a mental representation of that action by internally mimicking the experience of stubbing a toe. This signals the insular cortex (the pain center), particularly the anterior insula cortex,[4] to transmit information to our body and other brain areas, stimulating both a cringing sensation and empathically resonant feelings of another person's bodily pain.[5] This is how we can know the pain of another without having the direct experience of stubbing our toe.

Research has shown that people with autism and emotional dysregulation often suffer impairment in cognitive empathy; those with some forms of bipolar disorders and narcissistic personality disorder (NPD) experience impairment in affective empathy.[6] It was widely agreed that impairment in emotional empathy was a central feature of psychopathy. But several recent studies have questioned that assumption. Two preliminary studies showed increased affective empathy with higher psychopathy.[7] This implies that the ability to empathize—to construct a mental and emotional representation of what another thinks and feels—does not necessarily lead to wholesome thoughts and actions.

Western psychology has long assumed that almost everything humans do—even good and selfless acts—is ultimately motivated by egoic self-interest. However, infants 15 months of age choose cooperative altruistic behavior over aggressive competitive behavior.[8] Other studies suggest that when adults empathize with those in need they are more likely to offer help.[9] C. Daniel Batson and colleagues have spent three decades researching the empathy-altruism hypothesis and have tentatively concluded that "feeling empathic concern for a person in need does indeed evoke altruistic motivation to see that need relieved" (2011).

Buddhist psychology agrees with this proposition insofar as empathic knowing is the first step in accurately resonating with another's cognitive-affective states. But compassion and altruism are attributed to an intention to be of help. "Although empathy is probably a crucial step in the chain of emotional responses that lead toward feelings of compassion it is not the same: whereas empathy refers to 'feeling as,' that is, sharing the same affective response with the other, the latter concepts relate to 'feeling for'" (Singer, 2012). So empathy is being in resonance with another being. Compassion is a warm, loving feeling that leads to motivational concern for another.

Therapeutic Attunement

Intersubjectivity enables a psychotherapist to empathically use her or his entire psychophysical system to receive and mirror a patient's cognitive-affective somatic material. This form of empathy, known as *therapeutic attunement*, is the primary process through which a patient feels seen and heard. Although most schools of psychology agree that successful patient outcomes depend on a therapist's ability to create and maintain accurate therapeutic attunement, there is disagreement on how this is accomplished.

Older schools of Western psychology held a dualistic view of two separate subjective mind-worlds interacting through language and internally generated transferences and countertransferences. In other words, the therapist intentionally acts on the patient, almost hierarchically, while any influence the patient may exert on the therapist's psyche is noted as countertransference and then personally dealt with at a later time.

The intersubjective school of psychoanalysis augmented this conventional view by hypothesizing an intersubjective field—a mediating synchronized awareness of bidirectional knowing existing in and between two minds.[10] So, although an empathic therapist works to facilitate meaningful patient inquiry, intersubjectivity considers both parties to be equal influencers of the therapeutic container's empathic ebb and flow.[11]

Empathy Fatigue

When a psychotherapist refuses to acknowledge her or his vulnerability to a patient's suffering, empathic resonance can become overwhelming. If empathy is the only tool a clinician can bring to another's suffering, empathic responsiveness devolves into *empathic distress*—a withdrawal from rather than a movement toward suffering. Remember that the brain is wired to simulate another's suffering in order to understand it.

> Watching or imagining other people experiencing pain activates the central nervous system's pain matrix in the observer . . . repeated exposure to the suffering of others in healthcare professionals may be associated with the adverse consequences of personal distress, burnout and compassion fatigue. (Decety, 2010)

Neuroscientists Olga Klimecki and Tonya Singer argue that *the harmful effects of empathic over-arousal can be averted when one chooses an other-concerned but not self-identified compassionate response*. This has led them to suggest that what is commonly known as compassion fatigue is actually *empathy fatigue*.[12] Dr. Singer's group has demarcated two separate neural networks for empathy and compassion. The empathy networks primarily stimulate the brain's pain centers. Compassion activates brain regions previously related to connectedness and positive affect (medial orbitofrontal cortex, putamen, palladium and ventral tegmental area).[13]

Researchers agree that responding with empathic distress to a patient's suffering increases the likelihood of developing burnout symptoms. When healthcare professionals intentionally down-regulate their response to the pain of others, their negative arousal decreases and the ability to assist increases.[14] A 2009 study published in *JAMA: The Journal of the American Medical Association* showed that 60% of queried physicians reported exhaustion and burnout symptoms, including empathy withdrawal and decreased feelings of accomplishment. These findings were linked to reductions in the quality of care, more medical errors and greater patient dissatisfaction. After undertaking a 52-hour mindful communication program, participating physicians attributed improvements in quality of care and personal well-being to (1) mindfulness skills for attentiveness and emotion regulation, (2) reduction in isolation, and (3) attention to personal growth and well-being.[15] These results provide an incentive for all clinicians to add meditation and meaningful colleague interaction to their self-care regimen.

Lovingkindness: The Joy of Generating Well-Being for Self and Others (P: *mettā* S: *maitrī* T: *byams pa*)

Think: Happy, at rest, may all beings be happy at heart.
Whatever beings there may be,
May all beings be happy at heart.

Let none deceive or decry
His fellow anywhere;
Let none wish others harm
In resentment or in hate.

With good will for the entire cosmos,
cultivate a limitless heart: Above, below, & all around,
unobstructed, without enmity or hate.
Whether standing, walking, sitting, or lying down,
as long as one is alert,
one should be resolved on this mindfulness.
This is called a sublime abiding here & now.
From the *Karaniya Mettā Sutta* (SN 1:8)16

The Pāli word *mettā* means lovingkindness, friendliness and goodwill. *Mettā*, the first *Brahmavihāra*, is an altruistic aim to resonate a kind love unfettered by self-interest. In her classic book on lovingkindness, Buddhist teacher Sharon Salzberg describes *mettā* as a gentle rain, one that cannot choose where it falls "but simply falls without discrimination" (1995). The non-discriminativeness of *mettā* makes it a powerful antidote to hatred and anger. Lovingkindness is both a mindful application of non-violence and a spontaneous outpouring of benevolent love.

In the *Karaniya Mettā Sutta*, the Buddha beautifully describes lovingkindness as a *sublime abiding, here and now*, a serene, loving, awakened presence mindfully embodied and shared. This is our essential wakeful, loving nature.

The Buddha begins this teaching with a directive: *Think: Happy, at rest, may all beings be happy at heart.* Attentive and relaxed, know that all beings are deserving of joy and deep contentment. *Let none deceive nor decry or wish harm to any being.* Embrace the responsibility to renounce harming in all forms toward all beings. *With good will cultivate a limitless heart.* Non-preferential love is our aim; the immeasurable heart is the vehicle. *As long as one is alert, one should be resolved on this mindfulness.* At all times be attentive and rest in essence love. Mindfully resolve to cultivate lovingkindness.

In this *sutta* the Buddha outlines three distinct ways to practice *mettā*: (1) informally in daily life, (2) in meditation, and (3) as an unconditional expression of peace and universal love. *Ordinary lovingkindness* is preferential, extended to self and one's familiars. *Immeasurable lovingkindness* is non-preferential, encompassing all beings, everywhere. *Mettā* strengthens the connection to our innate loving nature. It liberates the heart-mind from preference and hatred.

The Self-Hating Western Psyche

Many before me have observed that the Western psyche has a penchant for self-loathing. This can make the simple act of offering lovingkindness to oneself quite challenging. I have witnessed patients enthusiastically wish loved ones great ease and then struggle to offer themselves even a meager amount of kindness. In the *Udana Nikāya*, King Pasenadi Kosala told the Buddha that he and Queen Mallikā claimed to love one another more than they loved themselves. The Buddha responded with this teaching:

> *Searching all directions with your awareness,*
> *you find no one dearer than yourself.*
> *In the same way, others are thickly dear to themselves.*
> *So you shouldn't hurt others if you love yourself.* (5:1)

A recognition of innate lovability is the foundation of non-harming. Offering both ordinary and immeasurable *mettā* helps us recognize that we, like all other beings, are eminently worthy of lovingkindness. *Mettā* melts self-and other-directed anger and nurtures a non-harming attitude that turns hostile persons into allies—even when we are our most hostile person!

I witnessed a profound case of this melting in a 50-year-old male raised by a violent alcoholic father and depressed victimized mother. He came to therapy with unrelenting depression and trouble expressing any emotion other than anger. As we worked together it became clear that deep within his psyche lived a staunch and unforgiving child-self, continually demanding perfection from this hardworking, loyal husband and father. When I introduced him to *mettā* practice, his heart melted as he wished happiness for his wife and child. But as soon as I asked him to offer kindness to himself, he froze in fear. Nevertheless, he insisted on continuing to do *mettā* practice because it allowed him to connect deeply with the love he felt for his family. Over time he was able to freely offer lovingkindness to himself. *Mettā* became an important ally as he worked to heal the trauma that had for so long been locked away in his mind and body.

Practicing lovingkindness informally in daily life stimulates positive emotions toward self and others even in the difficult moments when we most need to cultivate warm-heartedness. For this reason, as an adjunct to *kind recognition*, I informally introduce *mettā* in sessions when patients experience distress and are in need of wishing well-being for themselves or others.

Lovingkindness Meditation

Mettā meditation grounds us in the aspiration to live in joy. Like *ānāpānasati*, lovingkindness meditation is a concentration practice. A 2008 study showed that *mettā* meditation gradually augmented participants' daily experiences of positive emotions. These changes led to increases in mindfulness, life purpose and social support and predicted increased life satisfaction and reduced depressive symptoms.[17] Regular practice of lovingkindness meditation has been found to enhance vagal tone, feelings of social connectedness, pain tolerance and affect regulation.[18] In long-term lovingkindness meditation practitioners (for 5 years or more), more gray matter volume has been detected in brain areas implicated in the regulation of empathic response and anxiety.[19] Lovingkindness meditation also increases self-compassion and other-focused concern.[20] *Mettā* practice has also been shown to enhance recovery from negative symptoms associated with schizophrenia.[21]

Sustained *mettā* practice develops immeasurable lovingkindness—an all-embracing boundless love that transcends conditions, cultural affiliation and individual preference. "*Thus above, below, across, and everywhere, one dwells pervading the entire world with a mind imbued with lovingkindness, vast, exalted, measureless, without hostility, without ill will*" (SN IV iv:i).

Formal *mettā* meditation is a full-hearted active well-wishing of safety, health, well-being and ease. The practice uses phrases directed toward a series of individuals and then to all beings. Western practitioners traditionally begin lovingkindness meditation with someone they feel is easy to love. Many people choose a pet, child or benefactor. Since it is quite easy to open the heart toward those we love, I think of this as priming the pump. The practice continues with offering *mettā* for oneself, a neutral person, and a difficult person and, finally, immeasurable lovingkindness for all beings. This stepped approach introduces the practice under favorable conditions and progressively moves toward generating lovingkindness in less easy circumstances.

Biased Love: The Near Enemy of Mettā

Biased love—what one of my Tibetan Buddhist teachers calls 'greasy love'—is the gooey, wonderful, yet perilous personal love most people experience. "Biased love that we feel for only particular persons—which is often built merely on the fact that another person brings us pleasure—easily turns into consternation or flips to hatred when the person does not provide the familiar pleasure" (Hopkins, 2008).

Although the goal of *mettā* is to expand the heart *and* widen the circle of love, *mettā* meditation begins by wishing someone well whom we have no trouble loving. This is a necessary preferential beginning for people raised in a culture bound by the conditioning of biased love yet strangely averse to freely offering that love to themselves. But restricting well-wishes to the self, loved ones or those who have helped us or whom we consider deserving is biased love, not immeasurable lovingkindness.

As our circle of well-wishing expands to include those we find increasingly difficult, *mettā* practice can turn into grasping at lovingkindness to enhance our position, avert discomfort or try to gain another's love. These motivations are sham *mettā* born of intense wanting. Desired objects become exaggerated and objects of clinging to future happiness. Remember, *mettā* is universally non-harming and free from any self-interested motivation.

Hatred: The Far Enemy of Mettā

> *One whose mind all day and night*
> *Takes delight in harmlessness,*

Who has lovingkindness for all beings—
For him there is enmity with none.
The Buddha (SN I 10:4)

Rather than begin with a rousing call for fellowship and the renunciation of hatred, it seems best to go right to the root cause of enmity. I will let Shantideva, a renowned eighth-century Indian Buddhist monk, enlighten us:

> Finding its fuel in discontent, origination from an undesired event and from an impediment to desired events, anger becomes inflamed and destroys me. Therefore I shall remove the fuel of that enemy, for that foe has no function other than to harm me. (Wallace, 1997)

The fuel of discontent is clinging. Rooted in aversion and craving, discontent gives rise to the mental afflictions of anger, ill will and resentment. To what do we most cling? Self-identification, self-concern and self-cherishing—fundamental cognitive distortions generated by primordial ignorance (*avidyā*) and dispositional formations (*samskāras*).

While it is true that humans are wired to seek their own survival, human flourishing occurs when we recognize that our existence relies on countless interdependent micro and macro interactions. The illusion of an all-powerful self unto itself lies at the heart of all self-inflicted and other-directed anger and resentment. When the mind is engaged with self-cherishing thoughts of entitlement or exceptionalism, it clings to false notions of separate self-existence.

Alternatively, negative self-cherishing—the false belief in one's hideousness—is a profound impediment to recognizing innate love. Often an outcome of traumatic childhood maltreatment, negative self-cherishing becomes a continual source of unwarranted feelings of guilt and vileness.

Buddhist psychology makes a clear distinction between the healing emotions of remorse and atonement and the destructive emotions of guilt and denigration. We are human. Embracing mistakes with kindheartedness involves mending them with remorse and atonement—gestures that lead to personal and collective healing. Guilt exhausts the mind-heart with its recursive self-directed loathing, belittling and cruelty. Much like rumination, guilt leads nowhere and helps no one. It is, in the words of someone very dear to me, "a useless emotion."

Mettā is an unfolding, self-reflective process, akin to peeling back the layers of an artichoke to arrive at its heart. With its potent combination of mindfulness and heartfulness, lovingkindness meditation calms the mind, clears our perception and suffuses the heart with a limitless love. We don't need a new or different kind of heart. Just recognize that each moment is an opportunity to connect with the love that exists in every breath, every heartbeat, every smile, every tear, every opening.

Lovingkindness (*Mettā*) Meditation Instruction

Relax into a comfortable position. Let mind and body be at ease. Become aware of any agitation in the mind or body. Try not to fix it. Instead, soften your attitude toward physical or mental agitation. Kindly observe the phenomena just as they are. Let your wise heart know experience with gentleness.

Now let your attention be drawn to your heart—the part of you that swells with joy when you experience happiness. Rest awareness on this area. Imagine on your next in-breath breathing a soft, greenish light into your heart, and on the out-breath feel the warmth in your heart begin to expand. With each inhale let the light warm your heart. With each exhale feel your heart expand with love.

Now bring to mind someone very easy to love—a child, a pet, a benefactor, a dear friend or a loved one. Bring an image of this being into your warm, expanded heart. Attend to the experience of their presence in your heart. Now you will direct a series of lovingkindness phrases to this being, repeating the phrases quietly to yourself while actively wishing these intentions. Ride the waves of love in your heart as you send the *mettā*.

May you be safe from inner and outer harm. See this being safe, protected, free of harm from any source, including their own mind.

May you be free of hatred, guilt and shame. Actively see this being experiencing the freedom of knowing difficult experience with wisdom and compassion; able to respond with skill and ease.

May you live with the ease of an open heart. See this being contented and receptive, moving through life with a loving heart.

May you have a calm, clear mind and enjoy mental well-being. Even if this being currently has mental health challenges, see their mind at peace, wise, responsive and resilient.

May you enjoy physical well-being. Even if this being currently has health challenges, see their body glowing with health and vitality, strong and fit, resilient and alive.

May you go beyond your inner darkness and awaken to your true nature as boundless love and wisdom. See this being actively lessening mental and emotional affliction, walking the path to freedom from suffering.

Now rest for a moment noticing the condition of your heart. Enjoy the loving expanse emanating from the practice. You may repeat the phrases if you choose. If not, let their image be released from your heart.

Now bring an image of yourself to mind. This can be at any time in your life—now, as a child or at a time when you felt complete. Let that image be drawn into your warm, expanded heart. Be gentle and notice how easy or hard this is for you. Attend to the experience with kindness and generosity, not forcing anything. When you are ready, direct the *mettā* phrases toward yourself, actively wishing these intentions from deep within your heart.

May I be safe from inner and outer harm. See yourself safe, protected, free of harm from any source, including your mind.

May I be free of hatred, guilt and shame. Actively see yourself experiencing the freedom of knowing difficult experience with wisdom and compassion. Visualize responding with skill and ease.

May I live with the ease of an open heart. See yourself contented and receptive, moving through the world with a loving heart.

May I have a calm, clear mind and enjoy mental well-being. Even if you currently have mental health challenges, see your mind at peace, wise, responsive and resilient.

May I enjoy physical well-being. Even you currently have health challenges, see your body glowing with health and vitality, strong and fit, resilient and alive.

May I go beyond my inner darkness and awaken to my true nature as boundless love and wisdom. See yourself actively lessening mental and emotional affliction, walking the path to freedom from suffering.

Rest for a moment attending to the condition of your heart. Notice any difference between offering lovingkindness to a loved one and offering it to yourself. Be kind if you experienced difficulty; don't judge yourself harshly or get lost in blame or shame. Enjoy whatever joy emanates from the practice.

If at any time during the practice distressful emotions or disturbing thoughts arise, take a break and turn your attention to care for your own distress. Soften your attitude and compassionately observe. Clearly comprehend difficulty. You may repeat the phrases if you choose. If not, let your image be released from your heart. Take a few cleansing breaths by inhaling greenish light and expanding the love in your heart as you exhale.

Now bring to mind someone neutral, a person you see in life but do not know personally. When you envision this person clearly, bring their image into your warm, expanded heart. Don't force it to be there. Invite the image in as much as you can, respecting any resistance that might appear. Attend to the experience of this person's presence in your heart. Now direct the set of *mettā* phrases to them, repeating them quietly to yourself and actively wishing these intentions from deep within your heart. Notice how it feels to generate lovingkindness for a neutral person. When you are done, release them from your heart. Take a few cleansing breaths by inhaling greenish light and expanding the love in your heart as you exhale.

Now bring to mind a somewhat difficult person—someone who irritates or confuses you. When you envision this person clearly, see what it is like to gently bring their image into your warm, expanded heart. Don't force it to be there. Invite this person in as much as you can, respecting any resistance that might appear. With practice, resistance will dissolve. Attend to the experience of this person's presence in your heart. Now direct the set of *mettā* phrases to this person, repeating the phrases quietly to yourself and actively wishing these intentions from deep within your heart. Notice how it feels to generate lovingkindness for a somewhat difficult person. Care deeply for any distressing emotions you may have during this practice. Soften your attitude and compassionately observe. When you are done, release them from your heart. Take a few cleansing breaths by inhaling greenish light and expanding the love in your heart as you exhale.

Finally, bring to mind all beings everywhere. Envision all beings as clearly as you can, and gently bring each of them into your warm, expanded heart. Invite all beings in as much as you can, respecting any resistance that might appear. With practice, resistance will dissolve. Attend to the experience of their presence in your heart. Now direct the set of *mettā* phrases to all beings, as best you can, repeating them quietly to yourself and actively wishing these intentions from deep within your heart. Notice how it feels to generate lovingkindness for all beings equally. Repeat as many times as you like. When you are done, release them from your heart. Take a few cleansing breaths by inhaling greenish light and expanding the love in your heart as you exhale.

Compassion: Responsiveness to Human Suffering (P & S: *karunā* T: *snying rje*)

> *Compassion is the very essence of all the Dharmas.* (Lama Shabkar quoted in Ricard, 2013)

Most religions and philosophies consider compassion—often equated with empathy or sympathy—necessary for human survival and co-existence. Research literature describes compassion as a prosocial emotion that is (1) a mix of love and sadness or (2) a feeling that arises when witnessing another's suffering, sometimes linked with a motivation to help.[22] Charles Darwin conjectured that compassion (he used 'sympathy') evolved to motivate humans to note, care for and reduce harm and suffering in their vulnerable offspring. We are not alone. Similar caregiving impulses and behaviors have been observed in dolphins and primates.[23] The development of human compassion has also been attributed to sexual selection or a need for successful non-kin transactions.[24]

Social research shows that feelings of compassion are elicited in self-relevant or self-distinctive contexts. Perceived self-similarity and relational closeness foster feelings of equality, directly impacting levels of felt compassion and active cooperation.[25] It seems humans are primed to seek mitigation of suffering for those whose well-being we depend on or whose suffering is dissimilar from our own.[26] Deservingness also plays an important role in deciding who is worthy of compassion.[27] Those who are at fault or cause their own suffering receive less compassionate concern and pity or provoke anger instead.[28]

Self-report studies show that respondents link feelings of compassion with a motivation to end suffering and do distinguish these feelings from sadness or distress. Several studies were conducted where participants received an appeal for help and were then offered an easy escape. Those with higher levels of self-reported compassion helped more, while those with greater self-reported distress were less helpful.[29] So although empathic distress can occur alongside feelings of compassion, it clearly impedes compassionate action.

Until recent years, compassion research was primarily conducted on individuals with no access to contemplative compassion training and as such accurately reflected normative, conditional state (momentary feelings) and trait (tendencies toward) compassion. In the presence of unbearable suffering, who among us might not succumb to helplessness and empathic distress? Buddhist psychology views this conditionality—referred to as *referential compassion*—as a deficit in mental training rather than an insoluble insufficiency of the human mind-heart.

Compassion in Buddhist Psychology

Compassion (*karunā*) is the second *Brahmavihāra*. The Abhidharma classifies *karunā* as one of 52 mental factors but, because of its limitlessness, distinguishes it from other prosocial emotions. The Buddhist psychological definition of compassion underscores the inseparability of *karunā* and *prajñā* (wisdom): *compassion is a quivering of the heart in response to suffering imbued with clear comprehension (*samprajanya*) of suffering, inspiring a genuine determination to end suffering*. That may seem like an overwhelming task for imperfect beings like us. But regardless of limitation, we can each genuinely aspire to end human suffering.

The inseparability of compassion and wisdom differentiates *karunā* from other traditional conceptualizations of compassion. In Buddhist psychology, one who clearly comprehends the causes of unsatisfactoriness (*dukkha*) actively seeks to understand his or her own suffering and avert its arising. When other-related suffering is encountered, that being feels moved by a tenderheartedness (*anukampā*) toward others in distress. "They suffer as I suffer; lost in *samsāra*, they too endure the unsatisfactoriness of human experience as best they can." This deep relationality dissolves the conditional nature of referential compassion, transforming it into an *illimitable, non-referential compassion for all beings, with unimpeded willingness to help end suffering.*

When one is compassionately lessening suffering for those with intense pain or irrevocable outcomes, knowing that they desire happiness makes it possible to circumvent helplessness and empathic distress. It also removes any requirement of blamelessness and deservingness that would impede compassionate assistance to perpetrators who might otherwise elicit hatred or fear. For this reason, Buddhist compassion training is ideal for treatment professionals in medical, mental health and incarceration settings.

Compassion meditation is a powerful antidote to grasping at negative distortions about self and others. When we expand the circle of self-similarity, we stand in the truth that we are no more hideous or special than any other being. Their gifts and faults are our gifts and faults. We may not agree with unwise or harmful deeds, but that does not make those who perpetrate them any less worthy of compassionate understanding and kind regard.

Cultivating illimitable compassion liberates an essential love. Empty yet primordially present, this love is powerful enough to dissolve the ultimate cognitive distortion of a separately existing self.

How to Begin: Compassionate Recognition of the Difficulties of Human Life

Compassion and genuineness are inseparable, and authenticity is the fertile soil for compassionate response. Yet who among us does not fear showing up authentically in an unforgiving world like ours? Now add the thicket of trauma-induced or ego-related defense structures most of us live with that make genuineness feel like a leap of faith. Vulnerability requires softening of psyche-somatic armoring. When we are real with others, they are more likely to be real with us. The kind way to begin this softening is with compassionate recognition of the difficulty of being human.

Here is a beautiful example of what this process looks like in a therapeutic context.

> J and T entered couples therapy to heal the rage and disconnectedness undermining their relationship. J was a skilled upper-level manager who regulated her emotional responses at work but at home was given to uncontrolled raging. She had for many years struggled with perfectionism and overwhelming fears of abandonment. T was a research scientist who grew up with an abusive, distant father and a "saintly mother." Although T was a gentle, loving person, his intense fear of commitment triggered J's fearfulness and anger. Applying Buddhist psychological principles and interventions dramatically lessened J's angry outbursts, and soon they began working on the abandonment and commitment issues that had kept them from surrendering fully to the relationship.

Months into our work, T began a session by reporting that J had gone into a severe rage, the type of harmful over-reaction he had thought would not recur. As the session continued, it became obvious that J would not admit culpability or show remorse. Any admonition of her imperfection was simply intolerable.

I gently invited them to know the difficulty of that moment with a kind, compassionate attitude toward how hard it was to be in such pain, to soften their hearts and let a gentle warm-heartedness penetrate any hatred of themselves or each other. Gradually their faces softened and their bodies relaxed. Small tears flowed from their closed eyes. Compassionately recognizing their suffering provided an opening for authentic self-reflectivity devoid of harmful self-hatred. J realized how scared she was and that as long as she lived in self-hatred, she would be fully capable of harming herself and her partner with rage. Truly understanding the ramifications of harming self and others broke her heart open. The session ended with a heartfelt, solemn commitment to renounce further harm.

Referential Compassion (Attached or Reasoned Compassion)

> *I should eliminate the suffering of others because it is suffering. I should take care of others because they are sentient beings just as I am a sentient being.* (Shantideva, Bodhicaryāvatāra, VIII: 94)

All beings long to be free of suffering. Yet we are conditioned to seek the welfare of those we know and love, above all others' well-being. Most of my Buddhist teachers agree that *referential compassion* begins at home by developing tenderheartedness toward oneself. While this first step in compassion training can be challenging for people who have spent years steeped in the brine of self-hating narratives, ultimately they, more than anyone, appreciate the liberating fruits of compassion meditation. Studies have shown that people who exhibit greater levels of self-compassion have better relationships[30] and are more likely to exercise, eat healthy foods and smoke less.[31]

Compassion Meditation for Self and Loved Ones

Cultivating compassion for those we love may seem redundant, since we already regard them with great fondness and wish them all good things. But that love is often conditioned on how loving and kind we are to each other. We are imperfect beings and sometimes show up in ways that cause distress for each other. These difficult experiences present great opportunities to develop compassion.

Below is a self-or other-directed compassion meditation using the following standardized phrases from Theravada Buddhism:

> *May I (you) have compassion for my (your) pain and suffering.*
> *May my (your) pain and suffering be eased.*
> *May I (you) be at peace.*

Remember that the goal of compassion meditation is to generate a welcoming attitude toward suffering (*dukkha*) in all its forms. Be gentle with yourself. Set your intention to try as best you can, and know that that is the right effort, right now.

> Begin by resting in a comfortable seated position. Let your mind and body be at ease. Become aware of any agitation or fear arising in your mind or body. Try not to fix it. Instead, soften your attitude toward agitation and fear by compassionately observing it. Be gentle, and it will abate on its own.
>
> When you feel ready, decide whether to direct compassion toward your own suffering or that of a loved one, friend or benefactor. Bring to mind the object of your compassion, and let that person's image be drawn into your heart. See the person as they are now and let your heart-mind be filled with love. Observe them and the ways in which they are suffering. If it is you, observe actual distress occurring in this moment, or bring to mind a difficult experience from the past.
>
> Begin to say the phrases. *May I (you) have compassion for my (your) pain and suffering.* Know the humanness of this suffering, for it deserves compassionate recognition free of hatred and fear. Be loving, kind and caring. *May my (your) pain and suffering be eased.* This is not a demand. It is an aspiration born of clear comprehension that even this pain and suffering are impermanent. Let compassion ease the demand that pain and suffering end now. Instead, make friends with the impulse to be free of suffering and embrace *dukkha* as a teacher. Let compassionate recognition be the cause of awakening. *May I (you) be at peace.* Clearly comprehend *dukkha*. Know that peace is possible even in the midst of suffering. Let compassionate wisdom free you of delusion. Contemplate the possibility of a heart-mind liberated from self-grasping, self-delusion and self-harm.
>
> Continue repeating these phrases as long as you wish. At any time during the practice, if distressful emotions, painful sensations or difficult thoughts arise, soften your attitude toward them. Compassionately observe them using your wise heart. Use the waves of love and compassion to gently turn the heart-mind toward human suffering. End the practice by seeing the object of your compassion radiant, healthy and happy, even if that is not their present condition.

Pity: The Near Enemy of Karunā

Pity can be an immediate emotional response to suffering, especially when feelings of otherness, superiority, blame or uncontrollability are present. A homeless person afflicted with addiction and/or schizophrenia aimlessly walking the streets may appear incapable of helping himself/herself. Sadly, his/her plight is most often received with pity rather than compassion. Several factors may contribute to that response: (1) feeling sorry for another makes one avoid, not help, the person;[32] (2) pity is an ambivalent emotion and a convenient way to ease the distress of helplessness or an unwillingness to help;[33] (3) pity involving sadness and disrespect leads to inaction, dismissiveness or neglect;[34] and (4) downward comparisons arising from fear or feelings of dissimilarity generate distancing or, in extreme cases, expulsion.[35]

Compassion is expressive, connective and active. Pity is dismissive, avoidant and inactive. Pity arises when we misapprehend the nature of reality. To avert pity, one must wisely recognize that all beings are equally afflicted by the ubiquitousness of suffering. Cutting through entitlement and unlikeness elicits compassionate recognition of life's unsatisfactoriness and moves us to be of assistance. Here is an example of how a patient used compassion skills to work through feelings of pity for a dear friend.

> Traveling was not something M did very often, because of health issues. Yet I could sense M's excitement about an upcoming trip to the mountains with a friend. M spent the first part of the session talking about the friend's stressed life and lifelong inattentiveness to self-care. Spending a weekend together made M feel agitated, and then guilty and ashamed for pitying a friend. As we worked on kindly recognizing inner distress, M's body relaxed, and soon feelings of other-relatedness and self-similarity arose. M realized they both suffered in different ways. Then we focused on how to use compassionate recognition and mindful inquiry should distressful feelings arise on the trip. A week later M shared how enjoyable the weekend had been. Applying wise compassion even in the midst of irritation made the trip so much less stressful.

Cruelty: The Far Enemy of Karunā

According to Buddhist psychology, compassion and kindness lie at the root of human nature. Acceptance of that view has been an uphill battle for Western psychology, which considers aggression and self-directed desire the most basic evolutionary drives. As psychologist Paul Gilbert puts it, "We have grown in the shadow of beliefs that anything that is basic to human nature is *bad nature*" (2005). The unbelievable cruelty that continues to be a part of human experience might lead one to agree with that opinion.

Consider the irony of countless colossal displays of cruelty perpetrated in the name of religions espousing values of compassion and kindness, even those who call themselves Buddhists, strangely enough. Is this just a profound disconnect between religious ideology and its wise expression in the world? Or is there a fundamental relationship between a lack or misunderstanding of compassion and a mind convinced of the rightness of applying cruelty to ensure its brand of compassionate values?

The great Tibetan Buddhist yogi Lama Shabkar once said, "One with compassion is kind even when angry; One without compassion will kill even as he smiles" (2001). Buddhist psychology's proposition that cruelty is the far enemy of compassion is bolstered by research showing that prosocial acts and aggression represent opposite ends of a spectrum of behavior.[36] Where dignity is lacking, cruelty takes over.

In the early 1970s researchers at Stanford University conducted a now-infamous study called the Stanford Prison Experiment,[37] which concluded that potent social situations could persuade average young men to behave inhumanely toward one another.

Since then, *interactionism*—the belief that behavior is a product of the interaction of a person and her or his situation—has been largely accepted by social psychology. Interactionism has shown that people in compromising situations are able to choose prosocial behavior or avoid harming others.[38]

Other research has looked more closely at what internal conditions might lead to violence. An analysis of 20th-century mass killings showed that those with malicious dispositions might self-selectively join groups that perpetrated violent acts.[39] In addition, such people may share personality traits that organize the psyche around the following tendencies:[40] (1) dispositional aggression—a propensity toward anger, hostility and abusive acts;[41] (2) submissiveness to and agreement with socially sanctioned authoritarian aggression;[42] (3) narcissistic characteristics like power-craving, interpersonal exploitativeness and lack of empathy;[43] and (4) adherence to ideologies of superiority and social dominance.[44]

Compassion Meditation for a Difficult Person

> *Compassion has many faces. Some of them are fierce; some of them are wrathful; some of them are tender; some of them are wise.* (Halifax, 2010)

The true benefit of this practice is cultivating compassion for people in our private, professional and public lives we don't like, don't understand, or have caused us harm. Abusive family members or intimate partners, close friends that turn on us, bosses or co-workers who take credit for our work or demonstrate little appreciation: these are the ones who show us the healing power of compassionate recognition. Compassion is the supreme vehicle of non-hatred. The Buddha taught, "Hatred can never end hatred. By non-hate alone does it end" (Fronsdal, 2005).

It can be quite challenging to feel non-hatred for people we find difficult. Compassion does not imply condoning or agreeing with an action. We can abhor an act and still actively, compassionately, aim to end that suffering. Compassion meditation does not require forgiveness, nor is it even a part of the practice. Yet many find forgiveness naturally arising from compassion meditation.

Violence, jealousy, greed, hatred, abuse, manipulation, lies and theft: these are all manifestations of human suffering. Murder, war, rape, terrorist attacks and torture arise from the depths of egoic delusion and extreme *dukkha*. Only the healing power of *karunā* (compassion) and *prajñā* (wisdom) can rid our species of these horrific acts.

Begin by resting in a comfortable seated position. Let your mind and body be at ease. Become aware of any agitation or fear. Try not to fix it. Instead, soften your attitude toward agitation and compassionately observe it. Use your wise heart to clearly comprehend distressful experience. Awareness will abate its intensity.

When you feel ready, bring to mind a person you find difficult. You can start with a somewhat difficult person, someone who irritates, frustrates or confuses you or whose actions may have been unsupportive. (As you gain confidence in the practice you can offer compassion to those you find more difficult.)

As the person's image comes to mind, attend to your thoughts, feelings and body sensations. If you become distressed, soften your attitude. Use your wise heart to compassionately observe distress. If you feel unsafe, open your heart and offer *mettā* to yourself—*May I be safe and protected from internal and external harm*—until you feel settled once again. Then gently return your attention to the difficult person. See if you can compassionately recognize the ways in which they suffer. If they have problems that contribute to their actions, bring these to mind. Recognize that these are sources of suffering for them. Clearly comprehend how their distress may impact you both. Know this without falling into pity or hatred.

Begin to internally say the compassion phrases and actively send their heartful intention to this person.

May I have compassion for your pain and suffering. Know the humanness of their suffering and the distress it may cause. Rest in compassionate recognition with an aspiration to understand the nature of suffering, freed from hatred and fear. Be loving, kind and caring toward them and toward your own efforts to generate compassion for their suffering.

May your pain and suffering be eased. This is not a demand. It is an aspiration born of clear comprehension that pain and suffering are impermanent. Genuinely wish them freedom from their suffering. Aspire to embrace *dukkha* as your teacher and its compassionate recognition as the cause of awakening. See this difficult person as a catalyst for the blossoming of wisdom and compassion in your mind-heart. See your own awakening as a catalyst for the emergence of wisdom and compassion in the other person's mind-heart.

May you be at peace. See this person clearly comprehending *dukkha*, realizing that inner peace is possible even in the midst of suffering. See them freed of their own internal discord and confusion. Let compassionate wisdom free them from the illusion of separateness. Know that they, too, are a being that suffers and can be freed from suffering. Let the compassion in your heart lighten the distress you feel regarding this person and free you from grasping at feelings of sadness, fear and anger.

Continue repeating the phrases as long as you wish. Take a break in the phrases anytime distressful emotions, painful sensations or difficult thoughts arise. Turn your attention to caring for your own distress. Soften your attitude and compassionately observe. End the practice by seeing this person radiant, healthy and happy, even if that is not their present condition.

Therapeutic Compassion: Skillful Compassionate Care

> *Remember you are not trying to "fix" the pain of the world, only to hold it with a compassionate heart.* (Kornfield, 2008)

For many years, the Buddhist teacher Phillip Moffitt has held a free daylong retreat at Spirit Rock Meditation Center for caregivers. Its intent is to provide time for those who primarily care for others to deeply care for themselves with meditation, reflection and dialogue. Each year more than 300 people attend, and every year the number of clinicians rises. Throughout the day a dedicated team (including myself) offers 10-minute interviews for participants seeking individual attention. This year the majority of my interviewees were physicians and psychotherapists struggling with empathic distress associated with a need to fix suffering that was either unfixable or not theirs to fix. It was a marvelous opportunity to introduce them to the Buddhist psychological framework for *being with suffering without creating more suffering.*

Professional caregivers generally have very big hearts. Who else could bear unbearable suffering? However, a big heart is not necessarily a wise heart. *Prajñā* means to know things in their actuality, to clearly comprehend the nature of suffering, the causes of suffering and the means to end suffering. Clinician effectiveness rests on the capacity to discern what is ours, what is theirs and what constitutes wise action, all the while compassionately holding another being in unbearable suffering. I know that sounds almost superhuman.

When a clinician regulates emotional responses by distancing herself/himself, he/she loses the compassionate stance required for accurate attunement and containment. Roshi Joan Halifax, one of North America's most treasured Zen Buddhist teachers, has dedicated her life's work to bringing compassion into the medical system, most particularly to end-of-life care. Roshi Joan responded to a call for tools to prevent clinician burnout and secondary trauma by creating the *G.R.A.C.E. model* (2012)—five simple steps to help clinicians compassionately attend to patients while maintaining equanimity:

G—*gathering attention*: mindfully grounding and centering oneself
R—*recalling intention*: recollecting a motivation to embody integrity
A—*attuning to self/other*: securing accurate affective resonance
C—*considering*: exploring what will best serve the patient
E—*engaging*: ethically engaging and skillfully ending the session

The *G.R.A.C.E. model* helps clinicians remain compassionately present with their limitations and the discomfort these may cause. This averts a reflexive need to fix a patient's unbearable suffering. It also helps patients learn to compassionately recognize and hold their own suffering.

Offering help that is mutually liberating cultivates and facilitates *awakened presence*. This facilitation begins with a clinician's commitment to practicing compassionate recognition of the distress that arises in the presence of another's suffering. Recent brain studies show that cultivation of compassion develops new positive coping strategies even when one is confronted with others' distress.[45] This should encourage every clinician to engage in daily compassion meditation practice.

In session, clinicians can internally offer compassion to themselves or to patients using compassion meditation phrases. Formal or informal compassion practice can be taught to patients. It is deeply connective and empowering when clinicians and patients practice lovingkindness and compassion together. There is an indescribable joy in sharing effective tools for compassionately receiving pain with less mentally generated suffering.

Compassion for Trauma

Compassion is an important support for mental health and resilience because it develops kindness, mindfulness and feelings of commonality.[46] Each of these variables is of particular benefit to trauma survivors, addicts/alcoholics and the chronically depressed. Kindness undercuts self-judging.[47] Mindful compassion regulates the response to distress and reduces rumination, worry and negative self-narratives. Increased connectedness with humanity decreases isolation, shame and feelings of otherness.

Chapter 3 made a good case for the relationship between childhood trauma and onset of psychophysical diseases and substance use problems. Self-compassion has been shown to mediate the relationship between the severity of childhood maltreatment and adult emotional dysregulation.[48] "Compassion meditation is part of our trauma protocol. This promotes acceptance in that the individual stays with the sense of pain and the reality of the trauma event but does so with a sense of compassion" (Hinton, 2011).

Because select areas of the body can be a source of distress for trauma survivors, direct attention to the body may be overstimulating or feel unsafe. Physical and sexual abuse survivors may experience difficulty with mindfulness if their first taste is mindfulness of the body. Compassion and lovingkindness practices are excellent mind training tools for trauma patients because they calm the mind, soften the heart and heal the physiology, all without direct attention to the body.

Compassion is a marvelous instrument for self-soothing, a necessary skill for reducing relapse into addictions or depression. Compassion practices soothe the body by increasing vagal tone and lowering inflammatory responses.[49] Self-compassion increases capacity to cope with life stressors and tolerate distressful emotions,[50] thereby lessening anxiety, depression, rumination and social anxiety.[51]

Learning to compassionately hold recurring flashbacks or stimulus triggers can make all the difference for sufferers with post-traumatic stress disorder. A flashback is a full-body experience, and compassion is a full-body intervention. Compassion lowers amygdalic activity (the fear response), modulates the heart rate, lowers stress hormones and stimulates production of oxytocin (associated with feelings of love, generosity and compassion).[52] Each of those effects helps mitigate the terror of a flashback with a kindness that allows the psychophysical system to return to the safety of the here and now.

Finally, compassion cuts through the delusion of 'being damaged beyond repair.' I can't tell you how often I hear that phrase from patients suffering with trauma and/or substance use problems. So much of the pain they have endured or caused has cut them to the quick. Many have dealt with adversity from a tender age for sustained periods, at the hands of those who were supposed to love and care for them. Is it any wonder they feel permanently damaged and incapable of generating even a meager amount of self-regard? A heart-mind filled with compassion and lovingkindness is available to hold even the most damaged parts of the psyche.

A patient with a history of childhood trauma and chronic pain/an autoimmune disorder recently shared this experience: I arrived home from work to find my spouse completely agitated, flailing around the house trying to get chores done and not accomplishing anything. I asked if I could help, but that just made him angry. I tried again to get him to calm down and let me help. He just got more defensive and started yelling at me. I felt my whole body tighten and my mind fill with fear. In the past I would have frozen and taken the abuse or lashed out at him. This time

I decided to leave the house. I went to a café to get something to eat and tried to calm down. I sat there breathing love and kindness into my body. As I became calmer I noticed a woman out front pacing back and forth with a dog on a leash. My heart first went out to the dog being dragged around. Then I wondered about the woman and why she was so frantic. I went outside and asked her whether she was okay, whether she or her dog needed some water? She said yes to water and explained she was waiting for a friend. When I returned with the water, we sat down and she shared her story with me. As she expressed her distress, I felt increasingly calmer inside, and I could see her upset was lessening as well. I was shocked at how wise compassion not only helped me take care of myself in a traumatic situation but also let me notice another person's suffering and feel moved to reach out and help. When I returned home, I wanted to apply the same wise compassion to work things through. Unfortunately, my spouse was still mad and unwilling to talk. I decided to let it be without creating more distress for either of us.

Tsoknyi Rinpoche refers to the unconditional kindness and affection of compassion as *essence love*. He suggests a very easy method to experience essence love that is appropriate for everyone, including trauma patients—*relax, just relax, until you sense some spark of well-being.*[53] Know that essence love is inborn in every human heart, including yours. So right now—relax, just relax, until you sense some spark of well-being.

Clinical Compassion Protocols

There are currently four clinical protocols that deliver compassion and loving-kindness practices to patients. Buddhist compassion mind training informs most of the interventions offered for developing feelings of warmth, safety and self-soothing.

Paul Gilbert's *Compassion Focused Therapy* (CFT),[54] with its inclusion of Buddhist compassion principles, is illustrative of a clinical shift from thought-based cognitive-behavioral interventions to heart-based compassion interventions. This modality is primarily a therapist/patient intervention focused on the use of self-compassion skills to alleviate self-criticism, self-hatred and toxic shame.[55] CFT links the desire to be compassionate with the ability to tolerate emotions. It encourages development of reasoned compassion to stimulate the growth of courage and warm-heartedness, which leads to compassionate behaviors. CFT is showing effectiveness for a wide range of psychological conditions, including depression,[56] trauma,[57] schizophrenia-spectrum disorders[58] and eating disorders.[59]

Cognitive-Based Compassion Training, *Compassion Cultivation Training* and, most recently, the *Mindful Self-Compassion Program* are group interventions delivered in 8 weeks of 2-hour classes. Like other 8-week mindfulness-based group interventions, these include meditation instruction and home practice.

Geshe Lobsang Tenzin Negi, PhD, the creator of *Cognitive-Based Compassion Training* (CBCT), co-directs the Emory University–Tibet Science Initiative and the Emory University Collaborative for Contemplative Studies. CBCT is derived from *lojong* mind training. *Lojong* features a rich set of contemplative training practices aimed at liberating the mind from suffering through the cultivation of mindfulness, altruism, compassion and lovingkindness. This other-centered approach is dedicated to cutting through endemic self-centeredness. CBCT interventions inspire the sincere desire to free the mind-heart from suffering for the benefit of all beings. This 8-week group intervention teaches Focused Attention and Open Monitoring meditation along with practices to develop appreciation, gratitude, affection and compassion. Research shows that CBCT reduces depression and neuroendocrine and inflammatory responses to stress.[60] It is showing effectiveness as a prosocial intervention for foster care youth and at-risk adolescents.[61]

Geshe Thupten Jinpa Langri, PhD, Stanford University visiting research scholar at The Center for Compassion and Altruism Research and Education CCARE, president of the Institute of Tibetan Classics, and longtime translator for the Dalai Lama, is the creator of *Compassion Cultivation Training*. This 8-week group intervention is also grounded in the principles and practices of *lojong* and focuses primarily on helping participants understand the causes of suffering and cultivate self-compassion and compassionate regard for all beings. This is a relatively new program, and research is ongoing.[62]

The *Mindful Self-Compassion Program* is a new 8-week intervention created by Kristin Neff, PhD, and Christopher Germer, PhD. Neff is a premier researcher in the field of self-compassion, and Germer is a longtime specialist in mindfulness-based psychotherapy. Their program combines meditation practices common to most mindfulness-based group interventions with Buddhist-inspired, secularized compassion practices. This program is showing preliminary evidence of enhancing self-compassion, mindfulness and well-being.[63]

Non-referential Compassion (T: **dmigs med snying rje***)*

When compassion develops we see that every single being wishes to be happy. *Non-referential compassion* is an active cultivation of limitless affection untainted by personal preferences and boundaries. Non-referential compassion connects us with the mass of human suffering without causing us to fall victim to feelings of hopelessness or powerlessness. But you might wonder, in what way does non-referential compassion help anyone other than the practitioner?

Tibetan Buddhist teacher Mingyur Rinpoche answers in the following way:

> [Immeasurable compassion] fosters a sense of confidence that whatever situation in which we find ourselves and whomever we face, we have a basis

> for relating in a way that is not quite so fearful and hopeless. We can see possibilities to which we might otherwise be blind and begin to develop a greater appreciation for the possibilities within us. (2009)

So training the mind-heart to extend lovingkindness and compassion to all beings ends up grounding us in the practicality of being of value to anyone we might meet in our daily lives. It trains us to respond skillfully regardless of the conditions or means. A recent study found that,

> within the population of Tibetan Buddhist practitioners, those who endorsed the statement that the goal of meditation was other-focused (for the benefit of all sentient beings) were significantly lower in depression, empathic distress, and anxiety, and significantly higher in cognitive empathy (perspective-taking) compared to practitioners whose goal of meditation was self-focused. (O'Connor, 2012)

Tibetan Buddhist monk Matthieu Ricard has been involved in the neuroscientific study of meditation for many years—in and out of fMRI machines. He describes the actual practice of non-referential compassion as "generating a state in which loving compassion permeates the whole mind with no other consideration, reasoning or discursive thoughts" (quoted in Davidson, 2012).

A well-known fMRI study compared adept Tibetan Buddhist meditators (more than 10,000 hours of meditation) with novice practitioners. During compassion meditation, subjects heard emotionally difficult sounds (baby cries or screams for help). Both groups showed activation in the empathy network. But the adepts showed additional activation in the compassion network (right temporo-parietal junction and right posterior superior temporal sulcus). The adepts also showed increased emotional cardiovascular arousal indicative of neurovisceral coupling of the brain and heart.[64]

There are two primary practices for developing non-referential, immeasurable compassion. The first is Theravada compassion meditation practice: bringing to mind all beings everywhere and actively sending them compassion phrases. This is a beautiful way to end compassion meditation for the self, a loved one or a difficult person. It expands the heart, filling it with boundless love unhindered by individual preference. I recommend extending the phrases to all beings each time you practice compassion or lovingkindness meditation.

The second method is *sending and taking* (*Tonglen*) meditation. I cannot say enough about the power of *Tonglen* and its clinical value for eliminating fixation on personal suffering, especially when we are convinced we suffer more than or differently from others. That mind has forgotten that it, like all beings, wants to be happy and wishes to avoid suffering. Tsoknyi Rinpoche suggests that the ideal time to practice *Tonglen* is when we feel consumed by distressful emotions like helplessness, anger, despair, jealousy or self-directed negativity.

It might seem counterintuitive to think that receiving the suffering of others and offering healing to them could help a deeply depressed person or someone lost in addiction. But it is a powerful elixir for healing inner disturbance. I use *Tonglen* meditation in sessions with patients consumed with unremitting depressive or anxious symptoms. The process invites a shift from the incapacitation of self-suffering to the possibility of similar other-suffering. *Tonglen* actively engages the mind-heart in lessening other-suffering, thereby decreasing one's own suffering.

Tonglen *Meditation*

Find a restful position for your body and relax. Let your eyes find your surroundings. If you feel agitated, begin with a few minutes of Orienting practice to let your system settle. Now draw your attention gently to your breathing. Don't strain to keep your attention on the breath. Bring awareness to the sensual quality of breathing in and out. Surrender to this experience for a few minutes.

Now turn your attention to the quality of your thoughts, emotions and body. If you are in physical pain or feel distressed, sad, lonely, angry or anxious, whatever is there, let yourself know it as best you can. Notice your response to distress. If you hate its presence, compassionately recognize the humanness of that response. We don't like to suffer; we want suffering to end. Generate compassion for the humanness of your impatience with distress.

Reconnect with the in- and out-breath. Now engage your imagination. Whatever distress you are feeling, bring to mind all other beings suffering in this way, the countless numbers of people who are as lost as you are in this very suffering. Whether depressed, anxious, hurt, addicted, traumatized or in physical pain—recognize that they, too, may feel alone and hopeless. See them vividly, and open compassionately toward them and their suffering. Feel the desire to see them freed from suffering. Do this until your heart swells with compassion and wishes to end suffering.

Now imagine that all of their pain and suffering begins to pour out of their bodies. See this outpouring coalesce into a cloud of dark smoke rising between you and them. As you take your next in-breath, imagine your breath has the power to dissolve that dark, heavy smoke. Breathe in knowing that as the dark smoke dissolves, the intensity with which you grasp at your own suffering also begins to lessen. Feel the in-breath brighten the light of compassion growing within your heart. Use your out-breath to exhale this bright pure compassion toward the beings you see in front of you. Let them be nourished by your out-breath. See the light of your compassion lessen their suffering. As their dark smoke disperses with each in-breath, the wind of your breath fans the flames of compassion, further dissolving the darkness within you. With each out-breath more compassion pours forth, healing the beings before you and intensifying the essence love in your heart until the mind is fully permeated with boundless love and compassion.

Continue with this practice as long as you like. You may end by practicing lovingkindness, seeing all beings safe, happy, healthy and at ease—freed from suffering and then dedicate the merit of this practice to all beings everywhere.

(Tonglen can also be done preferentially for a dear one or a difficult person who is suffering. See this person and his or her pain and suffering before you. Allow that suffering to billow forth from them as black smoke. Use the same process shown above to dissolve their suffering and develop your compassionate mind-heart.)

Altruistic Joy: Rejoicing in the Happiness of Others (P & S: *muditā* T: *dgas ba*)

We have established that positive emotions are evolved adaptations, and empathic concern does invoke the altruistic motivation to help those who suffer or are less advantaged. But if we are honest, most of us might agree that feeling joy for another's happiness is conditioned on (1) how positively disposed we are toward them, (2) how supportive or kind they have been to us and (3) whether it involves competition. If it doesn't threaten my sense of self, I can be happy for your good fortune! That is an excellent example of the kind of egoic conditionality and obsessive self-grasping that impedes compassionate responsiveness.

Altruistic joy (*muditā*), the third *Brahmavihāra*, is non-preferential rejoicing in the happiness of others. *Muditā* is a simple practice, one that is easy to do for those we love and challenging to do for those we are indisposed toward. Theravada *muditā* practice involves contemplating the positive circumstances of progressively more difficult persons and rejoicing in their happiness. Generating joy for the happiness experienced by someone we find difficult requires us to confront the unfairness of life and the disturbing emotions it can elicit. Altruistic joy dissolves jealousy and resentment by cultivating selflessness and positive other-regarding emotions. In this way *muditā* expands our capacity to love without egoic constraints.

Frivolity is the near enemy of *muditā*. Frivolity is not bad, but it is not altruistic joy. Sometimes when we are practicing *muditā*, joyfulness does not come easily. We really are not acculturated to purposely feeling happy when others are doing well. So for some this practice can feel silly. Rather than expanding the heart, one can become flippant. That isn't harming, but it also isn't beneficial. When silliness arises investigate deeply the roots of that emotion. In general, frivolity is an indication of resistance to feeling real happiness for another's happiness.

Envy and *resentment* are the far enemies of *muditā*. Our society has a penchant for glorifying truly poisonous emotions. I have seen jealousy rip apart old friendships and end good working relationships. Coveting another's better outcome or begrudging her or his success can create distorted feelings of injustice or inferiority and feed depression and anxiety.[65] Cultivating positive responses to other-related happiness cuts through distorted views that keep us from compassionately holding the harsh realities of life's twists and turns. *Muditā* shows us truth while inspiring connectedness.

Muditā *Meditation Instruction*

This practice begins by bringing to mind someone who is naturally happy. It can be a role model, a spiritual figure or even a pet. Just feel this person's happiness and bask in their joy. Now bring to mind a loved one or friend who is enjoying the fruits of success or a relationship, or just taking pleasure in life. Feel this person's delight, and rejoice in their accomplishments. Let joy for their joy swell in your heart. Now engage in the same process for a neutral person, someone you don't know well but see occasionally in your life.

Then bring to mind a difficult person, someone you have competed with unsuccessfully or a person who may have rejected you, undermined your happiness or even caused you harm. See how much you can feel this person's happiness and rejoice in their accomplishments. Let joy for their joy swell in your heart as best you can. At any time during the practice, if distressful emotions or disturbing thoughts arise, take a break and turn your attention to caring for your own distress. Soften your attitude and compassionately observe, clearly comprehending difficult experience. Then return to *muditā* practice. The practice ends by imagining the happiness of all beings and feeling the joy for their joy swell in your heart.

Tibetan Buddhists practice *muditā* informally in two additional ways. Cultivating altruistic joy for the virtuous actions of others helps us recognize goodness in the world and revel in its expression. *Muditā* can also be cultivated by generating altruistic joy for the benefit of others. This is particularly healing when one is in the presence of another's inner suffering. Cultivating joy where there seems to be no joy gladdens a downtrodden heart and lightens a darkened mind.

Equanimity: Unconditioned Impartiality (P & S: *upekkhā* T: *btang snyoms*)

Equanimity (*upekkhā*)—neutrality toward all phenomena—is fundamental to genuine mental well-being. "Equanimity is absolutely indispensible. . . . From equanimity one may cultivate great lovingkindness and great compassion, and from these bodhicitta arises" (Wallace, A. B., 1999).

In Western psychology equanimity is the display of a balanced perspective and is considered necessary for resilience.[66] In Buddhist psychology equanimity (*upekkhā*), the fourth *Brahmavihāra*, is described as a neutral feeling tone of experience (*adhukkhamasukhā vedanā*) or a mental quality of impartiality or mental equipoise (*upekkhā*) cultivated through Buddhist mind training.[67]

Equanimity builds distress tolerance.[68] When craving and aversion arise in an equanimous mind, those impulses are known and released without undue resistance. Equanimity is also associated with the one-pointed concentration experienced during *ānāpānasati* and *mettā/karunā* meditation. A collected and unified mind initiates what is known as the resultant enlightenment factor of equanimity.

Indifference is the near enemy of *upekkhā*. The equality and impartiality of equanimity are not indifference or ambivalence. Equanimity uncouples active caring from fear and anger. When all beings are regarded equally, the desire to help flows freely in any direction. Many first responders attest to the effectiveness of maintaining calm, attentive neutrality in a crisis. *Craving* and *aversion* are the far enemies of *upekkhā*. An equanimous mind is less likely to avert or grasp at pain and pleasure.

*Equanimity (*Upekkhā*) Meditation Instruction*

There are several ways to do this practice. The first is based on the truth that all beings are the possessors of their deeds.[69] Theravada Buddhism recommends meditating on the following set of phrases: *All beings are the owners of their karma. Their happiness and unhappiness depends on their actions, not upon my wishes.* This meditation cultivates the equanimity of wise boundaries and right action. When others face difficulties, compassion inspires us to help, and wisdom grants us the strength to avoid feeling responsible for conditions beyond our control. When we hold with equanimity what we wish, alongside what actually is, we do not heap more suffering onto already existing trials and tribulations.

The other methods are based on the Buddha's instructions for practicing the four *Brahmavihāras*. Equanimity (*upekkhā*) is cultivated by practicing cognitive-affective neutrality toward all beings. This neutrality is devoid of egoic over-involvement and clinging. It arises from experiencing without resistance or preference.

Like *mettā* and *muditā*, meditation on equanimity (*upekkhā*) is accomplished using a succession of people. One begins by contemplating a neutral person. The felt-sense of neutrality is something akin to equanimity. Once we experience it, we can then bring to mind a dear one and then a difficult person, developing the same calm, impartial feelings toward them. Neutrality cuts through conditioned attraction and aversion.

At any time during the practice, if distressful emotions or disturbing thoughts arise, take a break and care for your own distress. Soften your attitude and compassionately observe. Then return to *upekkhā* practice. The practice ends by bringing to mind all beings with equal regard.

The Tibetan Buddhist practice of equanimity/equalness (*mnyam nyid*) is entirely related to the cultivation of immeasurable compassion (*snying rje tshad med*) and *bodhicitta* (*byang chub kyi sems*). Shantideva's *Way of the Bodhisattva*[70] and Langri Tangpo's *Eight Verses of Thought Transformation*[71] deliver superlative instructions for the developing equalness and boundless compassion that arise inseparably from emptiness. Because we are wired for an over-emphasis on self-cherishing, training in other-cherishing practices equalizes other beings and develops selflessness, humility and grace.

The actual technique begins with a simple truth—*all beings yearn for happiness and wish to be free of suffering*. One can perform this practice informally in daily life by remembering this phrase and acting harmoniously. One can also practice more formally using a Theravada-like method. Apply the recognition that *all beings yearn for happiness and wish to be free of suffering* to a series of increasingly challenging people, ending with all beings everywhere. As you bring them and their actions to mind, be with this truth and allow it to free you from afflictive response-reactions of adoration, ambivalence and hostility.

 *Bodhicitta*

> *There is born in you exceeding compassion for all those living creatures who have forgotten their true nature.* (Longchen Rabjam [Longchenpa] quoted in Kornfield, 2008)

Bodhicitta is a dedicated, heartfelt desire to fully awaken for the benefit of all other beings. It is the ultimate fruition of all the heartfulness practices. *Bodhi* means 'awake' or 'enlightened essence,' and in later Indian Buddhism *citta* means both 'mind' and 'heart.' *Bodhicitta* has two levels: *absolute* and *relative*. Absolute *bodhicitta* is the awakened mind-heart liberated from dualistic perception.

Relative *bodhicitta* is the path by which we realize absolute *bodhicitta*. This path has two aspects: *aspiration bodhicitta* and *application bodhicitta*. Intending to awaken for the benefit of all beings begins by aspiring to keep this goal at the forefront of one's thoughts and actions. Aspiration *bodhicitta* inspires us to be wise and kind even when it may feel hard to do. Application *bodhicitta* is the means by which we carry out our efforts to awaken all beings: meditation practice, life-affirming actions, efforts to heal psychophysical disease, every time we recognize suffering and choose to end suffering.

Bodhicitta reminds us that every moment is an invitation to awaken all beings by motivating ourselves to engage in other-regarding behaviors. The more we practice on the cushion and in daily life, the more absolute *bodhicitta*, immeasurable compassion and lovingkindness blossom from within and without. "When bodhicitta arises spontaneously and effortlessly, suffusing your entire lifestyle, then you are a bodhisattva" (Wallace, 1999). Never forget that you are the *awakened presence*—that unconditioned, boundlessly compassionate wakeful cognizance—that you and this world have been waiting for all along.

Notes

1 Fredrickson, B. L. (2001). The role of positive emotions in positive psychology: The broaden-and-build theory of positive emotions. *American Psychologist, 56*, 218–226.

2 Hein, G., & Singer, T. (2008). I feel how you feel but not always: The empathic brain and its modulation. *Current Opinion in Neurobiology, 18*(2), 153–158.

3 Iacoboni, M. (2009). Imitation, empathy, and mirror neurons. *Annual Review of Psychology, 60*, 653–670.

4 Craig, A. D. (2002). How do you feel? Interoception: The sense of the physiological condition of the body. *National Review of Neuroscience, 3*, 655–666.

5 Lamm, C., Decety, J., & Singer, T. (2011). Meta-analytic evidence for common and distinct neural networks associated with directly experienced pain and empathy for pain. *NeuroImage, 54*(3), 2492–2502.
Siegel, D. J. (2012). *Pocket guide to interpersonal neurobiology: An integrative handbook of the mind (Norton Series on Interpersonal Neurobiology)*. New York, NY: W. W. Norton.

6 Smith, A., & Hobson, R. P. (2013). Autism, borderline personality disorder, and empathy. *Emotion Review, 5*(2), 223–224.
Harari, H., Shamay-Tsoory, S. G., Ravid, M., & Levkovitz, Y. (2010). Double dissociation between cognitive and affective empathy in borderline personality disorder. *Psychiatry Research, 175*(3), 277–279.
Ritter, K., Dziobek, I., Preißler, S., Rüter, A., Vater, A., Fydrich, T., . . . & Roepke, S. (2011). Lack of empathy in patients with narcissistic personality disorder. *Psychiatry Research, 187*(1), 241–247.

7 Lishner, D. A., Vitacco, M. J., Hong, P. Y., Mosley, J., Miska, K., & Stocks, E. L. (2012). Evaluating the relation between psychopathy and affective empathy: Two preliminary studies. *International Journal of Offender Therapy and Comparative Criminology, 56*(8), 1161–1181.
Domes, G., Hollerbach, P., Vohs, K., Mokros, A., & Habermeyer, E. (2013). Emotional empathy and psychopathy in offenders: An experimental study. *Journal of Personality Disorders, 27*(1), 67–84.

8 Schmidt, M. F., & Sommerville, J. A. (2011). Fairness expectations and altruistic sharing in 15-month-old human infants. *PLOS ONE, 6*(10), e23223.
Hepach, R., Vaish, A., & Tomasello, M. (2013). A new look at children's prosocial motivation. *Infancy, 18*(1), 67–90.

9 Eisenberg, N., & Morris, A. S. (2001). The origins and social significance of empathy-related responding: A review of empathy and moral development: Implications for caring and justice by M. L. Hoffman. *Social Justice Research, 14*(1), 95–120.

10 Hopenwasser, K. (2008). Being in rhythm: Dissociative attunement in therapeutic process. *Journal of Trauma & Dissociation, 9*(3), 349–367.

11 Stolorow, R.D. (1994). Subjectivity and self psychology. In R.D. Stolorow (Ed.), *The intersubjective perspective* (pp. 31–41). Lanham, MD: Rowman and Littlefield.
12 Klimecki, O., & Singer, T. (2011). Empathic distress fatigue rather than compassion fatigue? Integrating findings from empathy research in psychology and social neuroscience. In B. Oakley, A. Knafo, G. Madhavan & D.S. Wilson (Eds), *Pathological altruism* (pp. 368–383). New York, NY: Oxford University Press.
13 Singer, T. (2012, April). Neuroscience, empathy and compassion. Paper presented at the International Symposia for Contemplative Studies, Denver, CO.
Klimecki, O.M., Leiberg, S., Lamm, C., & Singer, T. (2012). Functional neural plasticity and associated changes in positive affect after compassion training. *Cerebral Cortex*, *3*(7), 1552–1561.
14 Stebnicki, M.A. (2007). Empathy fatigue: Healing the mind, body, and spirit of professional counselors. *American Journal of Psychiatric Rehabilitation*, *10*(4), 317–338.
Decety, J., Yang, C.Y., & Cheng, Y. (2010). Physicians down-regulate their pain empathy response: An event-related brain potential study. *NeuroImage*, *50*(4), 1676.
15 Krasner, M. S., Epstein, R. M., Beckman, H., Suchman, A. L., Chapman, B., Mooney, C. J., & Quill, T. E. (2009). Association of an educational program in mindful communication with burnout, empathy, and attitudes among primary care physicians. *JAMA: The Journal of the American Medical Association*, *302*(12), 1284–1293.
16 Bodhi, B. (2000). *The connected discourses of the Buddha: A translation of the Samyutta Nikaya.* (B. Bodhi, Trans.) Boston, MA: Wisdom Publications.
17 Fredrickson, B.L., Cohn, M.A., Coffey, K.A., Pek, J., & Finkel, S.M. (2008). Open hearts build lives: Positive emotions, induced through loving-kindness meditation, build consequential personal resources. *Journal of Personality and Social Psychology*, *95*(5), 1045.
18 Hutcherson, C.A., Seppala, E.M., & Gross, J.J. (2008). Loving-kindness meditation increases social connectedness. *Emotion*, *8*(5), 720–724.
Fredrickson, B.L., Cohn, M.A., Coffey, K.A., Pek, J., & Finkel, S.M., 2008, 1045.
Kok, B.E., Waugh, C.E., & Fredrickson, B.L. (2013). Meditation and health: The search for mechanisms of action. *Social and Personality Psychology Compass*, *7*(1), 27–39.
19 Leung, M.K., Chan, C.C., Yin, J., Lee, C.F., So, K.F., & Lee, T.M. (2013). Increased gray matter volume in the right angular and posterior parahippocampal gyri in loving-kindness meditators. *Social Cognitive and Affective Neuroscience*, *8*(1), 34–39.
20 Boellinghaus, I., Jones, F.W., & Hutton, J. (2012). The role of mindfulness and loving-kindness meditation in cultivating self-compassion and other-focused concern in health care professionals. *Mindfulness*, 1–10. Retrieved May 2013 from http://dx.doi.org/10.1007/s12671-012-0158-6
Weininger, R., & Kearney, M. (2011). Revisiting empathic engagement: Countering compassion fatigue with "exquisite empathy."
In Irene Renzenbrink (Ed.). *Caregiver stress and staff support in illness, dying, and bereavement*. Oxford, England: Oxford University Press. pp. 49–61.
21 Johnson, D.P., Penn, D.L., Fredrickson, B.L., Meyer, P.S., Kring, A.M., & Brantley, M. (2009). Loving-kindness meditation to enhance recovery from negative symptoms of schizophrenia. *Journal of Clinical Psychology*, *65*(5), 499–509.
22 Goetz, J.L., Keltner, D., & Simon-Thomas, E. (2010). Compassion: An evolutionary analysis and empirical review. *Psychological Bulletin*, *136*(3), 351.
23 Shane, S.H., Wells, R.S., & Würsig, B. (1986). Ecology, behavior and social organization of the bottlenose dolphin: A review. *Marine Mammal Science*, *2*(1), 34–63.
Maestripieri, D., & Roney, J.R. (2006). Evolutionary developmental psychology: Contributions from comparative research with nonhuman primates. *Developmental Review*, *26*(2), 120–137.

24 Nesse, R.M. (2007). Runaway social selection for displays of partner value and altruism. *Biological Theory, 2*, 143–155.

25 Sober, E., & Wilson, D.S. (1998). *Unto others: The evolution and psychology of unselfish behavior.* Cambridge, MA: Harvard University Press.

Dovidio, J. F., Piliavin, J. A., Schroeder, D. A., & Penner, L. (2006). *The social psychology of prosocial behavior.* Mahwah, NJ: Erlbaum.

26 Bowlby, J. (1969). *Attachment and loss*, Vol. 1: *Attachment*. New York, NY: Basic Books.

Nussbaum, M.C. (1996). Compassion: The basic social emotion. *Social Philosophy and Policy, 13*, 27–58.

27 Nussbaum, M.C. (2001). *Upheavals of thought: The intelligence of emotions.* New York, NY: Cambridge University Press.

28 Rudolph, U., Roesch, S.C., Greitemeyer, T., & Weiner, B. (2004). A meta-analytic review of help giving and aggression from an attributional perspective: Contributions to a general theory of motivation. *Cognition and Emotion, 18*, 815–848.

29 Batson, C.D. (1991). *The altruism question: Towards a social-psychological answer.* Hillsdale, NJ: Erlbaum.

Batson, C.D., O'Quin, K., Fultz, J., Vanderplas, M., & Isen, A.M. (1983). Influence of self-reported distress and empathy on egoistic versus altruistic motivation to help. *Journal of Personality and Social Psychology, 45*, 706–718.

30 Neff, K.D., & Beretvas, S.N. (2012). The role of self-compassion in romantic relationships. *Self and Identity,12*(1), 78–98.

31 Terry, M.L., & Leary, M.R. (2011). Self-compassion, self-regulation, and health. *Self and Identity, 10*, 352–362.

Kelly, A.C., Zuroff, D.C., Foa, C.L., & Gilbert, P. (2009). Who benefits from training in self-compassionate self-regulation? A study of smoking reduction. *Journal of Social and Clinical Psychology, 29*, 727–755.

Magnus, C., Kowalski, K., & McHugh, T. (2010). The role of self-compassion in women's self-determined motives to exercise and exercise-related outcomes. *Self and Identity, 9*, 363–382.

32 Cuddy, A.J., Fiske, S.T., & Glick, P. (2007). The BIAS map: Behaviors from intergroup affect and stereotypes. *Journal of Personality and Social Psychology, 92*(4), 631.

33 Weiner, B. (2005). *Social motivation, justice, and the moral emotions: An attributional approach.* Mahwah, NJ: Psychology Press.

34 Pasupathi, M., & Lockenhoff, C. (2002). Ageist behavior. In T.D. Nelson (Ed.), *Ageism: Stereotyping and prejudice against older persons* (pp. 201–246). Cambridge, MA: MIT Press.

35 Cuddy, A.J., Fiske, S.T., & Glick, P., 2007, p. 631.

36 Eron, L.D., & Huessmann, L.R. (1984). The relation of prosocial behavior to the development of aggression and psychopathology. *Aggressive Behavior, 10*, 201–211.

37 Haney, C., Banks, C., & Zimbardo, P. (1973). Interpersonal dynamics in a simulated prison. *International Journal of Criminology and Penology, 1*, 69–97.

38 Blass, T. (1991). Understanding behavior in the Milgram obedience experiment: The role of personality, situations, and their interactions. *Journal of Personality and Social Psychology, 60*, 398–413.

39 Staub, E. (1989). *The roots of evil: The origins of genocide and other group violence.* New York, NY: Cambridge University Press.

40 Carnahan, T., & McFarland, S. (2007). Revisiting the Stanford Prison Experiment: Could participant self-selection have led to the cruelty? *Personality and Social Psychology Bulletin, 33*(5), 603–614.

41 Buss, A.H., & Perry, M. (1992). The aggression questionnaire. *Journal of Personality and Social Psychology, 63*, 452–459.

42 Christie, R., & Geis, F. L. (1970). *Studies in Machiavellianism.* New York, NY: Academic Press.

43 American Psychiatric Association. (2000). *Diagnostic and statistical manual of mental disorders: DSM-IV-TR.* Arlington, VA: American Psychiatric Publishing, Inc.

44 Sidanius, J., & Pratto, F. (1999). *Social dominance.* New York, NY: Cambridge University Press.

45 Klimecki, O. M., Leiberg, S., Lamm, C., & Singer, T., 2012.

46 MacBeth, A., & Gumley, A. (2012). Exploring compassion: A meta-analysis of the association between self-compassion and psychopathology. *Clinical Psychology Review, 32*(6), 545–552.
Neff, K. (2003). Self-compassion: An alternative conceptualization of a healthy attitude toward oneself. *Self and Identity, 2*(2), 85–101.

47 Van Dam, N. T., Sheppard, S. C., Forsyth, J. P., & Earleywine, M. (2011). Self-compassion is a better predictor than mindfulness of symptom severity and quality of life in mixed anxiety and depression. *Journal of Anxiety Disorders, 25*(1), 123–130.

48 Vettese, L. C., Dyer, C. E., Li, W. L., & Wekerle, C. (2011). Does self-compassion mitigate the association between childhood maltreatment and later emotion regulation difficulties? A preliminary investigation. *International Journal of Mental Health and Addiction, 9*(5), 480–491.
Leary, M. R., Tate, E. B., Adams, C. E., Allen, A. B., & Hancock, J. (2007). Self-compassion and reactions to unpleasant self-relevant events: The implications of treating oneself kindly. *Journal of Personality and Social Psychology, 92*, 887–904.
Sbarra, D. A., Smith, H. L., & Mehl, M. R. (2012). When leaving your ex, love yourself: Observational ratings of self-compassion predict the course of emotional recovery following marital separation. *Psychological Science, 23*(3), 261–269.

49 Rockliff, H., Gilbert, P., McEwan, K., Lightman, S., & Glover, D. (2008). A pilot exploration of heart rate variability and salivary cortisol responses to compassion-focused imagery. *Clinical Neuropsychiatry, 5*, 132–139.

50 Desbordes, G., Negi, L. T., Pace, T.W.W., Wallace, B. A., Raison, C. L., & Schwartz E. L. (2012). Effects of mindful-attention and compassion meditation training on amygdala response to emotional stimuli in an ordinary, non-meditative state. *Frontiers in Human Neuroscience, 6*(292), 1–15.
Neff, K. D. (2012). The science of self-compassion. In C. Germer & R. Siegel (Eds.), *Compassion and wisdom in psychotherapy* (pp. 79–92). New York, NY: Guilford Press.

51 Werner, K. H., Jazaieri, H., Goldin, P. R., Ziv, M., Heimberg, R. G., & Gross, J. J. (2012). Self-compassion and social anxiety disorder. *Anxiety, Stress & Coping, 25*(5), 543–558.

52 Rockliff, H., Karl, A., McEwan, K., Gilbert, J., Matos, M., & Gilbert, P. (2011). Effects of intranasal oxytocin on "compassion focused imagery." *Emotion-APA, 11*(6), 1388.

53 Rinpoche, T., & Swanson, E. (2012). *Open heart, open mind: Awakening the power of essence love.* New York, NY: Harmony Books.

54 Gilbert, P. (2010). *The compassionate mind: A new approach to life's challenges.* Oakland, CA: New Harbinger Publications.

55 Gilbert, P., & Procter, S. (2006). Compassionate mind training for people with high shame and self-criticism: Overview and pilot study of a group therapy approach. *Clinical Psychology & Psychotherapy, 13*(6), 353–379.
Gilbert, P., Baldwin, M., Irons, C., Baccus, J., & Clark, M. (2006). Self-criticism and self-warmth: An imagery study exploring their relation to depression. *Journal of Cognitive Psychotherapy: An International Quarterly, 20*, 183–200.

56 Allen, N. B., & Knight, W.E.J. (2005). Mindfulness, compassion for self, and compassion for others: Implications for understanding the psychopathology and treatment

of depression. In P. Gilbert (Ed.). *Compassion: Conceptualisations, research and use in psychotherapy* (pp. 239–262). London, England: Routledge.

57 Lee, D. A. (2009). Compassion-focused cognitive therapy for shame-based trauma memories and flashbacks in post-traumatic stress disorder. In N. Grey (Ed.), *A casebook of cognitive therapy for traumatic stress reactions*, 230–246.

58 Braehler, C., Gumley, A., Harper, J., Wallace, S., Norrie, J., & Gilbert, P. (2012). Exploring change processes in compassion focused therapy in psychosis: Results of a feasibility randomized controlled trial. *British Journal of Clinical Psychology, 52*(2), 199–214.

59 Gale, C., Gilbert, P., Read, N., & Goss, K. (2012). An evaluation of the impact of introducing compassion focused therapy to a standard treatment programme for people with eating disorders. *Clinical Psychology & Psychotherapy*. doi: 10.1002/cpp.1806

60 Pace, T. W., Negi, L. T., Dodson-Lavelle, B., Ozawa-de Silva, B., Reddy, S. D., Cole, S. P., . . . & Raison, C. L. (2012). Engagement with cognitively-based compassion training is associated with reduced salivary C-reactive protein from before to after training in foster care program adolescents. *Psychoneuroendocrinology, 38*(2), 294–299.

61 Reddy, S. D., Negi, L. T., Dodson-Lavelle, B., Ozawa-de Silva, B., Pace, T. W., Cole, S. P., . . . & Craighead, L. W. (2013). Cognitive-based compassion training: A promising prevention strategy for at-risk adolescents. *Journal of Child and Family Studies, 22*(2), 219–230.

62 Jazaieri, H., Jinpa, G. T., McGonigal, K., Rosenberg, E. L., Finkelstein, J., Simon-Thomas, E., . . . & Goldin, P. R. (2012). Enhancing compassion: A randomized controlled trial of a compassion cultivation training program. *Journal of Happiness Studies, 14*(4), 1113–1126.

63 Neff, K. D., & Germer, C. K. (2013). A pilot study and randomized controlled trial of the mindful self-compassion program. *Journal of Clinical Psychology, 69*(1), 28–44.

64 Lutz, A., Greischar, L. L., Perlman, D. M., & Davidson, R. J. (2009). BOLD signal in insula is differentially related to cardiac function during compassion meditation in experts vs. novices. *NeuroImage, 47*(3), 1038–1046.

65 Smith, R. H., Parrott, W. G., Ozer, D., & Moniz, A. (1994). Subjective injustice and inferiority as predictors of hostile and depressive feelings in envy. *Personality and Social Psychology Bulletin, 20*(6), 705–711.

66 Lundman, B., Strandberg, G., Eisemann, M., Gustafson, Y., & Brulin, C. (2007). Psychometric properties of the Swedish version of the Resilience Scale. *Scandinavian Journal of Caring Sciences, 21*(2), 229–237.

67 Bodhi, B. (1993/1999). *A comprehensive manual of Abhidhamma*. Onalaska, WA: Buddhist Publication Society.

68 Mohr, S. (2011). Integration of spirituality and religion in the care of patients with severe mental disorders. *Religions, 2*(4), 549–565.

69 Buddhaghosa. (1975). *The Visuddhimaga*. (B. Nanamoli, Trans.) Kandy, Sri Lanka: Buddhist Publication Society. IX:96.

70 Shantideva. (1997). *The way of the Bodhisattva: A translation of the Bodhicharyāvatāra*. Boston, MA: Shambhala Publications.

71 Gyatso, T., & Jinpa, G. T. (2000). *Transforming the mind*. London, England: HarperCollins.

6

Know Spontaneous Awakened Presence

 Emptiness Redux: *Madhyamaka* and Yogācāra

Nāgārjuna

> *Those who think in terms of essences and real differences, and who cannot recognize entities without essences, do not grasp the truth taught by the Buddha.* (Nāgārjuna 15:6 in Garfield, 1995)

Nāgārjuna and his chief disciple, Āryadeva, were the progenitors of the *Middle Way School* (*Madhyamaka*) of Indian Buddhism. Although Nāgārjuna is often called the second Buddha, little is known about his actual life. Modern Buddhist scholars tend toward a theory of two Nāgārjunas: a Southern Indian philosopher living sometime between 150 and 250 CE, and a later figure who was primarily a tantric alchemist/yogi.[1] During Nāgārjuna's lifetime, Northern India was beset with ongoing political strife and successive foreign invasions. Some of the extant narratives about Nāgārjuna suggest rampant socio-political turmoil influenced his decision to renounce a wealthy Brahmin lifestyle and enter monastic life. As a philosopher monk, Nāgārjuna mastered the existing Theravada and Mahāyāna literature and composed what would become the root texts of *Madhyamaka* Middle Way philosophy.

In the *Fundamental Verses of the Middle Way* (*Mūlamadhyamaka-kārikā*), Nāgārjuna rebuffed both the mysticism of the *Prajñāpāramitā Sutras* and the Abhidharma's implied essentialism. Through reasoned analysis Nāgārjuna refuted the intrinsic irreducibility of the four ultimate *dhammas*—consciousness (*citta*), mental factors (*cetasikas*), matter (*rūpa*) and liberation *(nirvāna)*—upheld by the Abhidharmists. He rationally explicated the empty (*śūnyatā*) nature of causation, temporality, impermanence, self and *nirvāna*.

Nāgārjuna adamantly rejected eternalism and nihilism. His arguments for emptiness rested on two principles: (1) things/selves in the world appear nominally, and (2) because of their impermanence, interdependence and insubstantiality, these entities lack any essential (*svabhāva*) nature. Nāgārjuna's movement away from the Abhidharma framework restored an analytical method of inquiry that the historical Buddha had favored.

> It [the Abhidharma] presented a final description of human experience which became an orthodoxy that could not be challenged any further; one that was a bit alienated from the actual cut and thrust of lived human experience. Nāgārjuna in particular, began to rebel against that and return us to something rather more direct and immediate. (Batchelor, 2013)

Madhyamaka

Nāgārjuna's analytical style of refutation—rational exposition, critique and debate—became the hallmark of *Madhyamaka* philosophy. Take an object, for instance, this book. If the book is self-existing, it could not be broken down into its parts—cover, paper, letters, ink, ideas, matter, particles, quantum information and so on. Inevitably, one arrives at the impossibility of the book's independent self-existence. It is no more than a so-called object, interdependently linked to nominal parts similarly lacking any essential (*svabhāva*) nature. The book can be held, dropped and so on, and therefore does have conventional or relative existence. But the book cannot be found to ultimately exist separately from its myriad parts.

Nāgārjuna used a similar line of reasoning to revision *Dependent Origination* (*pratītyasamutpāda*). He argued that the Abhidharma's sequential view of the 12 links (*nidānas*) implied their self-existence. By emphasizing their systemic multi-directionality and mutual reciprocity, Nāgārjuna rendered the 12 *nidānas* empty of inherent self-existence. Many psychotherapists would recognize this systemic view in the work of Virginia Satir and Salvador Minuchin. Family systems psychotherapy operates on the assumption that any psycho-behavioral change in one family member will ripple out and impact the entire family.

A debate opponent once asked Nāgārjuna to agree that if nothing has inherent existence, that would also include his arguments. He replied that although his arguments lack inherent existence, they nonetheless had the power to refute.[2]

Shantideva (eighth century) stands out as one of the most revered figures in Indian Mahāyāna Buddhism and *Madhyamaka* scholarship. Tradition holds that *Shantideva* was a forest yogi prior to entering monastic life at Nālānda University, where he steeped himself in the Buddhist *Sutras*. Unbeknownst to his fellow monks, who only saw him sleep, eat and defecate, *Shantideva* had used his time at Nālānda to author two texts of his own. Fed up with Shantideva's apparent indolence, the other monks challenged him to publicly recite a *sutra*. *Shantideva* asked whether he should recite an existing *sutra* or new one. The monks resoundingly replied, "New!" *Shantideva* shocked all the monks as he launched into a recitation of his original treatise, *A Guide to the Bodhisattva's Way of Life* (*Bodhicaryavatara*). This renowned 10-chapter tome represents the best of Buddhist ethics and includes one of the most succinct descriptions of *Madhyamaka* philosophy.[3]

*The Two Truths (*Satyadvayavibhāga*)*

Madhyamaka formalized its description of emptiness in the doctrine of the *Two Truths* (*satyadvayavibhāga*). Nāgārjuna based his defense of the Two Truths on the *Kaccayanagotta Sutta*. In this Pāli Sutta the Buddha explained the difference between conventionally accepted mental constructions about experience and direct comprehension of the ultimate truth of experience. Discerning this difference is a key component of genuine mental health.

"By & large, this world is supported by (takes as its object) a polarity, that of existence & non-existence. . . . By & large, this world is in bondage to cravings, clingings & biases. . . ." These are examples of *conventional* truth (P: *sammuti sacca* S: *lokasamvrtisatya* T: *kun-rdzob bden-pa*). *"But [a wise] one does not get involved with or cling to these cravings, clingings, fixations of awareness, biases, or obsessions; nor is she/he resolved on 'my self.' She/he has no uncertainty or doubt that just suffering, when arising, is arising; suffering, when passing away, is passing away."* Knowing experience devoid of fixation, bias or self-reference is how one recognizes *ultimate* truth (P: *paramattha sacca* S: *paramārthasatya* T: *don-dam bden-pa*). *"'Everything exists': That is one extreme. 'Everything doesn't exist': That is a second extreme. Avoiding these two extremes, the Buddha teaches the Dhamma via the middle"* (SN 12:15). And that middle rests firmly in the emptiness of Dependent Origination.

So although phenomena *conventionally* exist, they cannot be found to have *ultimate* existence. The Two Truths provide a psychological container to hold the empty nature of conventional existence. "Emptiness refers specifically to the emptiness of mind—the absence of mind's independent, intrinsic existence. In this context we can then say the ultimate creator of *samsāra* and *nirvāna* is the mind" (Gyatso, 2005).

Yogācāra

The rise of the Gupta Empire in the fourth century CE ushered in a 200-year period of peace, prosperity and cultural flourishing in Northern India. Great monasteries like Nālānda thrived as institutions of higher learning in Buddhist philosophy, arts and medicine. Pilgrims came from all over Asia to study at these universities.

Thanks to the efforts of *Asanga* and his half-brother *Vasubandhu*, *Yogācāra* philosophy gained popularity. Asanga and Vasubandhu began their monastic training in earlier Buddhist schools and later converted to Mahāyāna Buddhism. After his conversion, Asanga authored the *Yogācārabhūmi-śāstra*, a compendium of Buddhist terms and practices structured to fit Yogācāra principles. Prior to his conversion, Vasubandhu wrote a commentary on the *Sarvāstivāda Abhidharma* titled *The Abhidharmakośa*, which became the authoritative Abhidharma literature of Mahāyāna Buddhism. Both men authored authoritative commentaries on the first Yogācāra text, the *Sandhinirmocana Sutra*, written a century or two earlier.

The *Sandhinirmocana Sutra* (*Unraveling the Mystery of Thought*) and the later *Lankāvatāra Sutra* (fourth century) preached the primacy of mind/consciousness. Yogācāra means 'yoga practice,' in this case the meditative path to enlightened mind. Yogācārins were supremely interested in consciousness, mind and its functions, the processes of perception and knowledge acquisition, and karmic influence on the human psyche.

Yogācāra philosophy systematized the stages of the Bodhisattva path and introduced several important developments in the Buddhist philosophy of mind: *cognition-only* (*vijñapti-mātra*), the *three natures* (*trisvabhāva*), *the storehouse consciousness (ālaya-vijñāna)* and the *eight consciousnesses*.[4]

The *Sandhinirmocana Sutra* adamantly upheld the notion of the Buddha offering remarkably different teachings depending on an audience's level of understanding. According to this text, the Theravada—First Turning of the Wheel of Dharma (Nikāyas and Abhidharma)—and the Mahāyāna—Second Turning of the Wheel of Dharma (*Prajñāpāramitā* and *Mahāyāna Sutras*)—were incomplete teachings and in need of Yogācāra's further elaboration to obtain full understanding. The *Sandhinirmocana Sutra* declared its tenets and doctrines the definitive teachings of the Buddha, the Vajrayāna—Third Turning of the Wheel of Dharma.

Yogācāra has been called the *mind-only* (*cittamātra*) school of Buddhism and often criticized for its insistence on an ultimate mind cognizing/giving birth to all phenomena. However, some Buddhist scholars disagree:

> [Yogācāra] denies that it makes any sense to speak of cognitive objects occurring outside an act of cognition. . . . The mind doesn't create the physical world, but it produces the interpretative categories through which we know and classify the physical world, and it does this so seamlessly that we mistake our interpretations for the world itself. Those interpretations, which are projections of our desires and anxieties, become obstructions (*āvaraṇa*) preventing us from seeing what is actually the case. (Lusthaus, 2004)

*The Three Natures (*Trisvabhāva*)*

According to the *Sandhinirmocana Sutra*, anything that can be known has one of three natures: constructed, dependent or perfected. The *constructed nature* (S: *paraikalpitasvabhāva* T: *kun brtags*) includes all language-based appropriation. Conceptual at its core, this mental world of names and labels ascribes ultimacy to objects of cognition and reinforces subject/object dualism. Objects include both the experiencer and that which is experienced, or what is known in Yogācāra terminology as the *grasper* and the *grasped*. Constructive knowing codifies deluded perception and obscures the emptiness of self and objects.

The *dependent nature* (S: *paratantrasvabhāva* T: *gzhan bdang*) is the ever-shifting stream of interconnected, compounded internal and external objects, on which language-based constructions act. Dependent nature is purely and simply the 'just is' of phenomena. In our addiction to concepts, humans remain unaware of dependent nature and imprisoned by the confused alienation of the illusory self's subject/object dualism. Recognizing the dependent nature of our mentative constructions leads to direct knowing of emptiness.

The *perfected nature* (S: *parinispannasvabhāva* T: *yongs gsum*) is *suchness*, a term shared by all schools of Buddhism to designate enlightened perception or 'the way things truly are.' Even though the *Yogācārabhūmi-śāstra* seems to imply a real[5] mind of suchness, it would be incorrect to envision perfected nature as a reified, eternally existing, enlightened mind, separate from or primary to all other phenomena. The perfected nature is the "complete absence, in the dependent nature, of conceptualized nature" (Williams, 2008).

Yogācārins considered meditation the supreme vehicle to realize suchness—the empty, non-duality of experience and an experiencer's concepts:

> For Yogācāra thinkers a truly liberative meditative state must not be caught in the false distinction between subject and object. . . . the state must be *non-dual*, in that the experience is not structured by the duality of object and subject. (Dunne, 2011)

Therefore, perfected nature is merely the cessation of false perceptual constructions.

Psychotherapeutically Recognizing Constructed Reality

Recognizing constructive habits of perception is a common strategy of most psychotherapeutic modalities. When therapists reframe, they invite reconsideration of cognitive habituation. Cognitive behavioral therapy questions automatic thoughts and encourages discovery of less negative, more accurate alternative views. Depth psychotherapy provokes investigation of deeply embedded constructed assumptions hidden beneath the surface of defenses and symptoms. While these methods transform the sense of self and its relationship to the larger world, none dissolves the adventitious suffering of imputed existence or *wrong view*.

Buddhist psychology employs direct knowing of actuality to cut through wrong views, distorted cognitions and emotion dysregulation. This allows false constructions to dissolve on their own. By pointing out the Two Truths and the *Three Natures*, Buddhist psychology distinguishes habitual conceptualizations from the nonconceptual actuality of here-and-now experience. Purposefully embodying the actuality of experience cuts through wrong views and effortlessly lands us in the liberating viscerality of *awakened presence*.

Cutting Through Wrong View

H: I have this intense anxiety all the time (with a strained look on his face).

LDM: *What do you experience when you feel this anxiety?*

H: I get a terrible feeling here (hand on his chest).

LDM: *Can you describe the sensation you have in your chest?*

H: It's radiating out (fingers on the hand move out, the pained look on his face tightens more).

LDM: *Okay . . . Would you be willing to try something?*

H: All right.

LDM: *Let your attention be soft and open your senses . . . see and hear like an antenna; just receive things around you for about 30 seconds. Now let this same open, soft attention be drawn to that area in your chest. You don't have to close your eyes . . . The visual field is just here, like the sounds in the room. Don't dive into the sensation with intense focus. Just touch it lightly with awareness and explore the actual physical sensations with curiosity. Does it have movement? Is it dull or sharp? Try to get to know it.*

LDM: *What did you notice?*

H: It is buzzing, like electricity, but not like it shocks me (face softens a bit).

LDM: *Okay, can you hang out with that for a bit? Notice whether the sensations are pleasant, unpleasant or neutral.*

H: Well . . . kind of neutral, actually (a surprised facial expression emerges).

LDM: *All right, would you be willing to stay with neutral and see what happens?*

H: Yeah . . . (After a minute or two) It's still there and moving out into my arms and legs.

LDM: *How is that for you?*

H: Still kind of neutral.

LDM: *Okay, let that happen. (After a minute or two) How is your mind?*

H: Calm . . .

LDM: *Well, that is very interesting! Here you are with that sensation you called 'anxiety' and 'terrible,' yet your mind is calm.*

H: Yeah, I'm amazed. It's really like energy, and I am not afraid of feeling it. I don't necessarily want it, but I don't hate it either. I let myself get to know it for what it is, not what my mind was telling me it is.

LDM: *Would you still call it anxiety?*

H: No . . . I don't know what to call it.

LDM: *How about energy radiating out from the chest through the body?*

H: (Smiles.)

Table 6.1

Two Truths	
Conventional (selfing)	**Ultimate** (not-self)
I have anxiety all the time. I get a terrible feeling. I don't like it. I fear anxiety in my chest. I and anxiety are solid and separate.	Bare awareness of buzzing sensations. Sensation is not shocking or dangerous. The sensation is neutral. Mind is calm; anxiety cannot be found. Knower and known *interare.*
Three Natures	
Constructed (dualistic)	I, anxiety, all the time, terrible, catastrophe, aversion, fear, disembodied from actual sensation
Dependent (interdependent)	Embodied knowing of sensation devoid of distorted, appropriative mental labeling and affective responses to sensation
Perfected (non-dual)	Awareness of constructed and dependent natures that liberates from cognitive, affective and physical distress; resting in experience, embodied, unperturbed, awake

 Not-Self (*Anātman*), Part 2: The Multi-Layered Empty Self

Madhyamaka *and Not-Self*

In the *Samyutta Nikāya*, the Buddha defined not-self as any manifestation of the Five Aggregates, "*One sees them as they really are with correct wisdom thus: 'this is not mine, this I am not, this is not my self*'" (22:82).

Nāgārjuna further analyzed this teaching in the *Fundamental Verses of the Middle Way*:

> 18:1 *If the self were the aggregates, it would have arising and ceasing (as properties). If it were different than the aggregates, it would not have the characteristics of the aggregates.*

> 18:4 *When views of 'I' and 'mine' are extinguished, whether with respect to the internal or external, the appropriator ceases. This having ceased, birth ceases.*
> 18:7 *What language expresses is nonexistent. The sphere of thought is nonexistent. Unarisen and unceased, like nirvāna, is the nature of things.*
> 18:9 *Not dependent on another, peaceful and not fabricated by mental fabrication, not thought, without distinctions, that is the character of reality (suchness).*[6]

When false belief in an illusory self dissolves, so, too, does the associated suffering of self-referential cogitation and affective stickiness. Seeing beyond appropriation reveals the empty transparency of the Five Aggregates. Because of this clarity, emptiness is not nothingness; it is the total possibility of *suchness*: beyond thought, beyond words, inexpressible, unarisen, unceasing, unconditioned.

Yogācāra and Not-Self

Analytical disputation of the self was not enough for the Yogācārins. They wanted to know through meditative inquiry the what, how and why of the illusory self, particularly, answers to unresolved questions about the mechanisms of karmic legacy and the psychological structure of mind. "Yogācārins finalized a radically new model of mind in Indian Buddhism, one in which subliminal cognitive, affective, and even afflictive processes interact and co-exist with supraliminal processes" (Waldron, 2003).

Vasubandhu aligned with traditional Abhidharmists in describing awareness as the apprehension of an object, but parted ways with them about the manner in which objects are known. In the *Abhidharmakośa*, Vasubandhu postulated *objects arising in a continuum of luminous consciousness as mere appearances of that consciousness*. In fact, this consciousness was said to phenomenally construct experience *and* the subjectivity of experience from its own pre-reflective luminosity. While that may sound perilously close to positing an enduring 'self' residing beyond the flow of experience, it would apply only if 'self' and 'subjectivity' could not be differentiated from one another.[7] *Self* owns experience and defines itself by it; *subjectivity* experiences reflexively.

The Eight Consciousnesses

Yogācāra differentiated processes of self-reification from subjective conscious experience. The Abhidharma's model of five sense-consciousnesses (eye, ear, nose, touch and taste) plus mind-consciousness (*mano-vijñāna*) sufficiently explained cognition and processing of self and objects but failed to account for the complexity and interaction of the psyche's various conscious and unconscious characteristics. To bring clarity to these unaddressed issues, Yogācāra revisioned the sixth consciousness (*mano-vijñāna*) and added two more consciousnesses: the seventh consciousness/deluded mind (*klistamanas*) and eighth consciousness/storehouse consciousness (*ālaya-vijñāna*).

This new topology of mind radically departed from the Abhidharmic framework of six consciousnesses meeting objects that activate feelings (*vedanā*) and give rise to free-floating, karmically informed perceptive reactive distortions. The Yogācārins envisioned seeds of karma and purification housed in an unconscious mental stream (*ālaya-vijñāna*), giving rise to discrete consciousnesses interacting with the psyche. In this schema, awakening results from the gradual increase of purified seeds "until finally the *ālaya-vijñāna* and all of its mundane seeds are diminished in all of its aspects" (Waldron, 2003).

Yogācāra philosophy was also deeply interested in deconstructing the illusory self to better understand the relationship between unconscious drives and behaviors propelling human suffering. They differentiated two forms of self-view: (1) *mano*, a minimal self-sense shared by all life forms, which is karmically benign and co-existent with all conscious states; and (2) *manas*, the 'I'-making that simultaneously arises with *ālaya-vijñāna*, such that *manas* takes the *ālaya-vijñāna* to be itself. Together, *mano* and *manas* create a continuous yet afflicted self-identity integrated into each mind moment.

Ālaya-vijñāna*: The Buddhist Unconscious (T:* kun gzhi'i rnam shes*)*

The term *ālaya-vijñāna* (storehouse consciousness) refers to an uninterrupted stream of sentience and was first used by Asanga in the *Yogācārabhūmi-śāstra*. *Ālaya* means 'that which is clung to' or 'dwelling.'[8] It has embodiment as its proximate cause, and by 'sticking to' the six sense faculties it uses body and mind as its means of expression. The *ālaya-vijñāna* is portrayed as a continually arising basal consciousness activated by the five senses and mind. Informed by a predisposition to distortion, the *ālaya-vijñāna* resides unconsciously and was said to be *difficult to discern even by the wise ones of the world* (Waldron, 2003, p. 110)

The *ālaya-vijñāna* houses seeds (*bīja-bhāva*) of ignorance (*avidyā*) and volitional dispositions (*sankhāra*), such as cognitive-affective distortions and habitual reactive tendencies, and seeds of wholesome dispositions accrued through various forms of dharmic practice and purification. These seeds lie dormant, awaiting activation from contact with phenomena. Once triggered, a particular seed's karmic and psychological distortion arises in a discrete cognitive awareness (*pravrtti-vijñāna*) acting on the body and psyche and inclining one toward particular habits of cognition, emotion and behavior.

This notion of karmic seeds has resonance with Western psychology's theory of unconscious impulses. Those of you who have studied Freud may be having déjà vu. Freud postulated all manner of unconscious material acting on the psyche—repressed desires, distressful emotions, traumas and memories—located in an unconscious. Of course, he had detractors who outright rejected the idea of a separate unconscious. Today, most cognitive neuroscientists accept the existence of non-conscious processes and implicit memories but reject the notion of a singular unconscious habitat.

Mano-vijñāna: *Mere 'I' (T:* yid-kyi rnam-shes*)*

Mano-vijñāna, the sixth consciousness, is integral to the biological processing of experience. This basic subjectivity is a pre-reflective self-awareness with *minimal, first-person givenness* (basic self-referencing). *Mano*, a rudimentary receiving consciousness, routinely cognizes, characterizes and interacts, all ostensibly untainted by self-reified assignment, assessment or critique. It is a bare experiencer. For instance, *right now this awareness perceives hands extending from its body typing a keyboard.*

Philosopher Dan Zahavi argues that *first-person givenness* endows the minimal self with an egoic nature.[9] Other Western philosophers of mind disagree. Ludwig Wittgenstein bemoaned the global usage of 'I,' particularly in reference to the minimal self's basic here-and-now experience, which he did not necessarily regard as personal.[10]

Recall Antonio Damasio's postulation of a *proto-self* generating basic responses to objects and an intermediary *core self* creating primitive narratives about the *proto-self*'s responses. Neither of these selves has ego function. Yet together they provide a fairly accurate description of *mano-vijñāna*. From that perspective it seems somewhat misguided to equate *mano-vijñāna*'s bare 'I'-as-experiencer with the egologicality of grasping at an 'I'-as-object.

Tibetan Buddhist teacher Tsoknyi Rinpoche refers to the basic subjectivity of the minimal self as 'mere I' (*dak tsam*) and describes it as a primarily experiential form of consciousness, not unlike that of a preverbal child.[11] The felt-sense of 'mere I' has a childlike immediacy of joyful wonder and relaxed openness. Although it has ignorance (*avidyā*) as its cause, 'mere I' precedes reified higher-order concepts and biases and therefore discerns the stream of objects with cognitive spaciousness and benevolence.

Tsoknyi Rinpoche considers 'mere I' a form of healthy ego and suggests cultivating increased 'mere I' perceptivity.[12] He recommends *shamatha* meditation to quiet obsessive narratives that prevent the mind from resting in 'mere I' nowness of mere knowing. The Mindfulness of Breath meditation as taught in chapter 4 is exemplary for this purpose.

Klistamanas: *Reified 'I' (T:* nyon-yid rnam-shes*)*

Klistamanas means 'afflictive mentation,' specifically self-reified mentation. Most schools of Buddhism associate *manas* (mind) with the arising of the *kleshas* (afflictive thoughts and emotions). The benign subjectivity of *manas* is associated with the *four afflictions*—self-existence (*satkāya drsti*), the conceit of 'I am' (*asmimāna*), self-cherishing (*ātmasneha*) and self-confusion (*moha*)—by way of *klistamanas*. As *klistamanas* subliminally grasps the *ālaya-vijñāna*'s unconscious seed habits and their distorted cognitions (*pravrtti-vijñāna*), it subconsciously reifies the four afflictions by constructing an enduring, cherished 'I'—vaguely located in the body and requiring constant attention, protection and delimitation.

Caught in *klistamanas'* subliminal web of false *'I'dentity*, we accept its reified contingencies as definitions of the self and the world: 'I am' good/bad, worthy/unworthy, loved/hated, successful/a failure, smart/stupid, rich/poor, fat/thin, ugly/beautiful. 'Life is' kind/harsh, accommodating/limiting, accessible/restricted, like me/unlike me, loving/hateful, alienating/embracing, unfit/appropriate.

The more rigidly we adhere to these beliefs, the less we perceive the apparent phenomenality of our thoughts and feelings. Mere thoughts and feelings become monumental certainties we use interchangeably as the truth. Is it any wonder that we walk through our lives feeling vacant and confused?

Tibetan Buddhism divides *klistamanas* into two levels of reification. The first level is 'grasping at true self' (*dak tenpar dzin*). This describes the process by which *manas* takes the seeds of karmic habits to be itself, fixates on them and molds them into a solid, enduring *'I'dentity*. *Dak tenpar dzin* is a story of 'me' abstracted from experience and informed by patterns of assumptive expectational knowing, which we adapt to and eventually find comfort in. This is the dis-ease of dualistic perception—an addictive disorder of 'selfing' that tricks us into wholesale acceptance of the ego's mental constructions about the way things should be and therefore must be.

The next level is 'precious I' (*dak che dzin*), which is comprised of all the ego concepts and stories we hold to, even the ones that are self-destructive. 'Precious I' is a highly distorted, egoic lens through which all conceptions and perceptions about the self and the world are viewed. As its internal influence expands, so does the distance between phenomenal reality and reified reality. Direct contact with the open benevolence of essential humanness is forgotten, buried deep beneath an ego-consumed psyche suffering from its own deluded self-perpetuating concepts and fears.

Self-Cherishing and Narcissistic Wounding

> *Self-knowledge means courageously understanding all of your limitations, afflictions and mental habits. Meditation lets us look inside and see how deluded we really are, with utter honesty. And we have to remember we are not alone, the whole of humanity is our company.* (Thubten, 2013, May)

Developmental psychology has proved that consistent, loving parent–infant interactions are critical for healthy child development. Research shows that infants of mothers with postpartum depression and personality disorders exhibit higher levels of dysregulated behavior, depressed mood by the third month and disruptions in developmental and physical growth.[13]

Heinz Kohut (1913–1981), the founder of Self Psychology, theorized that early developmental disruptions contributed tremendously to narcissistic rage and injury. He and other object relations theorists viewed child narcissism as a defensive response to a parent's child-as-object orientation, which nullified the child's beingness to fulfill the parent's narcissistic needs.[14] Alternatively, Social

Learning theorists argued that a child's normative feelings of supremacy are reinforced and distorted by parental over-indulgence and lack of commensurate reward rules.[15] In either case, as the child defends against or grasps at the parent's relational distortions of self and other, identity wounding in the child's psyche reifies inflated notions of grandiosity or lowliness.

Kohut believed the distortions of self-organization and self-regard—characteristic of narcissistic wounding—were rooted in early separation from essential humanness. He considered this absence of connectedness a primary cause of narcissistic rage and injury.[16] The outcome is a psyche that grasps at narcissistic fantasies of perfection to defend against detection of its flaws, limitations, uncertainties and vulnerabilities. In Yogācāra-informed Buddhist psychology, the fundamental distortion of *positive self-cherishing* (narcissistic self-beliefs) is thought to similarly impede natural expression of mere humanness.

Buddhist psychological theory also posits the equally deleterious effects of *negative self-cherishing*. This is a reified fixation on one's basic badness—*mentally placing oneself at the center of all bad things*. Clinging to the self's inherent brokenness is as deluded as grasping at the self's inherent perfection. While neither is true, both forms of self-cherishing can effectively wall off vulnerable aspects of the psyche and protect them from direct contact with the world. This can be a powerful incentive to eschew self-reflection and remain psychically frozen in the pain of self-cherishing.

Healing narcissistic wounding can be accomplished through the application of wisdom and compassion. By facilitating insight into the conceptual nature of afflictive self-cherishing, humility and understanding can blossom within a patient's psyche. Cultivation of compassion for the self and others increases the capacity to meet and heal underlying fearfulness and self-loathing. As the psyche repeatedly touches on and builds tolerance for mere humanness, its essential connectedness returns. This allows the mind to rest in the open benevolence of 'mere I' subjectivity, unhindered by reified grandiosity. When the *conceptual doer* is calmed, the *human being* shines forth. The psyche can know its basic humanness: no more, no less, not other than, just human.

Through this process the psyche will begin to relate differently to its world. More than once a patient of mine has reported being on the street and suddenly realizing that he or she no longer automatically judges every passerby; the mind is calm, and the heart feels accessible and receptive to the world. The psyche no longer needs to live apart, protected and separated by delusions of grandeur or brokenness. When the psyche is freed from the fear of being, thriving arises from resting in connectedness.

The Ego Tunnel

One need not suffer narcissistic wounding to live a primarily constructed, conceptual existence. When direct contact with phenomenal reality is replaced by an inner world of concepts, the psyche experiences life locked inside what philosopher

Thomas Metzinger calls an *ego tunnel*.[17] Metzinger defines consciousness as the appearance of a world and claims we live inside an impenetrable tunnel of internal constructs, which can only be perceived as givens, not the constructions they actually are. Metzinger postulates that various methods of perceptive purification can break through the ego tunnel and its myth of separability.

Many years ago, on the heels of a devastating loss, I came face to face with the ego tunnel on a meditation retreat and spontaneously blasted through its impenetrable walls. This experience occurred 8 years prior to the release of Metzinger's book, and I had no knowledge of his ego tunnel theory. Below is a portion of an account I wrote describing that experience

> *Before last week I was not directly experiencing my own phenomenology. Imagine a tunnel, let's call it the Tunnel of Knowing—my *self* on one side, everything else on the other side. The tunnel is composed of ideas about what is on both sides. I resided in the tunnel, afraid of direct contact with what was on either side. So my perception of both was formed by ideas about both rather than any kind of real phenomenal relationship with either. The tunnel was a safe place to hide from what resided on either side. It was populated by decades of definitive thoughts, statements, ideologies, identities, symbols and signs. The tunnel was long enough that I could move closer or farther from either end, depending on who I needed to believe I was touching: me or the world. I could touch both but only indirectly. This last week my mind awakened to the phenomenological processes of thought. The tunnel was revealed and by questioning, following, emptying and releasing, the tunnel finally blew apart. What followed was nakedness—me in the world, unveiled and vulnerable, touchable and real for the first time. To say I feel free under-represents the enormity of what life devoid of the tunnel looks like now. It is so much more relaxing to just experience 'what is' than have to generate mediating principles and doctrines, meanings and causes for 'what is.'*

I did not grasp the difference between actuality and the suppositional reality of dualism until the illusory cognitive barrier between myself and 'phenomenal me,' and between the world and 'phenomenal me' was revealed and then obliterated. My prior relationship with the world was merely mental, barely phenomenological, and based primarily on false representations of the self and the world, not their actualities.

Tathāgatagarbha

When referring to himself, the Buddha often used the term *Tathāgata*. *Tathā āgata* means 'thus come,' and *Tathā gata* means 'thus gone.' Commentators on the Pāli Suttas explain his use of this term in the following manner. The Buddha *came* with the teaching of deathlessness, to which he had *gone* through his own practice.[18] So with this term the Buddha identified himself as *the deathless*—gone beyond self, beyond name and form. A passage in the *Majjhima Nikāya* (MN) hints at the later evolution of *Tathāgata* into *Tathāgatagarbha*: "Here a Tathāgata appears in the world, accomplished, fully enlightened, perfect in true knowledge and conduct, sublime" (27:11).

The Mahāyānist *Tathāgatagarbha Sutra* emerged in the third century and preached a specific doctrine—*all beings, though they suffer with greed, hatred and delusion, possess an innate pristine, undefiled Buddhanature*. Although the *Tathāgatagarbha* teachings were not directly associated with *Madhyamaka* or Yogācāra, the term was mentioned in the *Lankāvatāra Sutra* in conjunction with *ālaya-vijñāna*. The *Tathāgatagarbha* teachings are fully integrated into Tibetan Buddhism, where Buddhanature is considered the 'true nature of things' (S: *dharmatā* T: *chos nyid*) and the true nature of all beings.

 Non-dual Mindfulness

Non-dual mindfulness seeks to collapse perceptual dualism by exposing it directly from within the field of awareness. Non-dual meditative methods develop three important characteristics of genuine mental health: (1) receptivity to the flow of phenomena, (2) enhanced metacognitive surveying of mental processes, and (3) recognition of the innate reflexivity of awareness or what is known as 'awareness of awareness.'[19]

Open Monitoring meditation is the most basic non-dual practice. Theravada Buddhism prescribes this method to promote emotional regulation and cognitive decentering but, more important, to gain direct insight into the constructed nature of reality. Most Mindfulness-Based Stress Reduction classes teach their own brand of Open Monitoring, called *choiceless awareness*.

During Open Monitoring practice one attends to the stream of sensations, thoughts and emotions arising and passing within an expanded field of awareness, which to the observer seemingly exists in the 'background.' Noting objects of awareness is recommended. When a practitioner knows from within the clarity of awareness that 'sadness is here,' emotion decouples from the sticky autobiographical narratives of the 'reified I.'[20] Open Monitoring meditation regulates the emotions by lessening reactivity to aversion and clinging. Open Monitoring also develops the mind's introspective, reflective capacity, generating insight into the constructed nature of the self and phenomena. This increases and stabilizes with the practice of Open Presence meditation.

Open Monitoring Meditation Instruction

This practice begins with a period of *shamatha* meditation to settle the mind and then opens the field of awareness to all of what arrives through the five senses and mind: sounds, sights, smells, body sensations, thoughts and emotions. The practice is receptive and reflexive, effortful and effortless. While one exerts an effort to know phenomena, one does not control phenomena—there is nothing to make happen and nothing to stop from happening.

This practice will increase your capacity to discern objects of awareness with an attitude of curiosity and non-judgmentality. You will notice how the mind simultaneously labels external objects upon recognition of them. For instance, along with the sound of a car comes the word 'car.' Note this automaticity with interest. It will increase your ability to intentionally label thoughts and emotions.

Sit on a cushion or in a chair with both feet flat on the floor. Let your spine be long and upright but not stiff. Roll your shoulders up, back and down. Relax your arms slightly back and down. Feel as though you are a queen or king sitting regally on a throne. If you are on a zafu, make sure to soften your sitz bones and feel the spine rise up naturally from there. Rest your hands either folded in your lap or flat on your thighs or knees. Tuck your chin in slightly to ease any strain in the back of the neck. Let your eyes gaze diagonally down in front of you and then soften your gaze, not looking at anything in particular. If your eyes feel the need to close, that is fine as well.

Now draw awareness to the felt-sense of sitting in your chair or on your cushion. Feel the weight of your torso resting on the hips and the actual physical sensation of that weight sinking into the cushion or the seat of the chair. Now turn your attention to receive the actual physical sensation of your body breathing, *not what you think breath is like, but what is actually occurring in your body.* Notice the natural rhythm of your breath. There is no need to change your breath or make it anything other than what it is. Now draw your attention to the actual physical sensation of the air flowing in and out of your nostrils. Aim the attention at the soft, cool feeling of air entering the nostrils and the slightly warmer air exiting the nostrils. Maintain mindful awareness of the flow of air at the tip of the nostrils for at least 5–10 minutes or until the mind is sufficiently calm and stabilized.

If your eyes have been closed, allow them to open slightly and soften your gaze so that you are not looking at anything in particular. Now relax your attention and open to the field of awareness. Observe all of what arrives at your five senses: sounds, sights, smells, body sensations and tastes. Open to phenomena like an antenna and just receive. There is nothing to control, nothing to make happen and nothing to stop from happening. Discern the objects of awareness with an attitude of curiosity and non-judgmentality, noting how the mind automatically labels sense objects. Do the same with body sensations. Label them as they arise: tingling, burning, relaxing, tightening or pulsating. Whatever comes into the field of awareness let it arrive, know it, note it and allow it to pass away. Continue for at least 5–10 minutes.

Now open to the continually shifting landscape of thoughts and emotions. Do not let yourself become fixated on any particular thought or emotion. Do not see thoughts and emotions as something to continue or end. Simply note their attributes. For instance, if you find yourself planning your day, simply label that mental activity 'planning.' If you get lost in doubtful thoughts, simply label that mental activity 'doubting.' Whatever you feel, simply note it as present. Discern all phenomena of mind with an attitude of curiosity and non-judgmentality. There is nothing to control, nothing to make happen and nothing to stop from happening. Let the awareness know all occurrences from within the field of mind.

As you become more adept at Open Monitoring meditation, the need for labeling may fall away as moments when the mind is absent of thought increase. When this occurs, just rest and cultivate watchfulness. This indicates it may be time to try Objectless *Shamatha* meditation.

Open Presence Meditation

The next method of non-dual mindfulness is called *Open Presence* meditation or Non-dual Awareness meditation. "Open Monitoring is the beginning stage of Open Presence meditation. Over time, mental noting and labeling falls away, then engagement and disengagement falls away, and then one is just resting in open presence or nature of mind" (Vago, 2013).

The introductory Open Presence practice is *Objectless Shamatha.* During this practice one attends lightly to the flow of phenomena without specifically engaging or disengaging from objects. When the mind does not grasp at content, the ascertaining consciousness that accompanies every mind moment presents more prominently and objects recede into the background of awareness. Cultivating the skill of calm abiding in the midst of phenomena makes Objectless *Shamatha* an important stepping-stone to recognizing the mind's intrinsic clarity, *innate awareness* or *rigpa*.

The non-dual metaphor of mind is that of a mirror reflecting objects as mere appearances. A mirror reflects a red ball but does not become red. No matter what arises in the mind, awareness itself remains, like the mirror, unchanged and transparent.

As the practitioner progresses in Open Presence meditation, the nonconceptual luminosity of mind becomes more apparent. Eventually, the suppression or cultivation of content, or the application of special meditative techniques, is abandoned. In Indo-Tibetan Buddhism this is known as *non-meditation*—resting effortlessly in the mere clarity of knowing.

At a 2012 Mind and Life meeting, neuroscientist Richard Davidson bemoaned the fact that neuroscience does not have a good understanding of the neural correlates of clarity; whether clarity emerges from or is a feature of consciousness. His studies have shown a correlation between perceived clarity and the magnitude of gamma waves and increased neural signaling in the prefrontal cortex.[21]

What has become evident is that the cortex seems to have two global systems—an extrinsic, object-oriented task-responsive system and an intrinsic, default, self-oriented, non-task-specific system.[22] These two systems appear to be functionally anti-correlated.[23] For example, ruminating or mind wandering activity tends to cease when motor or sensory stimuli intrude on awareness. Some meditation researchers speculate that subject/object perception may be related to the functional separation of these two systems.[24] However, there is evidence of synchronized brain area activation between these two systems. Because of its context orientation, non-dual awareness seems to be a distinctly synergistic state of mind that lessens competition between the intrinsic and extrinsic cortical systems.[25]

Another very recent study using real-time fMRI neurofeedback and third-person data showed cognitive processing differences between 'trying to meditate' and 'effortless meditation:

> We found that for meditators, the subjective experiences of "undistracted awareness" such as "concentration" and "observing sensory experience," and "effortless doing" such as "observing sensory experience," "not efforting," and "contentment," correspond with posterior cingulate cortex (PCC) deactivation. Further, the subjective experiences of "distracted awareness" such as "distraction" and "interpreting," and "controlling" such as "efforting" and "discontentment," correspond with PCC activation. (Garrison, 2013)

Jon Kabat-Zinn described the difference between effortful mindfulness (Focused Attention or Open Monitoring) and effortless mindfulness (Open Presence and Non-dual Awareness) with a now-antiquated yet useful metaphor:

> In deliberate mindfulness, you could think of it as dial-up networking where you have to make an effort to get connected, where often the connection keeps getting disconnected and you have to reestablish it. In effortless mindfulness, the connection is always present. No dial-up is necessary. It just is. We are already connected. (2005)

Interview With John D. Dunne

To gain more clarity about the trajectory of *non-dual mindfulness* in Buddhism, I turned to Buddhist scholar and longtime Tibetan Buddhist practitioner John D.

Dunne, associate professor in the Department of Religion at Emory University. In his inimitable way, John brings together many of the early Buddhist principles and practices you are now familiar with and shows us the trajectory from effortful to effortless mindfulness.

What is non-dual mindfulness?

It is a term I use to distinguish certain styles of Buddhist practice from other styles of Buddhist practice. I call the other styles 'classical,' which come out of the Abhidharma account of the mind. The theory underlying those practices is that suffering is caused by *cetanā*, which means 'intention.' The mere presence of intention constitutes a mental action. This paradigm is trying to unpack with depth, a method where the practitioner would no longer have distorted intentions. But in order to do that the practitioner needs to calm the mind so its intentions can be observed.

This requires the three trainings of ethics, meditation and wisdom. In order to obtain wisdom—corrected distorted cognitions—one must have a certain level of meditative concentration. For that one needs an ethical life. For without an ethical life the mind is too disturbed. To change how distorted intentions (*cetanā*) arise requires correcting the cognitive flaws in the way the world is being perceived: taking the impermanent for the permanent, viewing selfless objects as belonging to an autonomous self and mistaking things conducive to suffering as conducive of pleasure. In classical mindfulness practice one is mindful of thoughts and impulses and restrains oneself.

One must also obtain the stability and clarity of mind to discern the actual nature of things: to detect their arising, see the cognitive distortions and correct them. Distortions are corrected through heedfulness (*appamāda*) and clear comprehension (*sampajāna*). This is called the *antidote model* (*prakti paksha*).

The movement from the classical approach involved a subtle shift in the Sanskrit term samprajanya, *from primarily seeing the nature of things to a monitoring function.* Meditative concentration—seeing things clearly and being aware of intention—requires two things: error checking and noticing what is happening in the background where distorted intentions first arise.

The shift into non-dual mindfulness occurs with Yogācāra and forward. Now the main source of distortions is the very structure that would permit an object to be presented. So it is more primitive. The distortion is not in intentions about objects. It is instead in intentionality (meaning subject/object structure). That dualistic structure makes it possible to conceive of objects as something one would want or not want. This is what now becomes the new target of practice.

Are you referring to primordial ignorance (*āvidya*)?

Yes, exactly. So certain aspects of the classical model now must be revisioned or abandoned, because they are about holding objects in mind. Holding objects in mind is problematic because one is just worsening dualistic habits of perception. The non-dual style of practice ends up as Mahāmudrā, which I treat as identical to Dzogchen for these purposes. Tibetan authors use the term *Chag Dzog* (*phyag rdzogs*).

The endpoint of this practice is *asmrti*, or non-mindfulness, because it is not focused on objects. Intentionality or subject/object structure always arises in the context of approach/avoidance behaviors—getting something or avoiding something. Even human agency and subjectivity are tied up in getting and avoiding. So to do something in meditation is falling back into that paradigm. Therefore, the actual practice is to learn how to release effort, to liberate any paradigm of getting and avoiding.

There is in every moment of consciousness an aspect of consciousness that is not caught up in getting and avoiding. It is what is the same for all aspects of consciousness—*awareness itself*. What is awareness itself? One metaphor is *prakasha* in Sanskrit and *selwa* in Tibetan, which means *luminosity* or the capacity to present content. Every moment of consciousness has this capacity to display content. That is knowingness. In that sense, the term *rang rig* in Tibetan, which means self-awareness or reflexive awareness, is a little misleading. It sounds like you are turning back and looking at yourself. What it really means is when you are aware of objects, awareness is not a searchlight that points at things. Awareness is more like a fully lit room. All aspects of the knowing process (thoughts, feelings, objects) are all in that room, being presented at once. We tend to get stuck on one slice of it even though we have access to all of it.

So reflexive awareness means that all aspects of awareness are presented simultaneously. When we see a beautiful sunset we are completely absorbed in it. Later on we may remember how we felt in the experience even though we may not have been paying particular attention to that. The feeling of it was being presented while we were absorbed in the sunset. In non-dual models one can be conscious without subjectivity. There are empirical claims [for non-dual awareness], like this is what occurs just before sleep or during orgasm or a strong shock or startle response.

Non-dual models say that to be aware is not to be an agent in this world, whereas all Western models are caught up in agency—acting in the world. The whole point of non-dual practices is *not* to be an agent in the samsāric world. This doesn't mean that some other kind of action cannot manifest, but it is not the action deliberately done by a conscious agent with volition. This is a very different paradigm, which can be very confusing for Westerners. Full-on non-dual mindfulness is not what people do generally.

There are two traditions in India distinguished by whether non-dual awareness has or does not have content. So one tradition views non-dual awareness as devoid of world, self and objects. Everything disappears. The other asserts one can still be interactive in the world and be in non-dual awareness. There are non-Buddhist traditions—Advaita Vedanta or Kashmir Shaivism [Transcendental Meditation is a modern example]—that will collapse the non-dual into a proto-subject and call it *Ātman*. Buddhism does not call this non-dual awareness 'a subjectivity.' Nāgārjuna said, *You are not bound by appearances. You are bound by subject/object experiences.*

In non-dual mindfulness the 'spy of mindfulness' now becomes associated with the monitoring aspect, reflexive awareness. This is awareness of subjectivity without taking the subject and making it into an object. That kind of mindfulness is non-dual because one is *not trying* to discern objects or abandon or get something. One is just allowing the mind's natural capacity to know.

A way to cultivate that is ramping up the monitoring aspect of awareness even while you are focused on objects. There is a famous verse the Ninth Karmapa cites, "On the basis of object focus, objectlessness arises." One learns to monitor the background while focusing on objects. Eventually one drops objects altogether. When I use the term non-dual mindfulness, I am referring to objectless *shamatha*.

In the context of Mahāmudrā practice and modern mindfulness practice one can look at the convergence of Zen, Vipassanā and Dzogchen practices that Joseph Goldstein writes about in his book *One Dharma.*[26] Features of that practice are similar to the Mahāmudrā practices. Open Monitoring encompasses choiceless awareness. There is a reason why when Joseph Goldstein after practicing *vipassanā* for 20 years heard Nyoshul Khen Rinpoche [a Dzogchen teacher] and lights flared brightly. There is an overlap between the modern style of *vipassanā* and objectless *shamatha*. You are not fully in a non-dual attitude. When objects arise they do so dualistically, but one is learning how to be aware of objects without fixating on them.

Objectless Shamatha *Instruction*

Start with 10 minutes of Mindfulness of Breath meditation. Then engage in 5 minutes of Open Monitoring meditation, noting and labeling internal and external phenomena, but do not let yourself become fixated on any particular object of awareness. Do not view body sensations, sensational objects, thoughts or emotions as something to continue or end. Know the presence of phenomena with an attitude of curiosity and non-judgmentality.

Now relax the labeling function to merely note the overall wholesome or unwholesome quality of your thoughts and emotions in response to external occurrences or physical sensations. Know the arising and passing of aversion and craving, without reactivity. No matter what occurs, cultivate watchfulness.

When you are ready, let go of noting altogether and simply rest in the mere knowing of objects coming and going. The differentiation of objects matters little. Arising internally or externally, they are equally mere phenomena. Observe and rest in the *emptiness* of phenomena—their continual arising, existing and passing away. There is nothing to control, nothing to make happen and nothing to stop from happening. Feel the freedom to experience everything that comes without acceptance or rejection, because its nature is to dissolve.

During periods when the shifting landscape of thoughts and emotions quiets, the clarity of knowing itself will become more present in your awareness. Rest easily in the luminosity of unobstructed mind, the pure presence of wakeful knowing.

 Mahāmudrā (T: *phyag rgya chen po*)

> *To cling to a concrete reality is to be as foolish as cattle. To cling to emptiness is even more foolish.* (Saraha, eighth-century Indian Mahāsiddha)

By the eighth century Indian culture was again in decline, and its northwestern frontier faced an onslaught of Arab invaders massacring, pillaging and forcing Islam on the Hindu and Buddhist populace. Amid this chaos, Vajrayāna Buddhism, with its potent tantric practices and profound non-dual Dzogchen and Mahāmudrā teachings, gained popularity. Mahāmudrā means 'great seal.'[27] Dzogchen Ponlop Rinpoche summarizes Mahāmudrā thusly: "It is often described to be like all-encompassing space; it rests nowhere and is free from all conceptions," (2010).

The Mahāmudrā teachings were elaborated in the writings of Saraha (late eighth century), Tilopa (988–1069), Maitrīpā (1007–1085) and Naropa (1016–1100). These Mahāsiddhas (great, realized beings) lived among the people as mendicant Buddhist yogis, teaching meditative practices to realize the innate, clear-light nature of mind.[28] Mahāmudrā made its way to Tibet through Marpa the Translator (1012–1097), the founder of the Kagyu Lineage of Tibetan Buddhism. Marpa taught the poet and yogi Milarepa (1052–1135), who taught Gampopa (1079–1153), who further established the Kagyu lineage by integrating the teachings of Atiśa, the great Bengali Buddhist sage into Mahāmudrā. Today Western practitioners are fortunate to have access to excellent Kagyu Mahāmudrā teachers such as Khenchen Thrangu Rinpoche,[29] Chökyi Nyima Rinpoche,[30] Dzogchen Ponlop Rinpoche[31] and Yongey Mingyur Rinpoche.[32]

The Kagyu Lineage prescribes two main approaches to realize Mahāmudrā. The first involves tantric methods and skillful means. The second is a *sutra*-based analytical meditative path to direct recognition. This methodology begins with Mahāyāna mindfulness and compassion meditation practices to calm the mind and heal disturbing emotions. These practices create the fertile ground to then directly investigate the nature of mind. In Mahāmudrā, *vipashyanā* (T: *lhag mthong*), or insight, leads to the realization of nonconceptual wisdom—the union of mind's innate clarity and emptiness.

The realization of Mahāmudrā is succinctly described by Saraha in his *Song for a King*:[33]

> *Mindfulness sees with certainty that all things are like an illusion.*
> *Self-arising and inconceivable, wisdom naturally abides within.*
> *These appearances have the nature of clarity; from the very first they are unborn. . . .*
> *Intellect, mind, and mental appearances have this very nature.*
> *All the worlds appearing in their diversity have this very nature.*
> *All the varieties of the seen and the seer have this very nature.*
> *Attachment, desire, aversion, and bodhicitta, too, have this very nature. . . .*
> *The ignorant are bound by mental categories.*
> *The inseparable, the co-emergent, is utterly pure.*

Unfindability: Looking for Mind

Up to this point, I have written quite a bit about mind and its function and dysfunction. I have invited you to engage directly with the mind-heart through meditative and analytical exercises designed to increase tranquility, prosocial emotions and insights into the nature of self and not-self. I hope you have availed yourself of the practices and gained some insight into your own cognitive and affective distortions and become aware of the mind's interpretive wonders and pitfalls. The time has come to inquire directly into mind itself, to try to actually find this entity called mind—that which we give so much credence and follow with such obeisance.

Tibetan Buddhism famously states that *not finding is the greatest finding*. In Tibetan, *lta* means both 'to look' and 'the view.' In the practice of meditative insight we do not infer what mind is. Rather than thinking about mind, we *look directly at mind* to know the actual nature of mind, which in Mahāmudrā and Dzogchen is *the view*. The following meditative inquiry is reminiscent of a methodology expounded by the Ninth Gyalwang Karmapa Wangchuk Dorje (1556–1603) and taught by Khenchen Thrangu Rinpoche.[34]

Practice Open Monitoring meditation for at least 10 minutes. Simply note the overall wholesome or unwholesome quality of your thoughts and emotions. Should you find the mind absent of thought, just rest in unobstructed mind. No matter what occurs, cultivate watchfulness. Tranquility will arise naturally from watchfulness.

Now you will engage in three exercises to gain insight into the mind. Take time with each one, investigating with curiosity and innate intelligence. If you find yourself over-analyzing or lost in conceptualizations, just rest in mere nowness and then try once again. Look directly as best you are able.

During periods of stillness, look at the mind without preconception. Genuinely inquire: where does this mind rest? What or who is at rest? Where did this mind come from, and where does it go? Try not to conceptualize these questions. Look directly to see if you can find a mind.

During periods of thoughts or emotions (movement of the mind), inquire with accuracy and precision: from where do thoughts come? When present, do thoughts reside in a location? To where do they go? Scrutinize and examine carefully to see whether a place of origin and cessation can be found.

Now turn this same precise looking in on itself. Can that which inquires into its existence or non-existence be found? Scrutinize and examine carefully.

When you have determined the unfindability of the mind, rest in the lucid certainty of the mind's empty nature. Feel free to look again and again at stillness, movement and the mind itself. Each time unfindability is determined, rest directly in the lucid certainty of emptiness.

Once the absolute conceptual belief in the 'thingness of mind' has been loosened, one can enter the path of Essence Mahāmudrā and receive direct *pointing out* of the nature of mind from a qualified teacher. This is the point where Mahāmudrā joins with and applies the experiential methodology of Dzogchen. Tibetan authors referred to this combined end-stage practice as *Chag Dzog*.

 Dzogchen

> *Naturally occurring timeless awareness—utterly lucid awakened mind—is something marvelous and superb, primordially and spontaneously present. It is the treasury from which comes the universe of appearances and possibilities, whether of* samsāra *or* nirvāna. *Homage to that unwavering state, free of elaboration.* (Rabjam, 2001)

Although it is not possible for me to point out *rigpa* (the nature of mind), my Dzogchen teachers have encouraged me to share the basic teachings on *rigpa* from a philosophical and clinical perspective. I do so now with great humility and only by virtue of their incalculable generosity.

Dzopa Chenpo (T: *rdzogs pa chen po*) *or Dzogchen* means 'great completeness' and is known as the yoga of primordial knowledge. Garab Dorje (55 CE) was the semi-historical first human teacher of Dzogchen (*rdzogs-chen*). Born in Oddiyana, he is said to have received the complete 6,400,000 Dzogchen verses from Vajrasattva, a celestial deity. Garab Dorje transmitted these teachings to Manjushrimitra, a learned Indian Brahmin from Bodhgaya, who later divided the Dzogchen teachings into three divisions: *Mind*—explicating innate lucidity; *Space*—explicating emptiness; and *Instruction*—explicating the inseparability of lucidity and emptiness. After his death, hidden teachings by Manjushrimitra were uncovered in Bodhgaya by his longtime disciple Shri Singha, who then further divided the Instruction section.

The Dzogchen teachings saw their greatest flowering in Tibet within two different Dzogchen traditions (Bön and Indian Buddhist). Bön claims its Dzogchen lineage was founded in Central Asia and brought to the Zhang-zhung region of Western Tibet five centuries before the historical Buddha lived by Buddha Tonpa Shenrab Miwoche. Bön Dzogchen is a rich collection of teachings. Tenzin Wangyal Rinpoche,[35] the foremost teacher of Bön Dzogchen in the West, has a longstanding interest in the intersection of psychology and Dzogchen. He continues to generously translate Bön Dzogchen teachings into practical strategies for healing the Western psyche and heart.

Indian Buddhist Dzogchen arrived in Tibet in 761 CE when King Trisong Detsen invited Śāntaraksita, an abbot of Nālānda University, to come to Tibet. Unfortunately, he was not well received by the Zhang-zhung factions and was forced to leave the country. Śāntaraksita then suggested the king bring Padmasambhava, a renowned Buddhist teacher from the Swat Valley, to clear the obstacles Śāntaraksita had faced. Once that was done, Śāntaraksita was able to return to Tibet, where he and Padmasambhava founded the Nyingma (*rnying ma*) 'ancient' school of Buddhism. Together, they supervised 108 translators in the largest transmission/translation of Indian Buddhist *Sutra* and Tantra, thereby firmly establishing tantric Buddhism in Tibet. These two men also founded Samye (*bsam yas*), the first Tibetan Buddhist monastery, where translators from the Chinese (Chan) Buddhist, Indian Buddhist and Zhang-zhung traditions worked together.

Padmasambhava left Tibet in 774 CE without completing the full transmission of Dzogchen teachings. It is said he buried *terma* (*gter-ma*) (treasure texts) to be found by later teachers when the time was right. In 779 CE King Trisong Detsen declared Buddhism the state religion and politically exiled the Bön Zhang-zhung. The king then sent a Tibetan monk named Vairochana from Samye to India. Vairochana returned with more texts and the great Buddhist teacher Vimalamitra, who further distilled the Dzogchen teachings on Mind (*sems sde*), Space (*klong sde*) and Instruction (*man ngag sde*).

Longchen Rabjam, 'Longchenpa' (1308–1364), was an abbot at Samye Monastery. An adept practitioner and scholar, he is still considered the most important Tibetan commentator on Dzogchen. During his lifetime, Longchenpa unified several systems of Dzogchen teachings into what came to be known as the

Longchen Nyingtik. Four hundred years later, Jigme Lingpa (1729–1798) received a vision of Longchenpa's teachings but kept it secret until years later, when in a retreat he received several visions of Longchenpa. Lingpa then transcribed all of these teachings and in 1764 released his cycle of the *Longchen Nyingtik* to the public. It remains the most widely practiced Dzogchen methodology.

Rigpa, *the Nature of Mind*

> *Our mind is primordially in the state of rigpa. Whatever state of mind we go through, whether it is a very heavy experience of ignorance or a very outrageous emotion of anger, we have never moved from the state of rigpa.* (Ponlop, 2006)

The basic tenets of Dzogchen can be distilled as follows: (1) The nature of mind is primordial wisdom (*ye shes*), and all phenomena arise from it as mere reflections; (2) direct realization of primordial wisdom is beyond all concepts; and (3) when one realizes *innate awareness* (*rigpa*)—the union of luminosity *selwa* (*gsal ba*) and emptiness (*stong pa nyid*)—experience and phenomena arise spontaneously as the compassionate expression of primordial wisdom.[36]

While there are countless Dzogchen teachings, to know it is to experience it directly. Therefore, Dzogchen has traditionally required contact with a qualified teacher who experientially points out *rigpa*—the primordially empty, lucid nature of mind.

Today in the West, one can receive *pointing out* instruction from superlative Tibetan Buddhist Dzogchen teachers such as Tsoknyi Rinpoche,[37] Anam Thubten Rinpoche,[38] Chökyi Nyima Rinpoche[39] and Sogyal Rinpoche.[40] I cannot emphasize enough the necessity of actual contact with a qualified Dzogchen teacher. In my hubris I thought decades of meditation and a mind full of concepts from books on Mahāmudrā and Dzogchen gave me the capacity to know *rigpa*. When I finally sat a retreat with Tsoknyi Rinpoche and received *pointing out* instruction, I realized nothing could have been further from the truth.

Tsoknyi Rinpoche generously agreed to answer a few questions about Dzogchen philosophy and practice.[41] Rinpoche has been teaching in the West for more than 25 years and is the author of several books on Dzogchen. His most recent book delivers the Dzogchen teachings with a distinctly modern focus on healing the systemic agitation and mental and emotional distress of modern life. He has high regard for Western psychology and is very enthusiastic about the blossoming of Buddhist psychology in the West.

Rinpoche, how can we understand emptiness from a Dzogchen point of view?

To think emptiness means something is totally void, or nothing at all, is a Western cultural perception. Someone looks at a glass with no liquid in it and thinks the glass is 'empty.' The Dzogchen view of emptiness is: the empty essence of mind is unified with cognizance. A person is not empty *or* cognizant. We perceive while the mind is empty; while the mind is empty it perceives. There is no separation. To understand emptiness we must recognize (from an ultimate point of view) that the dualistic way we perceive objects is mistaken. We typically view phenomena as existing or non-existing. Emptiness is empty of existence or non-existence. The Dalai Lama is fond of quoting Nāgārjuna: "That person who is not capable of [realizing, recognizing] emptiness is capable of nothing. The person who is capable of emptiness is capable of anything and everything."

Is Objectless *Shamatha* conceptual meditation?

Conceptual meditation involves a subject thinking of something (an object) and fixating attention on it. The breath is obviously something; a thought is also something. But there can be conceptual meditation even without a thought if your mind is the subject and it perceives space, the present moment or the 'ongoing flow of phenomena' as the object. What is it that prevents us from being as we naturally are? It's this basic subject/object fixing of attention. But there is also the possibility of an unfolding of awareness, independent of subject and object and totally unobstructed.

How does one recognize *rigpa*?

It's rather like Holi celebrations in India: people throw handfuls of colored pigment into the air, but none of it sticks onto the space through which it soars. When we hear *rigpa*, we should not try to picture empty essence, like trying to imagine what open space looks like. That kind of intellectual effort is unnecessary. Actually it's far easier than that. Just let your mind recognize itself by itself, and at once there's an open, aware feeling that knows. Whatever is experienced, don't hold onto any of that. Do not conceptualize anything perceived, not a single thing. When you simply let yourself be like that, recognition automatically unfolds.

Can you say more about illusory perception?

Illusory perception is practiced in Tibetan Buddhism because everything is considered dreamlike by its very nature. What we conceptually designate as the 'world' is a complex matrix of habitual concepts. We reify and attach to things and identities as if they were solid and real—not an illusion or empty appearance. We falsely cling to them as if they had a reality, which they do not possess. Not seeing how they 'merely exist' creates suffering. Illusory perception practice is designed to soften and release this grasping. To be with reality as it is. By experiencing all phenomena (including our ego) in a 'mere' or light way, we relieve the suffering caused by ignorant grasping and fully function in our lives.

What is the difference between mind/consciousness and *rigpa*?

In Tibetan, the mind/consciousness is called *sems*. It is fundamentally dualistic, constantly getting caught up in sensory, feeling or mental objects. *Rigpa* is the nonconceptual essence of mind, free of dualistic constructs and grasping. It is the natural mind, timeless awareness.

How does *rigpa* relate to 'mere I'?

'Mere I' is a subtle construct of 'I,' a light dualism fundamental to successively more complex 'I's. The open, playful quality of the 'mere I' acts precisely in varying roles without over-identifying with or grasping onto them. An example is how we hold things. If we squeeze a tissue it becomes distorted and not that usable. If we hold it too loosely it drops to the floor. Most of us hold our identity in that way.

'Mere I' is not *rigpa*. 'Mere I' is a dualistic ego construct, while *rigpa* is nonconceptual, egoless in essence and free of any form of conceptual limitation. *Rigpa* has no identity as this or that. Its union of emptiness and clarity accommodates all possibilities but does not impute their reality.

Notes

1 Williams, P. (2008). *Mahayana Buddhism: The doctrinal foundations*. New York, NY: Routledge. p. 64.
2 Bhattacharya, K., Johnston, E.E.H., & Kunst, A. (Eds.) (1978). *The dialectal method of Nāgārjuna (Vigrahavyāvartanī)*. Dehli, India: Motilal Banarsidass.
3 Wallace, V. A., & Wallace, B. A. (1997). *A guide to the Bodhisattva way of life*. Ithaca, NY: Snow Lion Publications.
4 Lusthaus, D. (2004). What is and isn't Yogacara? *Yogachara Buddhist Research Association*. Retrieved May 1, 2013 from www.acmuller.net/yogacara/articles/intro-uni.htm
5 Williams, P., 2008, p. 91.
6 Garfield, J. L., 1995.
7 Dreyfus, G. (2011). Self and subjectivity: A Middle Way approach. In Siderits, Thompson and Zahavi (Eds.). *Self, No-Self?* New York, NY: Oxford University Press. p. 114–156.
8 Waldron, W. (2003). *The Buddhist unconscious: The ālaya-vijñāna in the context of Indian Buddhist thought*. London, England: RoutledgeCurzon.
9 Zahavi, D. (2005). *Subjectivity and selfhood: Investigating the first-person perspective*. Cambridge, MA: MIT Press.
10 Wittgenstein, L. (1975). In Rhees, R. (Ed.). *Philosophical remarks*. Hargreaves, R., White, R. (Trans.). Hoboken, NJ: Wiley-Blackwell.
11 Rinpoche, T., & Swanson, E. (2012). *Open heart, open mind: Awakening the power of essence love*. New York, NY: Harmony Books.

12 Rinpoche, T. (May 2012). *A Dzogchen approach to open mind open heart*. Unpublished lecture presented at Spirit Rock,Woodacre, CA.

13 Field, T. (1992). Infants of depressed mothers. *Development and Psychopathology*, *4*(1), 49–66.
Conroy, S., Pariante, C. M., Marks, M. N., Davies, H. A., Farrelly, S., Schacht, R., & Moran, P. (2012). Maternal psychopathology and infant development at 18 months: The impact of maternal personality disorder and depression. *Journal of the American Academy of Child & Adolescent Psychiatry*, *51*(1), 51–61.

14 Horton, R. S. (2011). Parenting as a cause of narcissism. In W. K. Campbell and J. D. Miller (Eds.). *The handbook of narcissism and narcissistic personality disorder: Theoretical approaches, empirical findings, and treatments*, 181–190. Wiley Online Library. doi: 10.1002/9781118093108.ch16

15 Imbesi, L. (1999). The making of a narcissist. *Clinical Social Work Journal*, *27*, 41–54. doi: 10.1023/A:1022809314267

16 Mitchell, S. B. (1995). *Freud and beyond: A history of modern psychoanalytic thought*. New York, NY: Basic Books.

17 Metzinger, T. (2009). *The ego tunnel: The science of the mind and the myth of the self*. New York, NY: Basic Books.

18 Bodhi (Bhikkhu.) (Ed.). (1995). *The middle length discourses of the Buddha: A new translation of the Majjhima Nikāya: Translated from the Pali* (No. 49). Wisdom Publications Inc. p. 24f.

19 Raffone, A., & Srinivasan, N. (2010). The exploration of meditation in the neuroscience of attention and consciousness. *Cognitive Processing*, *11*(1), 1–7.

20 Lutz, A., Slagter, H. A., Rawlings, N. B., Francis, A. D., Greischar, L. L., & Davidson, R. J. (2009). Mental training enhances attentional stability: Beural and behavioral evidence. *Journal of Neuroscience*, *29*(42), 13418–13427.

21 Kabat-Zinn, J., & Davidson, R. (Eds.). (2012). *The mind's own physician: A scientific dialogue with the Dalai Lama on the healing power of meditation*. Oakland, CA: New Harbinger Publications.

22 Golland, Y., Golland, P., Bentin, S., & Malach, R. (2008). Data-driven clustering reveals a fundamental subdivision of the human cortex into two global systems. *Neuropsychologia*, *46*(2), 540–553.

23 Fox, M. D., Snyder, A. Z., Vincent, J. L., Corbetta, M., Van Essen, D. C., & Raichle, M. E. (2005). The human brain is intrinsically organized into dynamic, anticorrelated functional networks. *Proceedings of the National Academy of Sciences of the United States of America*, *102*(27), 9673–9678.

24 Soddu, A., Boly, M., Nir, Y., Noirhomme, Q., Vanhaudenhuyse, A., Demertzi, A., . . . & Malach, R. (2009). Reaching across the abyss: Recent advances in functional magnetic resonance imaging and their potential relevance to disorders of consciousness. *Progress in Brain Research*, *177*, 261–274.

25 Josipovic, Z., Dinstein, I., Weber, J., & Heeger, D. J. (2011). Influence of meditation on anti-correlated networks in the brain. *Frontiers in Human Neuroscience*, *5*(183), 1–11.

26 Goldstein, J. (2003). *One dharma: The emerging Western Buddhism*. New York, NY: HarperCollins.

27 Ninth Karmapa, *Mahamudra: The ocean of definitive meaning*. (E. Callahan, Trans.). US: Nitartha International.

28 For more on the Mahāsiddhas see Dowman, K. (1985). *Masters of Mahāmudrā: Songs and histories of the eighty-four Buddhist siddhas*. Albany, NY: State University of New York Press.

29 More information can be found at Pundarika Foundation. Retrieved March 2013 from www.rinpoche.com

30 More information can be found at Ka-Nying Shedrub Ling. Retrieved March 2013 from www.shedrub.org/teacherpage.php?tid=2
31 More information can be found at Dzogchen Ponlop Rinpoche. Retrieved March 2013 from http://dpr.info/index.htm
32 More information can be found at Tergar International. Retrieved March 2013 from http://tergar.org/
33 Thrangu, R. (2006). *A song for the king: Saraha on Mahāmudrā meditation*. Boston, MA: Wisdom Publications.
34 Rinpoche, K.T., & Namgyal, T. (2003). *The Ninth Karmapa's ocean of definitive meaning*. Ithaca, NY: Snow Lion Publications.
35 To learn more about Tenzin Wangyal, visit Lingmincha. Retrieved March 2013 from www.ligmincha.org/en/tenzin-wangyal-rinpoche.html.
To learn more about Bön Buddhism, visit Lingmincha. Retrieved March 2013 from www.ligmincha.org/en/bon-buddhism.html
36 Rabjam, L. (2001). *A treasure trove of scriptural transmission: A commentary on the precious treasury of the basic space of phenomena*. (R. Barron Trans.). Junction City, CA: Padma. p. xi.
37 More information can be found at Pundarika Foundation. Retrieved March 2013 from http://pundarika.org
38 More information can be found at Dharmata Foundation. Retrieved March 2013 from http://dharmata.org
39 More information can be found at Rangjung Yeshe Gomde California. Retrieved March 2013 from http://gomdeusa.org/
40 More information can be found at Rigpa. Retrieved March 2013 from http://rigpa.org/
41 Tsoknyi, D. (2013, August 30). Interview. (L. D. Miller, Interviewer).

7

Love Life Just as It Is

 The Buddhist Psychology of Happiness (P & S: *somanassa* T: *skyid*)

In Buddhism happiness (more accurately understood as *well-being*) is similarly thought to be a natural outcome of wise understanding, compassionate action and ethical conduct. The psychologist Thomas Bien sums up Buddhism's recipe for happiness in this pithy remark, "Happiness is being mindful" (2010). In this case, 'being mindful' is a virtuous dedication to developing the wakeful, compassionate presence that lies at the heart of genuine mental and emotional health.

Mindful engagement with wisdom and virtue endows us with the capacity to know which forms of happiness are and are not conducive to suffering. "It's our nature to want happiness and not want suffering, and thus Buddhists do not ask that one give up the pursuit of happiness but merely suggest that one become more intelligent about how it is pursued" (Hopkins, 2008).

Self-lessness (P: *anattā S: anātman*) and *non-violence* (S: *ahimsā*) are central to the intelligent pursuit of happiness. When one knows what intentions and actions facilitate an aliveness that is non-harming, the joy of being in the world is always available irrespective of causes and conditions. The Buddha offered two schemas for actualizing the well-being of non-harming and self-lessness in daily life.

The primary method, *The Eightfold Path*, is elaborated in the *Fourth Noble Truth*, *"And this is the path: the path with eight branches: right vision, right thought, right speech, right action, right livelihood, right effort, right mindfulness, right concentration"* (Batchelor, 2010).

The Eightfold Path can be divided into three categories of practice—wise knowing, *samādhi* and ethical conduct, each offering its own particular type of well-being. Meditative equipoise develops serenity and wise insight—the causes of liberation. Ethical conduct is the conduit through which liberative wisdom actualizes itself in daily life. The message is: *until you are fully awakened, mindfully endeavor to act in each moment with an aspiration to achieve the very awakening you seek.*

The second Buddhist framework involves ongoing cultivation of the *Perfections* (P: *pāramī* S: *pāramīta*), or complete virtuous action. Theravada Buddhism prescribes *10 pāramīs*: generosity (*dāna*), virtue (*sīla*), renunciation (*nekkhamma*), transcendent wisdom (*paññā*), energy/zeal (*viriyā*), patience (*khanti*), truthfulness (*sacca*), determination (*adhitthāna*), lovingkindness (*mettā*) and equanimity (*upekkhā*). Mahāyāna Buddhism stipulates *6 pāramītas*: generosity (*dāna*), virtue (*śīla*) patience (*ksānti*), energy/zeal (*vīrya*), one-pointed concentration (*dhyāna*) and transcendent wisdom (*prajñā*).

Two Kinds of Happiness

> *A person cannot have happiness unless they have some space, some freedom inside them.* (Hahn, 2013)

Because of the rise in popularity of positive psychology, research on happiness has increased exponentially. Until recently this research primarily measured life satisfaction, largely attributed to positive feelings about favorable circumstances. But studies increasingly show that conditional happiness turns out to be a poor indicator of inner well-being. Wealthier individuals report reduced levels of happiness derived from their wealth and impaired capacity to savor positive everyday experiences.[1] Furthermore, although increases in income up to $75,000 correlate to similar gains in emotional well-being and life satisfaction, no additional increases in emotional well-being occur above that amount.[2] It seems that more money does not necessarily equal more inner contentment.

Social science has differentiated happiness into two modes: (1) *fluctuating, hedonic happiness*[3]—the transient joy or relief derived from self-motivated seeking of pleasure and avoiding of displeasure; and (2) *sustainable, authentic happiness*[4]—a eudaimonic, resilient, non-egoic inner well-being resulting from inner development of wisdom (*prajñā*), compassion (*karunā*) and virtue (*śīla*).

When people say, "I just want to be happy," I believe they seek authentic happiness but may not know how to achieve it. Consumerism, materialism and fame-ism enslave us in a seemingly inescapable happiness trap of discomfort relief, pleasure seeking and maniacal becoming. Unaware of our captivity, we remain oblivious to the psyche's fixation on insufficiency and the painful pointlessness of incessant wanting.

Buddhism—with its insistence on the three trainings—wholeheartedly endorses renouncing self-centered, hedonic happiness for the self-less path of authentic human flourishing.

> *If by giving up a lesser happiness* [fluctuating, hedonic happiness]
> *One could experience greater happiness* [sustainable, authentic happiness],
> *A wise person would renounce the lesser to behold the greater.*
>
> The Buddha, *Dhammapada* 21[5]

Craving for the lesser happiness is sustained by the psyche's persistent denial of temporality and its false belief in certainty. No matter how painful the inevitable loss of favorable circumstances, a deluded psyche will still cling to false hope: 'next time it/they will be different, or it/they will work, or it/they won't end/leave.' Swinging between hope and fear the psyche remains fixated and captive in endless rounds of *samsāra*.

Buddhism's greater happiness is eudaimonic and results from embodying the practical wisdom of the three trainings. This inspires us to act wisely and virtuously with compassion, respect and regard for all beings. The greater happiness manifests in daily life as virtuous human flourishing.

Personal Exploration of Lesser and Greater Happiness

Exploring what makes us truly happy can be exciting *and* distressing. Realizing how much of what we think makes us happy actually leads to unsatisfactoriness can be frustrating. In the first part of the exercise, I urge you to be honest and kind. Non-judgmentality is your best friend. In the second part, focus on what you consider virtuous action. Again be honest and seek change that is doable. Over time small changes turn into big transformations.

Part 1: List your primary sources of happiness: family, intimate relationships, friends, work, service, hobbies, spiritual activities, leisure activities, community or political interests. Don't be afraid to list negative sources of pleasure like self-centeredness, irresponsibility, untruthfulness, addictions, infidelities, laziness, procrastination and so on. We do get something from the destructive habits we claim to dislike. Check the category of happiness it falls under. Contemplate and document what forms of suffering arise from it. Sources of greater happiness may have downsides and challenges too.

Table 7.1

Source of happiness	***Lesser***	***Greater***	***What kinds of suffering arise from this source?***

Part 2: Consider your current sources of happiness and the amount of suffering they contribute to your daily life. Now look at the following list of *pāramīs* (commendable virtues that cultivate authentic happiness): *generosity, morality, renunciation, meditation/wisdom, energy, patience,*

truthfulness, determination, restraint, lovingkindness and *equanimity*. Take some time to really sit with each of these virtuous qualities. Consider which virtues would generally increase feelings of well-being in your daily life. How might dedication to its practice specifically transform current positive sources of lesser happiness or replace destructive sources of hedonic happiness? Use the table below to document your chosen *Pāramīs*, the way in which they would increase well-being and a practice plan for their implementation in your daily life.

Table 7.2

pāramī	***What well-being would arise from it?***	***How will I practice this* pāramī *in daily life?***

Clinician's Exploration of Lesser and Greater Happiness

When clinicians inquire deeply into their desire for patient well-being, insights into self-cherishing can arise. Sometimes clinicians feel frustrated or defeated when change doesn't happen in line with their expectations. The goal of this exercise is to help clinicians discover which forms of encouragement and assistance to patients arise from an impulse to hedonically end the fear of another's suffering or ego-grasp at good outcomes. In the first part of the exercise, I urge you to self-reflect with kindness and curiosity. In the second part of the exercise, you will consider which of the *pāramīs* would aid in receiving suffering with wisdom and clarity.

Part 1: Bring to mind a few of your favorite interventions, preferably those that facilitate relaxation, stabilization, emotional expression or regulation, mental clarity or self-reflection. Now bring to mind one or two instances where a patient was visibly suffering and you chose to intervene with one of these techniques. Consider your own state of mind prior to offering that intervention, and write down what you remember. Then reflect on whether that impulse arose from a desire to ensure lesser happiness (ending distress or feeling self-glory) or greater happiness (wise, virtuous action). Also look deeply at whose suffering—yours or the patient's—was uppermost at that time.

Table 7.3

Intervention	***What were you thinking, feeling, wanting or experiencing prior to the intervention?***	***Lesser***	***Greater***	***Yours or theirs?***

Part 2: Now consider the following list of *pāramīs* (commendable virtues that cultivate authentic, durable happiness): *generosity, morality, renunciation, meditation/wisdom, energy, patience, truthfulness, determination, restraint, lovingkindness* and *equanimity*. Take some time to sit with each of these virtuous qualities. Which virtues would increase your capacity to recognize when you are caught in resistance to suffering? Which virtues would help you discern the appropriate timing for an intervention? How might dedication to its practice increase authentic well-being? Then document your chosen *pāramīs*, the way in which they would increase well-being and a practice plan for their implementation in sessions with patients.

Table 7.4

pāramī	***What well-being would arise from it?***	***How will I practice this* pāramī *in daily life?***

pāramī	***What well-being would arise from it?***	***How will I practice this* pāramī *in daily life?***

 Psyche/Soma Interdependence

Organismic Wisdom

Incarnation is an enactive, sensorimotor dance of body-mind-world engagement. But a thwarted capacity for attunement and self-regulation can severely undermine the joy of engaging with the world. These impediments often result from autonomic nervous system dysregulation, specifically chronic flight-fight-freeze response impairment. Despite what most mental health professionals think, we do not just work with minds; we work with minds dissociated from distressed psychophysical systems.

Genuine mental, emotional and physical health is unattainable when a dissociated mind absents itself from the body's homeostatic imperatives for metabolic and endocrine equilibrium. When the body signals 'NO!' but a disconnected mind continues to insist 'YES!' it exacerbates all manner of stress-related and freeze-physiology-related diseases—adrenal failure, chronic depression and anxiety, asthma, mitrovalve prolapse, fibromyalgia, chronic fatigue, irritable bowel syndrome, chronic pain and sensory processing disorders.[6] A disconnected mind—lost in its own repetitive conceptualizations and distorted narratives—cannot benefit from the body's innate *organismic wisdom*.

Steven Hoskinson, MA, senior international somatic experiencing instructor, describes the problems that ensue from ongoing dissociative habits of mind and the solution of mindfully attending to the body's innate capacity to heal itself:

> The notion of mind being an autonomous process is illusory. The function of mind is integrally related to biology in spite of what the mind thinks. The mind dissociates from the somatic experience, reifies itself and does not realize it is just reflecting organismic processes. . . . If we can see through the projection and in some way reclaim the projective process—in other words, stop literally believing what I think I am seeing and hearing—we might be able to relate somatically to experience and connect with phenomena rather than dissociate from it. Then something that irritates me can be experienced as an internal response to external phenomena; reflected upon, and known directly as the irritant it actually is without the self-narrative about it. That enables one to know the accompanying somatic response to an irritant (like tightness in the chest) and reintegrate it. When we are unaware of systemic responses, their activation persists. Only awareness facilitates a somatic response to reach its sufficiency and then naturally deactivate. (Hoskinson, 2013)

Somatically oriented psychotherapists help patients recognize how internal activation manifests in their particular system. Patients learn how to remain curious and present to activation states and the body's efforts to restore equilibrium. Any clinician can foster mind-body relatedness by teaching *Orienting* practice, an important skill for naturally decreasing activation by landing the mind where the body already lives.

Buddhist psychology has its own methods for reconnecting mind-body communication. Practicing *Open Monitoring* meditation directed toward the body furthers interoceptive capacity. *Objectless Shamatha* meditation promotes embodied awareness and enables the mind to rest more completely in the durable well-being of *awakened presence*.

Reconnecting mind-body communication can also be fostered in therapeutic sessions by combining mindful inquiry into body sensations with resting awareness effortlessly in body experience. Below is an example of the healing power of this method:

W: I can't tolerate my own mistakes. The thought of it is so terrible; even a small mistake will cause me to obsess about it for days.

LDM: *It is interesting how intolerant we can be toward our own humanness.*

W: When I was young I was afraid to cause trouble for others. I would hold in my feelings and pretend to be okay. No matter how difficult or scary the situation, I knew in my gut that things would be okay eventually. And somehow the true feeling in my gut got mixed up with my intense need to take care of everything myself.

LDM: *Shall we see what your gut has to say about your intolerance to imperfection?*

W: Okay.

LDM: *Bring to mind a recent time you had a strong reaction to making a small mistake. Now let your attention be drawn gently but firmly to your gut and see what shows up.*

W: A strong knowing said, *You deserve compassion too.* And then my thinking mind started going with critical thoughts.

LDM: *Yes, that is often the way when we are habituated to discursive thinking . . . Would it be okay to return awareness to the gut again and see what happens?*

W: (After a minute or so) There was less thinking this time. I could stay with my gut knowing . . . well, more like a feeling/thought coming from my gut saying, I love you. You don't need to figure out what to do or not to do. Just be with things as they are and that is right for now.

Moving meditation is also excellent for re-inhabiting the mind in the body. Although this is not the appropriate venue to discuss or teach yoga, tai chi or chi gong, I heartily recommend that everyone train in one or more of these body-centered practices to encourage genuine mental health. Chi gong is eminently adaptable and very healing for people with autonomic nervous system disorders or physical disabilities.

Walking meditation is a movement practice I can definitely share with great gusto. The basic idea is to let your awareness be drawn to and remain with the body as it moves in space. It is both concentration and insight meditation. Walking meditation can be done at any of three speeds, although it is best to start at the slowest pace, affectionately known as 'zombie walking.'

Walking Meditation Instruction

Stand with your feet together in a place where you can comfortably take about 15 steps. Begin by bringing awareness to the feeling of your body standing. Feel the weight of your body land in the soles of your feet, your spine upright and long, your arms hanging at your sides. Know the sensation of standing still. Experience how the body maintains balance and uprightness. Now slowly shift your weight into your left foot and mindfully notice how the right heel begins to lift. Keeping your awareness in the right foot and leg, slowly and mindfully lift it, swing the leg forward and place the foot down. As you do this notice the shift in body weight and the way the left heel naturally lifts to accommodate the forward movement. Now do the same with the left foot; lift it up, swing the leg forward and place the foot down, continuing to land your mind in the actual physical experience of the body moving. Mindfully take another 10–12 steps and then fully enjoy the complex movements required to turn the body around. Slowly and mindfully walk back to the point at which you started. Formal walking meditation can be done for a period of 20 minutes or more. If you are outside and something catches your attention, stop walking and mindfully attend to it. When you are ready, resume walking meditation. The second pace is a light stroll, and the third pace is a brisk walk. The faster you move, the more challenging the meditation. But definitely try a faster pace as you progress in your practice.

You can also do informal walking meditation in your daily life as you move around your office or from your car to the market. Zombie walking is not necessary in these instances because landing the mind in movement itself helps us meditate throughout the day.

Subtle Body Health and Healing

As Indian Buddhism progressed, so did attitudes about the body and its role in the process of awakening. Early Buddhism's insistence on renunciation of the body and its desires shifted with Vajrayāna Buddhism's recruitment of the body and desire as helpmates on the path to liberation. Vajrayāna and tantric Buddhism view the body as a microcosm of the dynamic interplay of energy, mass and cosmic intelligence. From the tantric point of view, enlightenment is a mind-body endeavor. Humans are tantric vessels, psycho-physical-spiritual beings with access to cognitive, affective, physical and subtle intelligences.

Along with the physical body, Vajrayāna and Tantric Buddhism postulate a gross energy body and a subtle energy body and emphasize their vital role in maintaining physical dynamism and psychological well-being. According to this model, the sensory/motor nerves and endocrine/metabolic systems condition the gross energy body. The subtle energy body consists of a complex system of energy-winds (S: *prāna* T: *rlung*)—motile, bio-energetic, animating life forces consistent with the proliferation of neural impulses.[7] These energy-winds are the precursors or conditioners for *kundalini* (T: *gtummo*), an awakening life force that rises up, activating *energetic hubs* (S: *bindu* T: *tigle*) located at the main junctions of the subtle body energy *channels* (S: *nadi* T: *tsa*). In Chinese medicine, the winds would be analogous to *chi* and channels to the meridians.

The principal determinants of subtle body health are the quality of mind and lifestyle. Persistent disturbing emotions, incessant worry and rumination, and physical and emotional trauma, coupled with a non-stop pace, over-activate the subtle body energetic system. This manifests as exhaustion, persistent jitteriness, restlessness or franticness, tightness in the abdomen or in the chest area, or pervasive buzzing sensations throughout the body.

Although most people label these effects 'anxiety,' it is actually the feeling of dysfunction in the subtle energy body. The upward-moving *prāna* has been drawn away from its natural resting place below the navel, to reside at the head, chest or upper abdomen. This improper residence over-stimulates and depletes the subtle energy body.

There are a variety of tantric 'wind' (*vayu*) meditation practices that stimulate and harness *prāna* and direct its flow through the *nadis* and *bindu*. Some of these techniques are breath-related; others employ visualization and yogic exercises. *gTummo* practices intentionally arouse body heat and have been studied by respected researchers like Herbert Benson and Sara Lazar.[8] Other 'wind' practices focus on the mind. In Tantric Buddhism, the mind is said to consist of wind-energy. These practices are specifically designed to induce psychophysical tranquility and promote emotional well-being.[9] Simple tantric practices like *Gentle Vase Breathing* return the upward-moving *prāna* to its proper home, restoring health to the energetic body and nervous system. The Tibetan Buddhist teacher Tsoknyi Rinpoche is a vocal proponent of offering subtle body healing practices to Westerners, who he insists suffer greatly from over-active *rlung*.

Gentle Vase Breathing Instruction

You may be familiar with diaphragmatic breathing, which encourages inhalation and exhalation from the lower diaphragm rather than the upper lung area. Its longer, deeper breaths are valued for inducing mind-body relaxation. Or you may have experienced yogic Ujjayi breathing or chi gong Tu-Na breath practices, which fill the lower belly on the in-breath and then intentionally move the breath up through the rib cage into the chest and throat areas.

Vase Breathing is similar to and different from Ujjayi and Tu-Na. Although there are Vase Breathing practices that induce heat and stimulate *kundalini/gtummo*, I will offer a gentle Vase Breathing practice to restore *prāna/rlung* to its proper resting place. This practice globally calms the nervous system and reduces the somatic and psychological effects of chronic stress and trauma.

Sit in a chair or on a meditation cushion in an upright but not stiff position. Let your awareness expand to take in the experience of sitting. Open all your senses; see what is before you, hear the sounds around you, feel the weight of your body resting on the chair or cushion. Give your mind time to land in your body and its environment. Gently notice your body breathing. Is the breath slow or fast, long or short? Let it be what it is without manipulating it mentally or physically. Gently scan around the body for any sensations that seem agitating, but let them be for now. Notice the quality of your mind. Is it agitated, calm, dull, restless, overwrought or racing? Let that, too, be as it is for now.

Vase Breathing is best done through the nostrils. When you are ready, inhale slowly and fully through the nostrils, filling your lower abdomen and letting it expand out as you inhale. Notice if you can take in a bit more air and do so. Then exhale slowly through the nostrils, allowing the abdomen to empty completely and compress back toward the spine. Do this a couple of times to get the hang of breathing from the abdomen. It should feel relaxing. If you have any discomfort, make sure you are not straining or forcing your breath. Try to be at ease and as gentle as possible. As you breathe, let yourself become aware of any buzzing, tight or pressured sensations in the head, throat or chest area. This is an indication of over-active *rlung*.

Now direct your attention about four finger-widths below your belly button. When full of air this area expands and is shaped like a vase, hence the name Vase Breathing. It may take some extra attention and intention to locate your awareness below the navel. So take your time if needed. When ready, inhale slowly and fully through the nostrils, expanding your lower abdomen. Use your attention to gently draw the breath down toward the vase area below your navel, and feel the vase expand as it receives the breath. Never force the breath to move downward. Intend the movement without pushing or straining. While drawing breath down below the navel, you will be holding the breath in the body for a few seconds. Be very gentle and slowly exhale through the nostrils when you are ready. Do this inhaling, drawing down and exhaling process about three times.

Now notice any *rlung* sensations residing in the head, throat or chest area. They may have lessened, indicating that *rlung* is naturally being drawn down with the breath to the vase area. Don't worry if the breath doesn't move all the way down below the navel. That will come in time.

The fourth time you inhale though the nostrils, draw the breath down, and as you exhale through the nostrils, try holding that last bit of breath in the vase area, intending to keep the *rlung* in its proper residence. Again do not strain to hold the breath, and always exhale slowly, without urgency. At first, the length of holding may be very short, but it will naturally increase with practice.

Continue Vase Breathing for about 10 minutes in this manner: inhaling, drawing down, exhaling almost completely, holding the last bit of breath in the vase area and then exhaling fully. When you are done, rest and notice how the body feels. Note the quality of your mind and emotions. Remember how you felt prior to beginning this practice.

 Why Desire Is Not the Problem

Prior to his awakening, Siddhartha Gautama experienced 28 years of over-indulgent palace life and 6 years of extreme asceticism as a forest yogi. After his awakening, the Buddha taught a Middle Way approach to desire.

Few of us realize that hedonic pleasures, which feel good while we have them, are actually *dukkha* producing—afflictive and agitating—not just in the wanting but equally so in the having. The Buddha vociferously argued this point in his teachings on craving (*tanhā*) and clinging (*upādāna*). He recommended renouncing unwholesome wanting for the serenity of non-clinging. But of course even that endeavor involves a desire to awaken. So the problem cannot be desire, for without it we would never awaken out of suffering.

I asked Buddhist teacher and scholar Stephen Batchelor what he thought was the difference between craving (*tanhā*) and desire (S: *chanda* T: *'dod pa*).

> Existentially, *tanhā* is just a modality of desire. Desire, if you get to the root of it, is the state we find ourselves in when we recognize a circumstance in which we wish for improvement. *Tanhā* is a desire that doesn't work—a gratification or solution that is bound to fail because of *tanhā*'s cognitive distortions. Abhidharmists went to a lot of trouble to delineate different kinds of desire. But I think it avoids the question that we are creatures of desire. I think the Vajrayāna is quite good on this point. It has this expression, *transform desire into the path*. I think there is honesty there, possibly arrived in exasperation at trying to fine tune good desire from bad desire. My sense is that the real problem with craving is that it blocks

us from blossoming and flourishing as humans. Egoism and self-image are problematic because they render life static, incapable of movement and growth because we are caught in patterns. *Samsāra*. The freedom from *samsāra* is not to get out of life but to get out of the cycle of suffering. The problem is the way we get locked into its cycles that reinforce our sense of ego. Where I would place the emphasis is on noticing reactive patterns as they come up and not identifying with them. Letting them go creates the freedom to embark on a response that is unconditioned by reactivity. This is what the Buddha was trying to impart. (Batchelor, 2013)

Get to Know Desire

I once heard the Venerable Ajahn Sumedho say, "The problem is not desire. Get to know desire; don't get rid of desire." Desire is our great teacher. It reveals our deepest longings and fuels creative actualization. Without desire life is passionless, sterile and bland. But desire is also a trickster and can at any time take on the false appearance of savior, master, friend or wise counselor.

By the time a person shows up in a therapist's office, he may feel disconnected from many aspects of his inner and outer life—including desire. Nevertheless, inquiring about desire relatively early in the work can be informative and fruitful. Don't be deterred if the first response is one of hesitation or confusion: something along the lines of "I am afraid to want anything" or "I don't know what I want anymore" or "what's the point, nothing goes right for me anyway." Past failures and losses often incite negative self-narratives that, when perseverated on, devolve into chronic hopelessness or helplessness.

Some come to therapy saddled with warped notions about desire and sensuality, often introjected from religious dogma or cultural/familial beliefs or as a result of abuse. These distortions restrict the psyche to a narrow, disgust-based world of self-imposed limitation and alienate it from its instinctual urge to enjoy the rich sensuality of human experience.

Getting to know desire—its destructive and transformative effects—is a process of discerning the difference between pure desires and deluded clinging to objects of desire. A wise psychotherapist can help patients rediscover, reclaim and reassert pure desires.

For example, a victim of repeated domestic violence continues to remain in an injurious relationship despite numerous therapeutic conversations about the need to exit. At the heart of every relationship—even the harmful, chaotic ones—is a pure desire to love and be loved. How that pure desire manifests in a particular psyche depends on the internal level of unawareness, volitional dispositions and external past or present circumstances. Although pure desire precedes the impulses and actions it begets, it can easily become over-coupled with subsequent clinging to objects of fulfillment—even harmful objects that will never satisfy the untainted desire's original intent.

In this example the harmful object of desire has become indistinguishable from the pure desire to love and be loved. Caught up in hoping for the harm to end or fearing what might occur if the partner is left, the mind clings to the false equation of harm and love. Suffering manifests as emotional confusion and an inability to secure one's own safety.

The first step in separating pure desire from its tainted manifestations is to name it. Reconnecting this domestic violence sufferer with the untainted desire to love and be loved will reveal desire's non-harming nature and help uncouple it from violence of any kind. The more the mind dis-identifies the harmful partner with the pure desire for love, the less clinging and suffering will occur. Buddhist psychology relies on facilitation of right seeing rather than repeated convincing; for wisdom is the path to awakening and its result.

Wholesome and Unwholesome Desires

Recently, a mid-30s Silicon Valley billionaire chose to be married in Big Sur, a pristine part of the California coastline. If you've visited the area, you may have felt the vast quietude emanating from Big Sur's awe-inspiring oceanscapes and old-growth redwoods. Who would not want to be married surrounded by such wondrous natural beauty? Did the couple choose one of several stunning, exclusive inns? No. They rented an abandoned campground in the old-growth redwoods and constructed an elaborate $4.5 million 'movie set' (with ruins, staircases, a stone bridge and enormous floral overhangs) without obtaining permits. Three weeks prior to the wedding the Coastal Commission ordered a stop to all preparations. The couple's claims of environmental sensitivity were met with a $2.5 million fine and reluctant go-ahead. Photos of the wedding site revealed their perverse vision of environmental sensitivity. The grand old growth redwoods were shrouded behind soaring, garish displays. In the end, the wholesome desire to celebrate the joining of two hearts was hijacked by unwholesome ego-driven wanting. The result was an astronomically wasteful $10 million hedonic event.

Psychiatrist Mark Epstein claims that desire forces us to face again and again the gap between expectations and reality.[10] I agree that this is absolutely true of unwholesome desires, which always lead to some form of disappointment or harm. But wholesome desires seem to narrow this gap. Wholesome desires are *self-less* (*anattā/anātman*) and *non-violent* (*ahimsā*), because their impetus and results reflect wisdom, humility and virtuous conduct.

Psychologist and Buddhist teacher Jack Kornfield offers the following advice: "To live in this world wisely, we have to go beyond the extremes of being numb to desire and being lost in desire. We need to release unhealthy desire and learn to hold healthy desire lightly" (2008). Kornfield further suggests that abundance, generosity and adornment naturally arise when one willingly lets go of greed, grasping and addiction. We can suffuse wholesome desire into all aspects of daily life through meaningful work, fairness, skillfulness, acts of caring and generosity, service, fidelity, honoring of parents, education of children and living in harmony with our environment.

Psychotherapeutic inquiry is an effective way to distinguish healthy desire from unhealthy desire. Many of us who use Motivational Interviewing with substance use sufferers know the power of meeting them in their addiction so they can reconnect with healthy desire and realize how antithetical it is to using a substance.

Buddhist psychology utilizes a universally applicable strategy for inquiring into wholesome and unwholesome desire—*expose self-cherishing and self-confusion.* More than any other cause, self-cherishing and self-confusion are the principal conditions that turn wholesome desire into unwholesome desire. Exorcising desire does not root out self-clinging. So we must hold the self lightly with an intention toward non-harming.

Discovering Pure Desire Exercise

(Psychotherapists please note: This exercise illustrates how I implement this inquiry with patients.) Choose a person, object or situation that has caused you suffering and that, for whatever reason, you've been unable to release. Try to pick something that has been confusing for you, or maybe that dear friends insist is unhealthy or wrong for you. When you have chosen something to work with, think back to how things were before it came into your life. Were you were feeling a lack of or longing for something like it? Was it surprising and unexpected, or were you actively seeking it? Take some time to sit with these questions.

Now remember how your life was impacted by its arrival. What did you feel? Were you open or cautious, impulsive or resistant? How strong was the attraction? How certain were you about the rightness of the object of your desire? How perfect did it seem in the beginning? Again, sit with this inquiry.

Now contemplate what desires you were hoping it would fulfill. List them below.

Which of these desires feels most authentic, wholesome and virtuous? Write it down and explain why.

____

____

____

Now remember when the person or the situation started to change or deteriorate. Was this authentic desire still being met? If so, in what way? If not, how did you cope?

Now come into the present and contemplate it with honesty and courage. Is this person, object or situation in opposition to that desire?

Have you lost sight of the authentic desire? Maybe there is a different pure desire that feels more pertinent to your current life. Kindly investigate the truth of these questions as best you can.

Imagine how your life would be without this object, person or situation. Notice whether what you imagine is primarily comprised of assumptions, hopes or fears. As you do this, observe your thoughts and emotions; let them come and go without clinging to them. Note the presence of negative or positive self-cherishing.

When you feel ready, bring to mind the pure desire or, if you have identified a new authentic desire, use that instead. Allow it to suffuse your mind, and let your heart open to it as well. Notice how it resonates in your body, and be curious about these sensations. Stay with this for a few minutes.

Before we finish, once again bring to mind the person, object or situation that has caused you suffering and that you've been unable to release. Notice how this feels in your mind, body and heart. Note the difference and then return to the authentic, pure desire. Rest in that for a few more minutes.

The Ultimate Desire: Being Good

A recent study measured the effect of mindfulness and compassion meditation on goodness and moral decision-making. Subjects were wait-listed or placed in either an 8-week mindfulness or a compassion meditation class. Upon completion each subject returned to the lab for 'cognitive testing.' The designated waiting area had three chairs, two of which were occupied by female confederates. Another confederate 'sufferer' entered on crutches. Seeing no empty chairs she winced and leaned against the wall. "To assess compassionate responding, we measured whether the true participant offered his or her seat to the sufferer to relieve her pain. If two minutes passed and the participant had not given up his or her seat, the trial was ended and coded as a non-helping response" (Condon, Desbordes, Miller, DeSteno, Hospital, & DeSteno, 2013 in press). The meditation group participants were five times more likely to offer their seats to the 'sufferer' than the wait-listed participants. The enhanced compassionate response was equivalent for the mindfulness and compassion protocols.

The Greek philosopher Aristotle placed great emphasis on the role of virtue in achieving the human goodness he considered central to living a happy life. For Aristotle, *eudaimonia*—the *human flourishing* that comes from goodness and its virtuous activities—was a sufficient goal for human life.

Buddhism agrees that fulfilling the fundamental human desire for happiness depends on the actualization of human goodness. But it goes one step further by determining that innate goodness has always been our true nature. The Buddha was adamant that although goodness is our birthright, embodying it requires intentional virtuous striving. Buddhist psychology maintains the centrality of virtue and goodness for psychological well-being. Thankfully, these days that view is finding increasing support in Western psychology.[11]

During the early part of the 20th century scientific psychology deemphasized virtue and morality in its study of the personality.[12] That bolstered Western psychology's existing tendency to favor individualism and contributed to its ambivalent relationship with morality, some might even say its *moral neutrality* with respect to the decent or indecent actions of patients.[13]

The desire to be good is not value-free proposition. Aligning oneself with a desire for wholesome action (*kusalā kamma*) and moral agency requires sustained intention and effort. Do not mistake this for a neurotic need to always be and do what one thinks others want. That 'trying to be good' comes from distorted perceptions (*saññā*) and mental proliferations (*papañca*) rooted in self-loathing and doubt. Hating oneself is anathema to moral agency and virtuous conduct.

I would like to pose some questions for clinicians to ponder. What role should psychotherapy play in the cultivation of a person's desire to connect with basic goodness? Can we find a universally agreed-upon standard for virtuous conduct and champion its value in sustaining genuine mental health? If mental health relies on cognitive and affective flexibility and resilience, why wouldn't psychotherapists offer skills to help patients connect with values and virtues that foster patience, willingness, restraint, thoughtfulness, tolerance, curiosity and openness?

It is not my place to insist that clinicians look within and question how willingly they reflect goodness to their patients. But I do think everyone would be better served if the meta-conversation about what a 'good life' or a 'good person' means took place openly and honestly. Being good is not just a matter of competence; it is the precious desire to seek the welfare and well-being of all beings, including ourselves, as best we are able. I firmly believe the powerful aspiration of *bodhicitta* could be a welcome addition to psychotherapy.

Bring Desire Onto the Path

> *"Bring everything onto the path" is a* Vajrayāna *Buddhist sentiment. Open your heart and hold this extraordinary attitude toward everything—crisis and loss too. Open your heart and take everything onto the path and through that awaken to your infinite nature.* (Thubten, 2012, July 29)

As Stephen Batchelor intimated, the instructions for how one meets and deals with desire vary among the three main schools of Buddhism. The Tibetan Buddhist monk and scholar Jamgön Kongtrul Lodrö Tayé (1813–1899) synthesized teachings from many Buddhist lineages in his renowned treatise

The Five Great Treasures. His instructions for dealing with desire combined skillful means from Theravada, Mahāyāna and Vajrayāna Buddhism. Each of these paths has merit and, depending on the situation, any one of their strategies may be the best choice for skillfully meeting a strong desire, overwhelming impulse or distressing emotion. The following information is loosely based on Jamgön Kongtrul Rinpoche's instructions.[14]

Theravada Buddhism seeks to abandon clinging to desire through clear comprehension and wise action. The goal is to intentionally realize the *samsāric* nature of all desires and mitigate their arising. In the presence of strong desire, analyze the object of your desire and your responses. Seek to recognize its impermanence, inevitable unsatisfactoriness and dependent constructed nature. Inquire into any self-cherishing or self-clinging that might be fueling intense wanting or aversion. Constant mindful attending and wise inquiry are recommended to increase wholesome desire, reduce the harm of unwholesome desire and lessen the psyche's tendencies toward mindless self-gratification. In the presence of overwhelming craving or distressful emotions, remember the internal and external harm these can cause. Endeavor to limit that harm with mindful, compassionate recognition of suffering and appropriate ethical conduct.

Mahāyāna Buddhism seeks to transform desires and afflictive emotions through Bodhisattvic means. Recognizing selflessness, emptiness and boundless compassion is emphasized in this method. When desire or disturbing emotions arise, Theravada methods for clear comprehension are recommended. While doing so, remain alert for any ego-driven grasping at the pride of being a 'good practitioner.' This is especially pertinent when working with disturbing emotions or unwholesome desires, which can catalyze strong aversion to one's own primordial ignorance and basic humanness. Remembering that all beings are afflicted by strong desire and disturbing emotions deflates pride and stimulates the Bodhisattvic wish to free all beings from similar suffering. Then one can freely practice Tonglen meditation with the Bodhisattvic intent to transform one's own suffering into liberation for all beings everywhere.

Dzongsar Jamyang Khyentse Rinpoche describes the value of this process:

> From a relative point of view what happens when you take on the suffering of others in this way? Fundamentally, you go against the wishes of your ego. So if your ego wants to be the holiest and most sublime of all beings so it can boast it has no desire or jealousy, this is exactly the practice you need to oppose and resist it. . . . If emotions were not inherently empty, transformation would not be possible because they would be "real." (2012)

Vajrayāna Buddhism seeks to know desire from within non-elaborative awareness. Rather than recommending the wholesale abandonment of desire and disturbing emotions, Vajrayāna suggests the skillful means of non-elaboration—resting awareness in these phenomena without following their dictates. Since effortless mindfulness is our ultimate aim, it is important to clearly understand the intent and right application of these instructions.

Because all phenomena are impermanent, what has arisen will naturally dissolve on its own. Remaining wakefully present in the actuality of intense desire or disturbing emotions allows us to recognize their appearance as transparent, shifting impressions of an illusory self. Letting be in the presence of internal disturbance loosens the discursive mind's compulsive, ego-driven need to construct, elaborate upon, or fix experience. This non-reactivity is the fertile ground for clear comprehension and wise action.

Elaborating refers to three conditions: falsely determining through afflictive thinking that internal or external phenomena are of the self or separately existent; emotionally grasping at ending or continuing experience for self-gain or self-soothing; or incorrectly identifying phenomena as anything other than a mere appearance of the innate luminosity of mind/consciousness.

When one looks into the nature of desire, the source of desire is known as the union of emptiness and awareness—*rigpa*, the nature of mind. Every desire, all afflictive emotions and thoughts, every experience (easy or hard, wanted or unwanted) is welcomed as a cause for the realization of primordial wisdom. Like a snake untying itself, clinging can spontaneously liberate itself from within the experience of desire. No longer driven by agitated reactivity, the mind dynamically responds from within the skillful play of *awakened presence.*

 Abandon Clinging to Hope and Fear

> *Being a bodhisattva means to be courageous and not to go looking for a perfect reality or spiritual 'lala land' for yourself . . . to have the courage to run into the samsāra—the life of messiness, pain and misery. True courage is to let go of all hope and fear.* (Thubten, 2012, December 23)

As a child, Yongey Mingyur Rinpoche suffered from anxiety, which exponentially increased when he left his family home and entered monastic life at the age of 11. In his books, Rinpoche recounts the mental anguish he lived with and kept secret during those first few months in the monastery. One day during a lesson with his teacher he finally shared his awful predicament. Saljay Rinpoche asked the novice monk to notice how his fearful thoughts came and went and then suggested he stop resisting his anxiety and make friends with it instead. While at first this didn't make sense to him, it soon became his refuge from the mental anguish of clinging to hope and fear.

> Words like 'attachment' and 'grasping' don't really capture the complexity of the underlying nature of this mechanism, which may best be described as a kind of balancing act between hope and fear: hope that things will either change or stay the same and fear of the same things. . . . One of the questions I am frequently asked in public teachings and private interviews is, 'How can I get rid of hope and fear?' The simple answer is, 'By not trying.' (Mingyur, 2009)

I think every psychotherapist has grappled with grasping at hope for a patient's healing and fear of continued suffering. Some clinicians keep hope alive for the hopeless or use fear to inspire change in the resistant. Trying to ameliorate or fix another's suffering by clinging to a wrong self-view ('I can change them') binds therapist and patient to the false legitimacy of powerlessness. 'Not trying' means being wakefully present, interested in and flexibly interacting with the stream of dependently originated intersubjective phenomena, clearly comprehending causes and conditions while skillfully, compassionately inspiring insight into the nature of suffering.

Dynamic Responsiveness

I tell patients that hope and fear fuel mental time travel and obstruct the mind's capacity for insight, intention and presence. Hope is ethereal. It lives in an undetermined imaginative future disconnected from personal accountability and intentionality. Fear belongs to the past but does not mentally stay there. Agitation in the psyche propels fearful mentation into the present, where its distress instantaneously transmutes fear into worry about the future. Consequently, much of our moment-to-moment inner experience is taken up with habitual rejecting and accepting. The result is the unsatisfactoriness of unawareness (*āvidya*) or what cognitive neuroscience calls cognitive-affective automaticity.

The cure for automaticity is awareness (*vidyā*), and awareness is a choice. When we actively choose to rest in awareness, its immeasurable display is revealed. Recognizing the luminosity of mind in the immediacy of experience dissolves dualism and with it internal fixation on hope and fear. Knower, known and knowing *interare*, and the psyche becomes an unobstructed vessel for spontaneous responsiveness and dynamic skillfulness. *This is the primordial wisdom of effortless mindfulness.*

A patient who came to therapy with childhood trauma-related post-traumatic stress disorder and alcohol dependence recently shared a pivotal experience of spontaneous insight and effortless responsiveness:

> I am becoming more comfortable with knowing what I need and noticing thoughts that before would have kept me from simply asking my son to take care of a task. I just did it without feeling any guilt or shame. That made it possible to take my time and drive to the social event in a relaxed way. When I arrived I was not feeling anxious, like I normally do. I poured myself a glass of ice water and started saying hello to people. It was so strange. I have known many of them for years and have intense opinions about them—lots of it negative or fearful. But I found myself not judging them, just being with them as they are. I let them talk and really listened without the stream of anxious negative self-talk. I was actually

with them! After some time, the hostess asked if I would like a glass of wine. Normally I would have already had at least one or two glasses of wine by that time to lessen the anxiety of talking to people. I said yes, but it didn't really make much of a difference in how I felt about them or me. I realized the story I had been telling myself about my anxiety and what alcohol did for me, why I needed it, was completely false.

Effortless Mindfulness: The Refuge of Resting in Awakened Presence

Effortless mindfulness (*rtsol med kyi dran pa*) is a technical term used in Mahāmudrā to refer to an advanced stage of meditative practice. I have chosen to use this term not because I am teaching an advanced-stage practice but more because it is the description I hear most from those who experience this practice. This insight meditation is the non-meditation of just being in the open, spacious clarity of knowing, holding onto nothing and resting effortlessly in experience. On the last retreat I attended with Ajahn Sumedho, he kept insisting we surrender into the deathless, which told me, without a doubt, that effortless mindfulness is exactly where Buddhist practitioners land in the end (regardless of their tradition). Once the limitless luminosity of mind is recognized, the mind will naturally be drawn to the peaceful abode of *awakened presence*. Certainly, that is a refuge every mental health clinician can immediately understand the value of helping patients cultivate in session.

What follows are a series of easy instructions for introducing the practice of effortless mindfulness in your life and in the midst of psychotherapy.

From Within the Body

> *The concrete presence of mind means that it resides in the center of the body. . . . This is the fundamental awareness present in the body. It is the abolition of all fictions.* (Guenther, 1976)

Draw your attention to your gut from within the gut. Attend to the actual physical feeling of the upper abdomen, rib cage and stomach. Rest your awareness in the actuality of how the upper abdomen, rib cage and stomach feel. You may notice the discursive mind label and critique, or the ego having its opinions. Know these phenomena as the mentation of self-clinging; don't grasp, hold or fixate on them. Remain instead with the gut—awareness of the gut. Now let go of any effort to hold attention to the gut and instead *surrender the awareness that knows the gut completely into the gut.* Rest spaciously, knowing that which illuminates the experience of the gut.

From Within Rumination

You realize you are obsessing on the past, running scenarios and mentally berating yourself. Locate the awareness that is witnessing rumination. Intentionally watch the mind's activity, scenarios running on like a movie. Know these phenomena as the mentation of self-clinging; don't grasp, hold or fixate on them. When you notice thoughts cease, let go in knowing itself. Awareness of no thought is the same as awareness of thought. No matter what occurs in the field of mind, rest spaciously, effortlessly knowing that which illuminates all mentation and non-mentation.

From Within Agitated or Worried Mind

You realize you are worrying about the future, running scenarios that mentally grip you in fear. Locate the awareness that is witnessing a worried and agitated mind. Know these phenomena as the mentation of self-clinging; don't grasp, hold or fixate on them. Instead, draw awareness into the body, and find any agitated sensations in the body (buzzing or tightness in the chest or gripping in the stomach). Don't dive into them. Let awareness be open, receptive and at ease—awareness resting at the edge of agitated sensations. Let the mind be soft and surrender into sensation without hoping it will end or fearing it will not end. Let be in phenomena, allowing them to come and go on their own. Rest spaciously, effortlessly knowing that which illuminates all sensation, thought and non-thought.

From Within Craving and Aversion

You realize you want something you cannot or should not have, avoiding or negating something painful. Know these phenomena as the mentation of self-clinging; don't believe, grasp, or fixate on them. Use awareness to get to know the actual experience of attraction and repulsion. Is it physical? If so, bring awareness to the body's positive or negative sensational response. Don't dive into sensations. Let awareness be open, receptive and at ease—awareness resting at the edge of aversive or longing sensations. Let the mind be soft and surrender into aversion or wanting without hoping it will end or fearing it will not end. Let be in the experience, resting spaciously, effortlessly knowing that which illuminates aversion and wanting.

Is your craving or aversion merely mental or emotional? Are you gripped in thinking about it obsessively or emotionally over-wrought? Locate the awareness that is witnessing thoughts and feelings of wanting and aversion. Intentionally watch the mind's activity as you would a movie. Remain interested and awake. Know these phenomena as the mentation of self-clinging; don't grasp, hold or fixate on them. When you notice thoughts and emotions cease, let go in that which knows. Awareness of no thought or neutrality is the same as awareness of distressing thought and over-emotionality. No matter what occurs in the field of mind, rest spaciously, effortlessly knowing that which illuminates all mentation and non-mentation.

From Within Awareness Itself

Open your awareness wide; take in as much as you can of what is actually occurring in you and around you. Don't fixate on anything in particular. If you are doing, just do, and rest awareness effortlessly in the doing. If you are sitting in meditation, let go of any reference point, including fixation on the self. Let be in the wakeful freshness of awareness—the mereness of all phenomena—with no effort to make anything happen or not happen. As Chökyi Nyima Rinpoche instructs (2002):

> *Allow your mind to be in the natural state,*
> *The unity of being empty and cognizant.*
> *Not fixating on anything,*
> *Not forming any conceptual attitude,*
> *You arrive at the innate nature.*
> *At that moment, no negative or positive attitude is present.*
> *There is nothing to be accepted or rejected.*
> *This is the natural state itself.*
> *For a short while*
> *There is total freedom from samsara,*
> *Total freedom from karma and disturbing emotions.*
> *Even though it is so short,*
> *How utterly amazing!*
> *For a brief moment we have awakened*
> *From the sleep of delusion.*

 *Lojong*: Daily Life Training in Awakened Presence

> *Lojong mind training is a powerful and practical teaching. The essential meaning of lojong is expressed in two phrases: stop placing blame on others or outer circumstances and embrace all unfavorable conditions as the path to awakening.* (Thubten, 2013, March 13)

The Tibetan term *lo* means 'mind,' 'attitude' or thought,' and *jong* means 'training,' 'familiarization' or 'purification.' Atiśa (982–1054), the revered Bengali Buddhist teacher, brought *Lojong Seven Point Mind Training* to Tibet after receiving these teachings from a Sumatran Buddhist master. Because of its universal applicability, *lojong* is a preferred method for cultivating awakening in daily life. One of *lojong*'s main tenets is: *If we truly cherish our happiness, we must seek the welfare of others.*[15] This makes the Seven Point Mind Training particularly useful for clinicians, who, by definition, are constantly engaged in seeking the welfare of others, and for patients, who come to alleviate their suffering.

Like crisis intervention, the first step in *lojong* mind training is delineating one's primary area of mental or emotional affliction. To alleviate that suffering, *lojong* specifies contemplative training in discerning self-reflection, compassionate renunciation, vigilant mindfulness and self-restraint. As with the *Eightfold Path*, the ultimate goal of *lojong* is the realization of emptiness through wisdom, compassion and virtue. But *lojong* mind training differentiates itself by encouraging contemplation of the dreamlike nature of mind, self and experience as a means to realizing the 'mereness' of phenomena. This right seeing enables us to regard all aspects of the human condition (even the most despicable) as our precious teacher and bring them onto the path of liberation.

Lojong is engaged Buddhism. It encourages us to courageously heal our own suffering so we can be free to intelligently, compassionately and energetically heal the world's suffering.

> One of the central themes running throughout the mind training instructions is the notion of genuine courage . . . a courage rooted in a clear understanding of the complexity that is our human condition. . . . The vision is this: a carefree mind rooted in a deep joy. (Jinpa, 2011)

What follows is a practical overview of several aspects of Seven Point Mind Training, with attention to its applicability for developing effortless mindfulness in daily life. I urge you to study *lojong* in depth and highly recommend Thubten Jinpa's classic text *Essential Mind Training* for this purpose.

Choosing to Live in Awareness

The Tibetan master Longchen Rabjam (Longchenpa) wrote, "*Wherever I go I am always arriving at the truth; wherever I reside I am always residing in the truth,*" (2001). That truth is the clear comprehending, without any doubt, of the myriad ways in which we create suffering for ourselves and others. Arriving at and residing in this truth is possible only when we choose to live in awareness (*rigpa*)—wakefully present to causes and conditions, curious and willing to wisely and compassionately avert or end suffering.

D: My mind was quiet. It was the strangest feeling, because normally my mind is talking 'at' me a thousand words a minute. What did this new quiet mean? At our next session, I told Lisa about this new development. She smiled and said, "That is *awakened presence*." The difference I've noticed between mindfulness therapy and traditional talk therapy is the focus on what is happening inside the body and mind versus the mind's story about what is happening. This *inside-out approach* gives relevance to whatever it is I'm feeling and gives me permission to just sit with whatever is happening. By quieting myself and really listening to and feeling what my body and mind were telling me, I was able to come to some realizations and finally heal some very old wounds. Being present is an amazing feeling! The focus and openness to the world and myself has been a true gift, one for which I am so grateful.

Lojong mind training begins with the cultivation of *The Four Recollections* and *bodhicitta*. To awaken the mind-heart, one must first become aware of the preciousness of human birth and its impermanent nature. These recollections combined with *shamatha* meditation comprise preliminary training in mindfulness and clear comprehension (*smrti samprajanya*). The second preliminary training arouses the desire for *bodhicitta*, the awakened heart. One investigates the principles of absolute *bodhicitta*—the dreamlike nature of self and objects and the unborn nature of mind—and practices relative *bodhicitta* through *Tonglen* and the *six pāramītas*.

Contemplating the dreamlike nature of existence invites us to open to the mystery of perception. The thoughts and feelings that carry so much weight and seem so real are merely dreamlike appearances of the mind. Embodying perception in the five senses allows us to truly see, hear, touch, smell and taste life as it is. The more we can recognize the difference between embodied awareness and the dreamlike nature of mentation, the greater our capacity to joyfully receive experience in all its vividness and to lightheartedly interact with causes and conditions as the cosmic play of an embodied mind-heart.

Living in Interdependence

> *Seek for the Buddha nowhere else than in primordial freedom itself, which is rootless and groundless—the pure fact of being aware right now.* (Rabjam, 2000)

Lojong was created for practitioners who wish to be free of internal strain while living in a world filled with negativity and hardship. When life rips away our delusions of primacy through the sudden death of a loved one, a serious disease, a massive betrayal, a random act of violence or natural disaster, the groundlessness of existence is exposed. Fixating on 'Why do bad things happen to me?' and wrongfully placing blame on outer circumstances or others is a uniquely human inaccuracy. We seem to partake in our lives while remaining unaware of how we participate in creating circumstances that lead to unwanted distressful events. This is a pervasive and destructive outcome of primordial ignorance (*avidyā*).

Because we can't magically make life conform to our wishes, the only workable solution is to bring adversity onto the path of awakening and transform our unskillful responses to suffering. That is the third step in *lojong* mind training. No one can know the full ramifications of his or her actions. Nor can anyone comprehend all the causes and conditions that lead to the harmful actions of others. Blaming difficulties on circumstances or on others prevents us looking deeply into self-clinging, the true source of all affliction.

Emptiness, groundlessness, freaks out the ego. "The sense of groundlessness leads to great defensive maneuvers to regain ground or *significance*" (Schneider, 2013). Because destructive emotions that feed blaming—like resentment, anger and vengeance—are primarily fueled by the ego's strong belief in its own significance, we must recognize self-centeredness as the main hindrance to personal and collective well-being.

To diminish self-centeredness, *lojong* suggests mind training in kindness, humility and tolerance toward all circumstances and all beings (including ourselves). Here are a few suggestions for how to accomplish this:

> Don't jump to conclusions.
> Be open-minded and listen.
> Share thoughts and feelings with honesty and truthfulness.
> Be generous in the presence of mistakes—yours and others.
> Compassionately recognize that every human being endures unsatisfactoriness.

But, above all other strategies, *lojong* mind training advises us to *bring all blames to the single source.*[16] That source is self-cherishing: (1) putting one's benefit above all others' and (2) grasping at ego-delusions and self-idealizations that, whether we know it or not, cause, contribute to or maintain self-and other-suffering. When we see how self-centeredness hurts us, we can understand how others' self-centeredness hurts them.

Integrating *lojong* mind training into psychotherapy shifts the focus from altering the self-view to transforming the root causes of self-suffering. For instance, traditional talk psychotherapy might help a patient feel less insecure by focusing on self-worth. If a patient can recognize insecurity as a mere collection of thoughts and feelings, which the mind reactively rejects as bad or accepts as true, insecurity is no longer something that is happening to them. It is a habitual mechanism of suffering that they are now empowered to follow or not follow. By discerning the dependent nature of insecurity, the patient's right seeing becomes the antidote to clinging to negative self-cherishing. To further dissolve the self-hatred at the core of insecurity, one can generate the *pāramīta* of generosity toward oneself or bring to mind all others who similarly suffer and practice *Tonglen*.

Making Friends With Samsāra

> *If you can tolerate anything, whatever you do brings happiness;*
> *If your mind rests where it's placed, you can journey anywhere.* (Sumpa Lotsāwa, quoted in Jinpa, 2011)

I work in a field where every day is a chance to contribute joy to the world. I have also had the good fortune to work with people who continually inspire me. They bring such courage and fortitude to freeing themselves from forms of suffering that would make most of us recoil or give up altogether. Here is the story of one person who triumphed over tremendous adversity by making friends with her *samsāric* existence.

L was raised in an adverse childhood environment. Despite ongoing emotional distress she managed to do well in high school. After she graduated from university, worsening depression and anxiety undermined her personal and professional independence. Within a few years she returned to her parents' home severely depressed and unable to work full-time. Her decline worsened after a failed surgery undercut her mobility. In-patient and out-patient psychotherapy had not lessened her emotional dysregulation. She struggled day to day with massive pain, working part-time at two jobs and spending the rest of her hours collapsed in bed. When L entered therapy with me, she had endured 10 years of ongoing autoimmune disorders, chronic nerve pain, severe suicidal depression and anxiety. Unsuccessful medical interventions had left her with an intense fear of doctors. Defeatism, self-loathing and exhaustion pervaded every cell of her body and psyche.

The first year of our work was challenging for both of us. L interpreted any pain as a sign that nothing would get better. Her long-held inner story of ugliness and unlovability was pervasive. Complex trauma, intense fearfulness, anger and psychophysical sensitivities to most drugs and neutraceuticals required a slow and gentle approach. Toward the end of our first year she was using mindfulness and compassion skills on her own with some good effects and began to consider the possibility of medical intervention.

Our second year of work was astonishing. L finally agreed to see a complementary pain specialist. As her body responded to pharmacological and nutritional treatment, her ability to implement awareness, inquiry and compassion dramatically increased. She spent less time collapsed in bed, joined a weekly chi gong class and was working more hours. With less cognitive and affective suffering, L realized how extreme clinging to hope for a cure and fear of no cure had obscured a life rich with possibility. Around the two-year mark, after her first successful trip in years, she came to a session and announced, "I am happy for the first time in years. I am not physically or mentally perfect by any means, but I don't hate my body or myself like I used to. I still have chronic pain, but it no longer rules everything I think and do. I have more energy to be helpful to others, which really makes me happy. And I feel beautiful for the first time in my entire life."

Befriending Your Greatest Challenges Exercise

Let's begin with some sage advice from Dr. Judson Brewer, "You're already awesome. Just get out of your own way!" (2013). In other words, get doubting, comparing mentation out of your way.

I am a big fan of faith and encourage everyone to generate faith in their inborn capacities to beat the odds. The potential to develop everything you need to meet any challenge already resides within you, and the Dharma is the supreme vehicle for nurturing that potential. The Eightfold Path and/or *lojong* mind training help us internally unite around moral principles, which promote right seeing, right action and right mindfulness, under all conditions—especially in challenging situations.

I imagine every mental health clinician has faced the difficulty of working with someone who is averse to or ambivalent toward challenge. Avoidance and resistance are common first responses to challenge in those who suffer from freeze physiology, depression and anxiety. Conversely, lashing out or spiraling out is a common reaction for those overwhelmed by anger, impulses or emotion dysregulation. The failure to thrive can often be rooted in existential fear of one's power and a resulting loss of will.

To encourage self-empowerment and lessen cognitive-affective resistance and fearfulness, I recommend breaking challenges down into digestible parts by examining *motivation, intention, values and commitment*. Doing so clarifies objectives and increases determination or 'guts'—sometimes referred to as 'fearlessness' by my Buddhist teachers. Contemplating these four attributes reimagines purpose, stimulates personal investment and steers skillful execution and achievement. This method is especially useful when successfully meeting a challenge necessitates acquiring new skills or greater resources or enduring difficult conditions.

The following exercise will help you analyze a current challenge and create a plan to meet it successfully by exploring motivation, intention, values and commitment. When commitment falters or doubts arise, reconnecting with motivation, intention and values will promote determination and follow-through. As you successfully work with this particular challenge, remain open to new challenges or the realization that what you thought was hard did not turn out to be very challenging in the end. Consider carefully any hopes and fears that may have distorted your perception of what you are capable of achieving, and let them go. Use this process to practice meeting life's challenges with greater courage, humility and, of course, *awakened presence*.

Choose a current life challenge.

____

Motivation

What motivates you to meet and master this challenge?

____

____

____

____

What skills, knowledge and resources do you already possess that will help you?

____

____

____

____

What skills, knowledge and resources do you need to accumulate?

____

____

____

____

Take some time to consider the following questions:

How would meeting this challenge impact your sense of purpose or meaning?

How would surmounting this challenge transform the way you show up in the world?

How would mastering this challenge alter the way you feel about yourself?

Intention

What intention will inspire the courage to meet this challenge?

____

____

When your motivation wanes, what intention will reconnect and reinvigorate motivation?

____

____

What intention will inspire you to persevere in times of difficulty, fearfulness or doubt?

____

____

What is your intended outcome?

____

____

What compromises are you willing to make to ensure a mutually beneficial outcome?

____

____

What is non-negotiable?

____

____

Values and Virtues

What values and virtues are important to embody as you meet this challenge?

____

____

____

____

What values and virtues will help you cultivate resilience, creativity and the ability to successfully meet obstacles along the way?

____

____

____

____

How will meeting this challenge contribute to the well-being of others?

____

____

____

____

Commitments

Get started with small steps to meet this challenge to build confidence in your abilities:

Choose one easily achievable goal:
____________________ and have it accomplished in _____ days.

Investigate a more challenging goal:
____________________ and have that accomplished in ______ days.

What allies and resources can you commit to gathering in the next ____ day/weeks?

____

____

Pick an activity for developing one of these resources and do it in the next ____ days/weeks.

____

____

On a scale of 1–10 (1 = not confident at all, 10 = totally confident), how confident were you before this exercise in your ability to face this challenge? ___ And now? ___

Notes

1. Quoidbach, J., Dunn, E. W., Petrides, K. V., & Mikolajczak, M. (2010). Money giveth, money taketh away: The dual effect of wealth on happiness. *Psychological Science, 21*(6), 759–763.
2. Kahneman, D., & Deaton, A. (2010). High income improves evaluation of life but not emotional well-being. *Proceedings of the National Academy of Sciences, 107*(38), 16489–16493.
3. Ryan, R. M., & Deci, E. L. (2001). On happiness and human potentials: A review of research on hedonic and eudaimonic well-being. *Annual Review of Psychology, 52*(1), 141–166.
4. Dambrun, M., & Ricard, M. (2011). Self-centeredness and selflessness: A theory of self-based psychological functioning and its consequences for happiness. *Review of General Psychology, 15*(2), 138.
5. Fronsdal, G. (2005). *The Dhammapada: A new translation of the Buddhist classic with annotations.* Boston, MA: Shambhala Publications.
6. Scaer, R. (2012). *8 keys to brain-body balance.* New York, NY: W. W. Norton.
7. Dale, C. (2009). *The subtle body: An encyclopedia of your energetic anatomy.* Boulder, CO: Sounds True. p. 4.
8. Benson, H., Malhotra, M. S., Goldman, R. F., Jacobs, G. D., & Hopkins, P. J. (1990). Three case reports of the metabolic and electroencephalographic changes during advanced Buddhist meditation techniques. *Behavioral Medicine, 16*(2), 90–95.
   Lazar, S. W., Bush, G., Gollub, R. L., Fricchione, G. L., Khalsa, G., & Benson, H. (2000). Functional brain mapping of the relaxation response and meditation. *Neuroreport, 11*(7), 1581–1585.
9. Lutz, A., Dunne, J. D., & Davidson, R. J. (2007). Meditation and the neuroscience of consciousness: An introduction. In P. D. Zelazo, P.D., M. Moscovitch, & E. Thompson (Eds.), *The Cambridge handbook of consciousness* (pp. 499–551). New York, NY: Cambridge University Press.
10. Epstein, M. (2003). *Open to desire: The truth about what the Buddha taught.* New York, NY: Gotham. p. 58.
11. Burns, J. P., Goodman, D. M., & Orman, A. J. (2013). Psychotherapy as moral encounter: A crisis of modern conscience. *Pastoral Psychology, 62*(1), 1–12.
12. Bellah, R. N., Madsen, R., Sullivan, W. M., Swidler, A., & Tipton, S. M. (1985). *Habits of the heart.* Los Angeles, CA: University of California Press.
13. Fowers, B. J. (2012). Placing virtue and the human good in psychology. *Journal of Theoretical and Philosophical Psychology, 32*(1), 1–9.
14. Khyentse, J. (2012). *Not for happiness: A guide to the so-called preliminary practices.* Boston, MA: Shambhala Publications.
15. Jinpa, T. (Ed. and Trans.). (2011). *Essential mind training.* Boston, MA: Wisdom Publications. p. 8.
16. Rabjam, L. (2000). *You are the eyes of the world.* (K. Lipman, Trans.). Ithaca, NY: Snow Lion Publications. p. 58.

8

Nirvāna as Skillful Action and Transformation

 Being a Light in a World of Darkness

When someone gives us the privilege of witnessing their inner work, that honor should be met with a commitment to full presence: sensorial, affective, cognitive and intuitive. Western psychology's parameters for correct psychotherapeutic presence have seen many iterations. For a Buddhist-inspired psychotherapist full presence means deep listening, compassionate attunement, wise containment and conscious inquiry.

Psychotherapy as Inner Pilgrimage

Psychotherapy has been envisioned by many Western modalities as an inner pilgrimage to reclaim the authentic self. Even Jack Engler, an analyst and longtime Buddhist practitioner, famously theorized that one must have a self before one can lose a self.[1] I question the necessity of accepting the psyche's ego-reifications (in other words, 'having a self') in order to realize the inherent fallaciousness of all self-conceptions. Maybe at this point in the book you concur. I remain skeptical of how repeated psychotherapeutic instantiation of self-clinging can free a psyche from primordial ignorance (*avidyā*).

Buddhist psychology proposes to decrease the mass of human suffering by seeding the world with quiescent, wise and compassionate people who move through their lives awakened and present to suffering and non-suffering. I imagine that many mental health clinicians resonate with that vision and believe their work aligns with similar objectives. So what makes Buddhist psychology different?

The Buddha asserted that *liberation comes from seeking unconventional truth—the unconditioned existential awareness of our innermost beingness.* Since unconditioned beingness is devoid of self-reified narratives and personal/transpersonal identities and is beyond all conceptualizations, it cannot be arrived at through psychodynamic, content-driven, narrative-focused or conceptually based psychotherapeutic methods. A Buddhist psychological approach would have to offer something more.

Envisage an inner pilgrimage designed to strip away the habitual conventionality of selfing, a form of psychotherapeutic inquiry that encourages a self to deliberately, fearlessly interact with the unconventional truth of its own emptiness. That inner pilgrimage would likely consist of interventions aimed at exposing the self's utter transparency—an insight-driven process of *not finding as the ultimate finding.*

If *not finding* elicits a sense of discomfort or inconceivability, see whether you can know the phenomenality of that uneasiness. As you do this, try to find a self, existing apart from the discomfort. You may experience the feeling of an identifiable self or the thought of a self, but an actual, separately existing self-entity can never be found. That is emptiness. "If you can make friends with emptiness, it will lead you to the unconventional truth, the ultimate truth, the truth of who you are—your original face, which is limitless. You will lose all your ideas of who you are; guilt, pride, and doubt. That is liberation" (Thubten, 2013, July 21). That liberation is the heart of Buddhist psychology.

 Wise Understanding

Toward the end of my interview with Judson Brewer, I asked him what he would most want clinicians to know about Buddhist psychology. His reply exemplifies wise understanding:

> Don't shove it into concepts of current cognitive therapy, because it is not that. Don't try to make mindfulness fit into your concept of cognitive therapy because it is not. *My experience is that it doesn't get much better than just resting in awareness.* All clinicians should do some meditation practice; actually, do a lot of meditation. I was most dangerous about two or three years in—a proselytizer not knowing what I was talking about. Now I know enough to know what I don't know and I am very happy to learn anything I can. (2013)

Wise understanding (*vidyā*) is the fundamental goal of all Buddhist psychological interventions. It is the process of arriving at the following truths:

1. The fundamental purpose of human life is to end suffering by recognizing the dependently originating appearance of all internal and external phenomena.
2. All human minds are negatively influenced by primordial ignorance and volitional dispositions. Thus every human being is the owner and heir of her or his perceptions, thoughts, emotions and actions (*karma*).
3. Because of the immeasurable luminosity of awareness, every moment of human existence is endowed with the potential for full liberation from afflicted perception.

Right view (*sammā ditthi*) and *right intention* (*sammā sankappa*) are the means to accomplish wise understanding.[2] Right view, or right seeing, is knowing things in their actuality. Right intention is the ongoing commitment to attain right view. In daily life right seeing and right intention are achieved through clear comprehension of causes and conditions and the active pursuit of mindful thought, speech, emotion and behavior. Right intention has three components—*good will*, *renunciation* and *harmlessness*.[3]

In Buddhist-inspired psychotherapy, good will is a genuine shared aspiration for freedom from suffering. Clinicians can hold this intention and actively extend lovingkindness to a patient by envisioning them free from suffering and harming. We can energetically encourage a patient's embrace of warm-heartedness and facilitate compassion practice.

Renunciation (*nekkhamma*) helps Buddhist-inspired clinicians lightly hold the *samsāra* and *nirvāna* of psychotherapy. Unhooked from suffering, not grasping at liberation is the way to remain present and available to activation and distress. This is how we model wakeful presencing to patients. We can also do our best to renounce 'why' in favor of '*What is arising, and how is it being met?*' Inquiry into 'what' and 'how' reduces fixation on habitual narratives and opens us to the immediacy of experience.

Non-harming (*ahimsā*) is a mutually beneficial intention. A Buddhist-inspired clinician never wants to jeopardize another being's potential for healing and eventual release from suffering. Their liberation is our highest aim. But grasping at any means to accomplish such liberation is unwise and harmful. Harmlessness is embodied in a clinician's determination to avert harmful responses. Cultivation of right seeing and right knowing is the key to actualizing *ahimsā*. Clinicians can hold the intention for wise understanding while extending *ahimsā* to the patient. We can encourage and instill a commitment to non-harming in patients and facilitate their practice of *ahimsā* phrases for self and others. This is particularly useful for healing suicidal and homicidal ideation. *May my body, mind and heart be safe from every form of inner and outer harm. May all beings be equally safe from all inner and outer harm. May I be peaceful and loving in all my relationships. May I respect and uphold the right of all beings to live a safe and happy life.*

Assessing Right View and Right Intention

The Eightfold Path and *lojong* mind training are excellent armatures for Buddhist-inspired psychological treatment planning. Below is an assessment tool for documenting a patient's presentation, self-and-other ideations, capacity for insight into the causes of suffering, and desires/goals/intentions for therapy.

Reason(s) for coming into psychotherapy at this time:

____

____

____

____

Is there a vision for how life would change if current struggles/problems were alleviated?

____

____

____

____

Is there sufficient awareness of the causes of suffering? Y ____ N____
Is there sufficient awareness of the causes of non-suffering? Y ____ N____
Has the patient accurately assessed the causes and conditions of suffering? Y ____ N____

If not, what needs to be explored to increase awareness of contributing causes of suffering and non-suffering?

____

____

____

Circle the level of identification with narratives of self-suffering: low/average/high

Describe the patient's self-ideation:
Rate on a scale of 1–10 (1 = non-existent 5 = average 10 = inflated)

Self-respect ____	Self-pity ____	Self-dissociation ____
Self-compassion ____	Self-doubt ____	Self-perfectionism ____
Self-loathing ____	Self-judgment ____	Self-awareness ____
Self-negativity ____	Self-criticality ____	Self-acceptance ____
Self-absorption ____	Self-woundedness ____	Self-honesty ____

Describe the patient's responses to others:
Rate on a scale of 1–10 (1 = non-existent 5 = average 10 = inflated)

Respectful ____	Disconnected ____	Critical ____	Anxiety-producing ____
Compassionate ____	Ambivalent ____	Envious ____	Over-attentive ____
Loathing ____	Judgmental ____	Connected ____	Generous ____
Idealized ____	Threatened ____	Suspicious ____	Non-empathic ____

Patient inquiry questions:

What changes are you seeking now?

____

____

____

What would constitute genuine well-being?

____

____

____

What is your intention for participating in treatment?

____

____

____

Set three goals for transforming/healing/ending suffering:

1. ____
2. ____
3. ____

Patient Presentation:
Cognitive-affective presentation: (Check all that apply.)

Thoughts: Logical ___ Loose ___ Tangential ___ Rigid ___ Confused ___ Scattered ___

Narratives: Delusional ___ Obsessive ___ Fearful ___ Ambivalent___ Hopeless ___ Narcissistic ___ Persecutory ___ Negative___ Hopeful ___ Self-involved ___ Other-obsessed ____ Blaming ___ Generous ___ Selfless ___ Codependent ___

Affect: Depressed ___ Blunted ___ Manic ___ Angry ___ Anxious ___ Fearful ___ Labile ___ Joyful ___ Optimistic ___ Sad ___ Dysregulated ___ Grieving ___ Shy ___ Open ___

Neuro-cognitive disorders:______________________________

Traumatic brain injury ___

Hallucinations: Visual ___ Auditory ___ Other ______________

Memory: Immediate ___ Recent ___ Remote ___ Dementia ___

Insight: Poor ___ Fair ___ Good ___ Excellent ___

Discernment: Poor ___ Fair ___ Good ___ Excellent ___

Somatic presentation: (Check all that apply)

Energy level: Lethargic ___ Agitated ___ Tense ___ Relaxed ___ Hyper-vigilant ___

Pain: Muscular ___ Skeletal ___ Nerve ___ Joint ___ Chronic ___ Fibromyalgia ___

Central nervous system tendency: Fight ___ Flight ___ Freeze ___

Motor Behavior: Slowed ___ Hyper ___ Normal ___ Other ____

Speech: Quiet ___ Pressured ___ Affected ___ Normal ___ Other ___

Oriented to: Person ___ Place ___ Time ___ Dissociated ___ Inwardly occupied ___

Physical Illness: Thyroid hypo ___ hyper ___ Diabetes I ___ II ___ Pre-diabetic ___ High BP ___ Cancer ___ Other ___

Stress level: Low ___ Med ___ High ___ Chronically high ___

Medications: ____

____

Trauma, addiction and mental health histories:
Trauma: (Check all that apply)

Adverse childhood environment Y ___ N ___ PTSD Y ___ N ___

Abuse: Childhood ___ Adulthood ___ Familial? Y ___ N ___

Sexual ___ Physical ___ Verbal ___ Emotional ___ Neglect ___ Combat-related ___ War-related ___ Race- or gender-related ___ Gang-related ___ Accident-related ___ Surgery/anesthesia-related ___ Loss-related ___

Acute stress disorder ___

Adjustment disorder: ___ Depressive ___ Anxious ___ Both ___ NOS ___ Chronic ___

Incident notes:

____

____

____

____

Family trauma history:

____

____

____

____

Addiction: (Check all that apply.)

Tobacco ___ daily intake ___ Caffeine ___ daily intake ___
Cannabis ___ daily intake ___

Street drugs

____

Prescription drugs

____

Alcohol: Beer ___ Wine ___ Hard liquor ___

Binge usage ___ Daily usage ___Weekly usage ___

In withdrawal: Y __ N __ In need of detox or inpatient rehab? Y __ N __

Sober: Y __ N __ Previous rehab ___________ Previous sobriety ______
Involved in: 12-step ___ Smart Recovery ___ LifeRing ___ Dharma ___
Punx _____

Successfully implementing harm reduction strategies? Y __ N __

Struggling with cravings/urges? Y __ N __ Anti-use or anti-craving medication ___

Food: Restricting ___ Binging ___ Expelling ___ Obese ___
Under weight ___

Abusing or dependent on: Gambling ___ Sex ___ Internet ___ Porn ___ Video games ___

Personal and family addiction history:

___

___

___

Mental Health: (Check all that apply.)

Medication:

___

Major depressive episodes: ___ How many? ___ First at what age? ___ With psychosis? ___
Manic episodes: ___ How many? ___ First at what age? ___ With psychosis? ___
Bipolar I or II last episode: Depressive ___ Manic ___ Rapid cycling ___ Partial/full remission ___

Schizophrenia: ___ First at what age? ___ Paranoid ___ Catatonic ___ Schizoaffective ___

Suicidal risk: Low ___ Med ___ High ___

Homicidal risk: Low ___ Med ___ High ___

Anxious disorders: Phobias ___ Panic ___ Generalized ___ Social Somaticized ___

Sleep: Apnea ___ Insomnia ___ Parasomnias ___ Sleep cycle-related ___ Nightmares ___

Attention disorders: Childhood ___ Adult ___ Specify:

___

Spectrum disorders:

___

Attachment style: Secure ___ Ambivalent ___ Avoidant ___ Insecure ___ Disorganized ___

Family mental health history:

___

___

___

 Wise Conduct

A young monk (sounding much like today's youth) approached the Buddha and asked for the 'CliffsNotes' version of Buddhist training. The Buddha replied,

> First establish yourself in the starting point of wholesome [cognitive-affective] states, that is, in purified moral discipline (*sīlakkhandha*) and in right view (*sammā ditthi*). Then, when your moral discipline is purified and your view straight, you should practice the Four Foundations of Mindfulness. (SN 47:3)

The Eightfold Path starts with right view (its fruition) and ends with meditation, the technique used to attain a direct experience of right view. Sandwiched between wise understanding and wise concentration is the skillful means of ethical conduct (*sīla*)—a framework for living wisely in the midst of ignorance and unsatisfactoriness.

Sīla is associated with *samādhāna*, or 'harmony.'[4] Acting harmoniously manifests generosity and produces beneficial results for all beings. Bhikkhu Bodhi describes this harmony as having four expressions: social, psychological, contemplative and active. Bringing the moral discipline of *sīla* into the therapeutic process is very beneficial. Relational ethics promote collective, responsive engagement and easeful conflict resolution. Aligning with moral principles stimulates measured thinking and diminishes unwholesome mind states. It also purifies afflictive tendencies and prepares the mind for contemplative practice.

Right Speech (Sammā Vācā)

My first clinical supervisor was a gifted and kind psychologist and analyst who early on in my tutelage looked me in the eye and said, "Your patients will tell you untruths, partly because they want you to like them, partly because they are merely repeating the lies they constantly tell themselves." From that moment on I dedicated myself to the pursuit of purposeful, truthful psychotherapeutic dialogue.

Right speech (*sammā vācā*) is Buddhist psychology's method for encouraging meaningful dialogue. Right speech entails the renunciation of false, slanderous, harsh and idle speech. Minding the arising of these forms of speech during therapeutic inquiry increases the possibility of insight and the probability of real change.

Buddhist psychological inquiry is much more than a simple set of questions. It is a path of genuine interest taken by *don't know mind*. The ego thinks it knows. But most of its knowing merely reflects distorted mental constructions. A wise mind values *not knowing* for its power to root out inaccurate mentation and reveal truth.

The Seven Principles of Effective Inquiry

These principles facilitate curiosity and honest therapeutic dialogue about challenging life issues, internal confusions and disturbing responses—the very material some patients (and even some therapists) may avoid.

1. *Speak truthfully.* Truth is more than factual correctness. It is a resonant awareness that lights up the eyes, permeates the bones and stirs the heart. When the mind is filled with doubt, avoidance or confusion, the body is tentative or agitated, and the eyes are distant. You can see someone struggling to find or hide truth. When this occurs, shift inquiry away from narrative conceptualizations and into the body. Directing patients to here-and-now experience exposes cognitive distortions. [Therapist:] "When you hear yourself say ___, what do you notice is happening in the body?" or "I can see you struggling to remember. Maybe shift your awareness into the body and see what it tells you about _______," or "You seem to really believe that is true. Let's see if the body sensations you are experiencing right now resonate with that story."
2. *Speak with care.* Difficulties happen to good people. Good people also create difficulty. We all have volitional habits, and each of us is subject to the karmic tendencies of others. Honest psychotherapeutic inquiry about difficult events can be done with kindheartedness toward ourselves and those who have harmed us. It is more healing to express anger, resentment, disappointment or disgust without resorting to defamation or blame. Clinging to hatred perpetuates emotional self-violence. [Therapist:] "I can see how upset you are with your wife's decision, how much you blame her for hurting you. See if you might be able to hold these feelings of anger with kindheartedness toward your upset . . . What do you notice when you let yourself feel anger from within a kind heart?" [Patient:] "I feel more sad and less like I want to hurt her back." [Therapist:] "Maybe we could take some time to let you care for your sadness."
3. *Speak in a timely manner.* Unfortunately, people are habituated to the idea that psychotherapy means digging up the past. 'Timely' means engaging with whatever is actually showing up in the moment and inquiring into that experience. Buddhist-inspired psychotherapy is interested in 'what is' right now, even if that is a memory of a past experience. Patients derive little insight from retelling the past when they are unaware of their here-and-now experience in the telling. So a patient can know the complexity of systemic responses to a past experience if the therapist concurrently inquires into awareness of feelings, thoughts, images and sensations/impulses. This process is slower and sometimes initially frustrating for patients because it is less ego-centered. But slower and self-less is the path to authentic insight. It also trains us in how to remain aware of moment-to-moment internal responses to events in daily life.

4. *Speak purposefully.* Speaking purposefully is primarily a directive for clinicians. Don't get lost in your own narratives and opinions. Deliberately consider whether you are self-disclosing for your benefit or for the patient's benefit, and don't do it if it is for you. Eschew ambivalent responses. If you get bored, get interested in body posture, voice tone and somatic responses. Actively query the patient about what you are noticing. While it is true that anything in psychotherapy can lead to something important, don't waste valuable time on small talk unless it is being used as an intentional rest space between challenging cycles of therapeutic work.
5. *Question the arising of mental constructs and emotional exaggerations.* Noting inconsistencies and plot/phrase divergence is the easiest way to recognize a mental construct. People will relate an incident by alternating between event narration and commentary about an event. Distorted internal views—typically fast-spoken, emotionally laden, assumptive opinions about the self and others—often show up at various points in the telling of a sequence of events. When these inconsistencies arise, point to them and help the person inquire into their veracity. If a therapist can maintain a stance of curiosity and interest, divergences can be exposed without belittling or criticizing. [Patient:] "Seems like every day my mother calls and leaves a message asking how I'm doing. I avoid the calls because she wants me to say I'm fine, but I am not. I feel so guilty for hurting her because I can't be what she wants." [Therapist:] "Sounds like she cares about your well-being." [Patient:] "Only if I am fine." [Therapist:] "Has she said that directly?" [Patient:] "Well, no, but I know it's true. Why else would I feel guilty all the time?" [Therapist:] "Well, I would love to explore that question. Because if you weren't saddled with guilt you might be able to set limits with your mother and receive her caring attention in a way that works for both of you."
6. *Inquire into self-cherishing.* The arising of self-cherishing is a constant occurrence in psychotherapeutic dialogue. Although psychotherapy is supposed to be all about the patient, self-cherishing causes much of the suffering that people come into therapy to alleviate. So it is a psychotherapist's duty to vigilantly notice the arising of self-cherishing, point it out and initiate a form of inquiry that encourages engagement with self-lessness. [Patient:] "Our customers were about to arrive for an important meeting, and one of my young direct reports starts telling me his great idea for altering one of our procedures . . . which does need to change, but I tried that approach at another company and it failed miserably. But I didn't have time to go into all that. Then he goes to my VP to complain about how I don't listen and now I'm the bad guy. Can you believe that?" [Therapist:] "How did you respond to him?" [Patient:] "I just shot it down. There was no time to explain . . . and who does he think he is anyway?" [Therapist:] "What is a director's responsibility to their direct reports?" [Patient:] "Oversee delegated work, set their budget, you know . . ." [Therapist:] "What about

mentoring or developing their talent?" [Patient:] "Well, that too . . ." (with some softening of frustration). [Therapist:] "What would have happened if you had been less reactive, able to acknowledge his idea and suggest discussing it at a more appropriate time?" [Patient:] "I was too absorbed in my own anxiety about the meeting. The words came out without thinking. I guess I need to work more on that awareness thing so I can be less in my head and more with what's happening around me."

7. *Bring all confusions, beliefs and assumptions onto the path of liberation.* Every occurrence is an opportunity to realize how things actually are. Every symptom, all failures and successes; every self-description and self-sentiment; all cognitive-affective distortions: no matter what is brought into therapy, that suffering can be fearlessly, judiciously and caringly queried and ultimately understood in its empty, dependent nature. This is how liberation grows in one's mind and life.

Right Action (Sammā Kammaññatā)

Buddhist monastics adhere to a strict code of conduct from which right action naturally springs forth—*non-harming, non-stealing, no sexual misconduct, wise speech and non-intoxication.* I try as best I can to adhere to these precepts in daily life. However, rather than dictate a specific set of rules, I wish to share three wholesome intentions for wise, harmonious living.

Aim to be a light in a world of darkness. "Without stick or sword, conscientious, full of compassion, one is desirous of the welfare of all sentient beings" (AN 10:176). Although every moment of life is an opportunity to illuminate human goodness, it is most potent to do so in the midst of hatred, greed and delusion. Striving to act wisely helps us find clarity and compassion, especially when we feel challenged or in distress. If we aim to meet suffering with a peaceful, wise and compassionate mind, our own inner contentment becomes a source of healing for others in distress. Aspiring to be a source of upliftment gives meaning to activities—even mundane, unfulfilling or stressful undertakings—and allows us to tolerate life's difficulties with patience and grace. When psychotherapists actively model this Bodhisattvic intention, patients know non-suffering is a reality, not some pie-in-the-sky wish.

Be mindful and temperate. Temperance cannot be underestimated as a source of mind-body health and healing. Dysregulation of emotion and impulses and the hedonistic harming they cause occur in the absence of temperance. Temperance is associated with the deliberate cultivation of *heedfulness* (P: *appamada* S: *apramāda* T: *bag yod pa*), a calculated awareness of sensations, feelings and thoughts. It is a moment-to-moment determining of what is and is not beneficial and the deliberate choosing of benefit over harm. The Buddha taught heedfulness as a means to, "*Break through to your benefit,*" (SN 3:17). This expression exemplifies the motivation one must have to abandon afflictive tendencies. Although many people blame over-emotionality, impulsiveness and addictions on uncontrollability, afflictive habits reign supreme only as long as they have perceived benefit. Once equanimity, moderation or abstinence is embraced as the true benefit, deliberately choosing temperance becomes a no-brainer. I have seen this happen for so many patients who have successfully liberated themselves from emotional dysregulation, persisting anxious/depressive symptoms and substance or food addictions.

Be thrifty and generous. So much of what we are told to want is irrelevant or detrimental to happiness. Inquiry into unheedful longings exposes our confusion about what actually produces contentment. Selfishness and greed make us crazy; they agitate the body and mind with incessant wanting and distract us from purposeful accumulation and contribution. Frugality is a form of self-compassion that unhooks us from materialistic values and the wiles of advertising. Generosity is compassion and selflessness in action. Studies show that compassion increases generosity even for those with no religious affiliation, and it predicts increased generosity across a variety of economic tasks.[5] *Taking only what is offered* is another way to practice generosity toward others and proliferate trust in a world that continues to glorify stealing and fraudulence.

Generosity also breeds connectedness. Actively contributing to the healing of our collective woes shifts our attention away from obsessive self-concern. I try my best to encourage patients to give away what they do not need and give back by volunteering for causes that matter to them. Ultimately, renouncing selfishness and extravagance to ensure the sustainability of the environment is our highest collective responsibility.

Right Livelihood (Sammā Ājīva)

The Buddha taught that wealth should be acquired legally, peacefully and honestly: without exploiting, over-charging, deceiving or disrespecting employees and patrons. This is the path of karma yoga—work as a dedicated practice of virtue, humility and effectiveness. I would like to come at right livelihood from two perspectives: the clinician's and the patient's.

Clinicians: The reality of the psychotherapeutic environment is this: it is a closed and hierarchical system. What happens in the therapy room is private and occurs between an assumed expert and a supposed novice. Clinicians can knowingly or unknowingly blunder or deceive, manipulate or abuse a patient in the name of treatment. This possibility remains largely undiscussed in our profession, and we are the worse for it. It certainly makes a difference when clinicians are aware of their imprudent impulses. Not following these impulses requires restraint and virtuous action. To counter the detriments of psychotherapy's closed system, psychotherapists must adhere to the highest ethical, legal and relational standards, seek out excellent supervision and elicit patient feedback. I encourage patients to share what does and doesn't work for them—both in the moment and during periodic check-ins where they analyze their progress *and* my effectiveness.

Then there is the myth of coming to therapy to get fixed. Patients do not need to be fixed. By acting as the fixer a psychotherapist colludes with a patient's abdication of responsibility for the quality of their mind-heart. Whatever troubles they may have, the solution is ultimately in their own consciousness. Rather than fixing, a skilled psychotherapist is a mindful attendant to a patient's inner work. The patient is the tour guide, the psychotherapist the observant companion. Our role is to mind the unfolding cognitive-affective activity, pointing out what the inhabitant overlooks or ignores. Once aware, the patient's co-curiosity will give rise to engagement and eventual healing. Rest assured that this non-fixing *is* the greatest fixing.

Another issue for clinicians is overwork. 'Unaffordable' is how some clinicians and mental health settings view moderation and therapist self-care. Believe me, I have seen more than enough burnt-out psychotherapists and physicians in my private practice. When a psychotherapist tells me she or he sees over 30 patients a week for 50 minutes each, I become concerned about their quality of presence and engagement. Being with a patient and delivering effective inquiry and interventions takes effort, no matter how much one might be resting in awareness. So we must learn to set limits, take care of our physical and mental health and mindfully practice the equanimity we preach.

Patients: Work is an integral part of maintaining genuine mental health. "Meta-analyses of 87 longitudinal studies and natural experiments endorsed the assumption that unemployment is not only correlated to distress but also causes it" (Paul, 2009). Repeated unemployment during one's working life is associated with greater psychosocial distress, which persists through one's retirement years.[6] Working may prevent premature mortality among young adults.[7] Retirees who lack venues to offer their talents experience more isolation and depression.[8]

In January 2013, the US Department of Labor launched a campaign to encourage employers to rethink what people with disabilities can achieve and to consider encouraging young people with disabilities to pursue their personal and career goals. This is an important step in the direction of empowering people with mental health disabilities to be contributing members of society. Every human being has the right to experience the joy of purposefulness, and everyone has something to offer. Several of my disabled patients have chosen to work part-time. Others volunteer for organizations like the National Alliance on Mental Illness (NAMI), teaching classes or facilitating groups for those who live with similar mental health disabilities. Being of service deeply supports genuine mental health for them and their families.

Right livelihood suggests finding some measure of work/life balance, no doubt an intractable yet decisively first world problem. I live in a part of the US where working full-time means a 60–80-hour workweek. Many workers here feel they have no choice, because overworking is the zeitgeist of this fast-paced, highly competitive business culture. You either agree to it or don't get hired.

But overworking in Silicon Valley is no more right livelihood than overworking at a low-wage factory job in a third world country. It just appears more tolerable because of the high wages and in some cases onsite free meals, gym, daycare, stress-reduction classes and more. No matter where one is expected to overwork, it is exploitative and unhealthy for the workers, their families and the community in which they live.

This brings us to the final aspect of right livelihood—applying oneself to the best of one's ability in all forms of work, from the most menial to the most highly specified or critical. When we free the mind of self-cherishing, work is no longer a way to bolster self-identity. It becomes the Bodhisattvic embodiment of virtue and service to others, freely offered as a means to seed happiness. This principle is embodied in the proverbial Zen sweeper who mindfully clears the sidewalk with dedication and dignity so others may walk it safely. Although his task appears menial and unimportant, the sidewalk sweeper works unburdened by egoic unsettledness or low self-esteem. This identitylessness is extremely important because we all have had or will have times in our lives when we must work at a job that is sub-optimal or not our first choice. The principles of right livelihood help us navigate tough work situations with dignity while we gain more skills or seek out better opportunities. Three thousand clinical internship hours for no pay? Three years' worth for me.

 Wise Concentration (*Sammā Samādhi*)

We have arrived at the final three factors of the Eightfold Path—direct mental training. All of the meditation practices featured in this book have already been offered in previous chapters. This section summarizes the various informal and formal practices and their delivery to patients.

Right Effort (Sammā Vāyāma)

Every aspect of Buddhist training involves effort. Even effortless mindfulness requires the determination to rest effortlessly in awareness. *Viriyā* or *vīrya*—a mixture of enthusiasm and diligence—is the energetic zeal of effort. Without the zeal to awaken, Buddhist training would not be undertaken.

In Buddhist psychology, the most basic form of right effort is developing the zeal to break the mental habit of suffering. For that to happen, one must understand the nature of suffering and know there is a path to end suffering. This should always be a Buddhist-inspired psychotherapist's first inquiry with a patient. Once knowledge of suffering is established, we can determine which forms of inquiry and which informal mindfulness and heartfulness skills will help a patient experience some immediate leveling off of distress. *Relief is a powerful catalyst for zeal.* It builds enthusiasm for intentionally shifting attention away from unwholesome to wholesome mind states and allows a patient to feel the efficacy of easing his or her suffering.

To make this process visible, I have created a general guide outlining which forms of inquiry and informal mindfulness and heartfulness skills are appropriate for what symptomatic presentation. One need not deliver every listed intervention or present them in the order they are shown. Always rely on your best clinical judgment. However, most of these interventions should be offered prior to instruction in formal meditation practice.

At the heart of the Buddha's teachings on right effort are techniques to meditatively train the mind to produce and maintain wholesome attention. During meditation and post-meditation periods, the Buddha recommended practitioners apply effort in four ways:

1. To avert the arising of unwholesome mind states (*akusalā dhamma*), one mindfully attends to preventing the five hindrances and/or rests in awareness.
2. To release already arisen unwholesome mind states, one applies an appropriate antidote or rests in awareness, allowing the hindrances to dissolve on their own.
3. To stimulate wholesome states of mind (*kusalā dhamma*), one undertakes daily practice of mindfulness and/or compassion meditation and engages in virtuous conduct.
4. To maintain and refine already arisen wholesome states, one recognizes and effortlessly rests in awareness itself.

Table 8.1

1. Inquiry into suffering and non-suffering
2. Inquiry into humanness
3. Orienting
4. The Four Reflections
5. Just Hearing
6. Resting in physical sensations
7. Noting the feeling tone of experience
8. Kind recognition
9. Inquiry into constructed nature of thoughts
10. Vase Breathing

Depressive/anxious symptoms	1, 2, 3, 4, 5, 6, 7, 8, 9, 10
Emotional dysregulation	1, 2, 3, 4, 5, 6, 7, 8, 9, 10
Recent traumatic event	1, 2, 3, 4, 5, 6, 7, 8, 10
Trauma	1, 2, 3, 4, 5, 6, 7, 8, 9, 10
Substance use problems	1, 2, 3, 4, 5, 6, 7, 8, 9, 10
Major depressive, manic or bipolar episode	1, 2, 3, 4, 5, 6, 7, 8,
Chronic pain	1, 2, 3, 4, 5, 6, 7, 8, 9, 10
Relational difficulties	1, 2, 3, 4, 7, 8, 9
Loss and grief	1, 2, 3, 4, 5, 6, 7, 8, 9, 10

Right Mindfulness (Sammā Sati) *and Right Concentration* (Sammā Samādhi)

The beauty of mindfulness is that it is not a one-size-fits-all cognitive-behavioral intervention. So we can start from where the patient is and tailor delivery of these skills to suit a particular propensity of mind. This is precisely why I have featured different forms of meditation, non-meditation and a host of ways to recognize emptiness.

That said, when it comes to right mindfulness, the Buddha was fairly clear about what that meant: *from within awareness, anchoring the mind in actuality as it presents itself moment to moment and simply noting the arising, existing and passing away of all inner and outer phenomena.* From this simple instruction comes every insight into existence and non-existence, self and not-self, mind and no-mind, non-awareness and awareness. Therefore, the insight-driven process of *not finding as the ultimate finding* is none other than right mindfulness.

At the end of my interview with Buddhist teacher Phillip Moffitt, I asked what he most wished that mental health professionals would know about mindfulness:

> If you are a mental health professional teaching mindfulness, at some point ask yourself this question: Is there a non-objecting aspect to mindfulness? If so, what is it like to know what is true and not object to it? Mature mindfulness is non-objecting. I teach mindfulness as fully receiving, investigating and fully knowing the impersonal nature of experience. I have taken more and more to calling this compassionate mindfulness. People need to have clarity about what they are teaching when they teach mindfulness. If they don't have any experience of what it is like to be with experience in a non-objecting way, even for the briefest of moments, they do not understand mindfulness. (2012)

The traditional meditative practice of right mindfulness is *vipassanā* meditation, which focuses awareness on each of four areas of interest—the body (*kāyā*), feelings (*vedanā*), mind/consciousness (*citta*) and mental contents (*dhammas*)—simply noting the arising, existing and passing away of phenomena.

Right concentration is the total unification of the mind with an object of attention. As we have seen, *samādhi* is a unified, wholesome state of mind that is one-pointed (*ekaggatā*) and unperturbed. Although there are various forms and levels of Buddhist *shamatha* meditation, most practitioners begin with Mindfulness of Breath meditation. I chose to teach the full *Ānāpānasati Sutta* to provide clinicians with meditation instruction in both right mindfulness and right concentration.

The ultimate fruition of right mindfulness and right concentration is *awakened presence*. This is the right effort of recollecting (*sati*) our true nature, which occurs when we mindfully attend to awareness itself (*rigpa*) and rest in its empty luminosity. Maintaining this awareness is the supreme concentration of effortless mindfulness.

Below is general advice for clinicians on what meditation practices to offer to whom. If your goal is to teach *shamatha, vipassanā, Brahmavihāra*, Open Monitoring or Objectless *Shamatha* meditation to patients, you must first be a dedicated daily practitioner. Take this as seriously as it is meant.

Table 8.2

Beginning meditation practices	***Further meditation for non-symptomatic patients***
Mindfulness of Breath Steps 1–4	Mindfulness of Breath Steps 5–16
Lovingkindness	Tonglen
Compassion	Open Monitoring
Sympathetic Joy	Objectless Shamatha
Equanimity	Looking for Mind
Walking	Effortless Mindfulness from within awareness
Effortless Mindfulness while aware of:	
Body	
Rumination	
Agitated mentation	
Craving and aversion	

Skillful Means

Buddhist psychological interventions are now utilized in hospitals and in-patient programs with highly symptomatic patients. My dear friend and colleague Jose Calderón-Abbo, MD, integrates practical Buddhist psychology into general psychiatry and addiction medicine. He is an assistant professor of clinical psychiatry with Louisiana State University School of Medicine, a clinical faculty member of Tulane University's Department of Psychiatry, and consultant to Harvard University's Program for Refugee Trauma and is the Mexican Minister of Public Safety. Jose teaches mindfulness at Saybrook University and is a national faculty member of the Center for Mind-Body Medicine.

Interview With Psychiatrist Jose Calderón-Abbo, MD

How have Buddhism and Buddhist Psychology informed or transformed your practice of psychiatry?

I started practicing psychiatry with a narrow focus on understanding the mind's healthy and pathological states. Fifteen years of Buddhist practice have broadened my agenda of service from merely reducing symptoms of depression, bipolar, addiction or schizophrenia to lessening human suffering. My practice now includes a wellness model with an emphasis on healthy lifestyles and skillful choice making.

Biomedicine and psychiatry favor brain-centered, biologically driven approaches. Evidence-based psychiatry is fantastic but limited. Until recently the body has been largely forgotten. Also, patients are put into a passive role. Doctors make general recommendations of exercise and diet, but the patient is left to his or her own devices.

Mindfulness (*vipassanā* meditation) inquires deeply into mind, emotions and the body. Buddhist psychology has numerous helpful techniques I use with co-workers, patients and myself. . . . it has changed my role as a practitioner.

Do you offer specific Buddhist psychological interventions for particular mental health issues?

I offer everyone—patients, the treatment team, myself—compassion, self-care, lovingkindness, forgiveness and inquiry into shared humanity. We all strive for happiness, but we still harm ourselves, knowingly or unknowingly. *In general, I think we suffer from an insufficiency in compassion, not serotonin.*

In our in-patient unit we hold bi-weekly group meetings for patients and staff together. When a patient voices doubt about his or her ability to achieve a treatment goal, I ask, "Who in this room is struggling with something they wish to change in their life?" All hands rise, including the staff's. That patient sees she is not alone. This is shared humanity. I offer tools for specific outcomes: mindfulness (from the *vipassanā* tradition), Tonglen meditation and body awareness practices. Grounding in the body is most helpful for patients in withdrawal or in highly agitated psychotic/schizophrenic states. The body provides a place of refuge.

Most Buddhist contemplative practices can be used when appropriately applied. Scattered or agitated patients may have difficulty with sitting breath meditation, but they can follow breath during mindful movement. If a patient has trauma in the body or feels stuck, I may begin with movement to ease him or her back into the body. Chronic pain sufferers can mindfully scan the body to shift awareness away from painful experience. Inhabiting the body is useful for everyone. I start with the body and then move to other mindfulness practices.

How are you instructing patients in Tonglen? Do they take in the suffering of others?

I teach a modified Tonglen practice. In general, I don't ask patients to breathe in other people's suffering. Instead, we practice by stating an intention to practice for the benefit of others and relieve their suffering. Then we move into transforming the suffering by opening the heart, breathing in difficult emotion and exhaling transformed emotion.

Can you say more about the bi-weekly meetings with patients and staff? Did you start that?

Yes. It takes place in the acute in-patient unit for addictions and mental health disorders at LSU's University Hospital. It started with traditional Community Meeting groups common to many psychiatric in-patient programs, where staff address resident issues. Post-Katrina, these evolved into a healing venue for everyone. We were all displaced and homeless—staff and patients. Staff were often in worse shape than patients! It was crucial to help all of us find an inner place to rest in the midst of our homelessness, worries and pain.

I lead two hour-long groups a week. During the evacuations we held two a day. We—staff and patients—all sit together, because in Buddhism suffering is the great equalizer. I wanted to blur the distinction between them and us. This elicits compassion for each other. These meetings have alleviated much of the ongoing power struggling that occurred on the unit. There is more understanding of what the other is going through. We start with meditation and then do a brief check-in. I may pose a question and invite discussion. For instance, if there has been violent arguing, I might ask, "How do we hold emotions skillfully?" We then do movement or Tonglen and close with a poem or story. Clinical interns and residents found it awkward at first to share in front of patients. So I would share something first. That made it easier for them. The clinical directors also attend the group but not many doctors. Other psychiatrists see it as a valuable tool but are happy to let me do it.

You had some very intense clinical and personal experiences after Hurricane Katrina. How did your Buddhist practice aid your mental health during that time?

Viewing Katrina as the impermanence of things helped me reframe and reduce my apprehension about uncertainty. There was a lot of struggle and strong emotions—sadness, shock and loss of the illusion of material safety and financial security. Buddhism allowed me to keep a perspective that all of this was an invitation to practice contemplation on impermanence. New Orleans has hurricane season and non-hurricane season. It reminds you that anything can end at any time. So stay focused on what is truly important in life and celebrate it.

Please share your vision for bringing this work to México.

As you know, México has struggled since it declared war on the drug cartels. The cartels have retaliated with their own war to secure trade routes and expand black markets. This has resulted in almost 70,000 deaths and tens of thousands of orphaned children. People are polarized into 'them' and 'us.' There is strong rhetoric of war and combat—as if we could solve the problem by surgically removing the perpetrators. I thought there was a need to change the political rhetoric from war to reconciliation by helping people realize we are all affected and we are all part of the solution.

People do not understand that drug crime and violence are related to a system that has not offered them opportunities for sustainable meaningful life. If you ask an 8-year-old who lives out in the Sierra what he or she wishes to do when they grow up, they may say pilot, attorney or nurse. By the age of 12 or 13 they will say they want to be in the drug trade because they don't have role models or any opportunity to go to university. Violence occurs as benign neglect. If I have not provided for my fellow citizens, then I have contributed to that violence.

I joined a think tank two years ago to advise the Mexican government on how to change the conversation, how to communicate and implement measures to address the effects of trauma in the general population. Our work has changed the government's rhetoric to a politic of restorative justice and reconciliation. We are planning to bring Mindfulness-based Stress Reduction (MBSR) and mind-body skills groups—heavily based on mindfulness and Buddhist psychological practices—to trauma victims, first responders and reporters who have been significantly traumatized.

New Orleans is also strongly divided by race and socio-economic realities. Half the population is struggling with daily violence. Ninety percent of African American children have seen someone shot in the streets. The other half, mostly Caucasian, middle and upper middle class, turn their heads and blame the struggling population, their lack of education and addiction problems. They do not recognize interdependence. So we are doing this reconciliation work in New Orleans as well.

What happens when these diverse class-cultures meet in your in-patient units?

When they arrive they are symptomatic and often disinhibited, so racial slurs and defensiveness can arise. But as they start to get better and begin sharing and spending more time together in the groups, they begin to experience their shared humanity and slowly it normalizes. We all breathe; we all aspire to health and happiness for our loved ones and us.

How do you apply these principles and practices in cases of serious mental illness such as psychosis, schizophrenia and suicidality? Are there contraindications?

During meditation the mind wanders to a mental image or a narrative. Hallucinations are just another narrative in the brain. We instruct patients to let the hallucinations come and go in a non-judgmental way. Depending on the level of symptomatic intensity, we may meditate for only 5 minutes or do moving meditation for 10 minutes. The principle is self-care and compassion toward self and others. We have not had any difficulty nor seen intensification of agitation or psychosis as a result of mind-body practices. As far as contraindications, I see none; perhaps some cautions. When practicing mindful movement, we emphasize skillful yoga practice so they won't hurt themselves.

In the case of Buddhist practitioners who have serious symptomatology and could benefit from pharmacotherapy but are resistant, do they hold a false idea that medication would impede their meditation practice or their ability to achieve liberation?

Recently, a young man with severe depression who started a *vipassanā* meditation practice came for a consultation. He was taking an antidepressant and wanted to know if it would impede his meditation. Medication can reduce reactivity and flight or fight activation, so it can help one settle during sitting meditation. But too much medication dulls the mind and/or emotional experience. Fine tuning a dosage is a joint effort.

What is it about emptiness and the nature of reality that seems pertinent in your life and in your practice of psychiatry?

This has been a struggle for me because I am a father of two small children. There is nothing solid about it, but how does one communicate that? I spend a great deal of my day pulled into the illusion of solid individuals whom I love deeply, yet in a way these are constructs. Not-self shows up in personal meditation practice and working with patients. I had a patient who was planning a huge event and was very stressed. I asked, "What part of you is planning?" In that moment the construct of a unified solid self fell apart, and different aspects of the psyche were revealed. The same thing works for distressing emotions, "What part of you is angry?" They may say, "Well, my ego." And I will ask, "What part of your ego?" That inquiry allows a shift in their relationship to emotion and the self who is having the emotion. Who is meditating, having the thoughts in meditation? I learned this technique from my *vipassanā* teachers.

What would you most wish other psychiatrists to know about the efficacy of Buddhist psychology for themselves and their patients?

This is a two-way street; the transformation of others leads to personal transformation. I wish we could go back 40 or 50 years in psychiatry, when there was a willingness to inquire into yourself and your life, which I think led to psychiatrists being more empathetic and humble. If we are truly talking about the cessation of suffering for our patients, then what is needed is a fierce personal engagement with introspection through therapy, meditation or the like; they are all evidence-based. Just prescribing and/or giving people tools leads to all kinds of difficulties, let alone the risk of burning out while treating chronic psychiatric conditions. It is important to know that people can heal and help themselves. I want to be a part a journey of healing and meaning, one focused on reducing suffering, not just alleviating symptoms.

What does cessation mean to you? If that is our goal, what would that look like in a mental health model?

Cessation in the mental health model is a controlled symptom that just disappears or enters remission. You can retire into the *nirvāna* of eternal happiness! Real cessation, as I understand it, is value, service, meaning and equanimity. It means having a balanced life. Where one remains dedicated to transformation and healing in the world and is not easily overcome by the twists and turns of daily life. It means looking beyond the brain to the causes and causations of their predicament in order to identify solutions and places that need skillful action.

I would like to share a case to help people better understand practical application of Buddhist psychology. I have a patient who suffers with Crohn's disease—an inflammatory autoimmune condition of the bowel—who came for help with depression, panic and pain management. Crohn's intense flare-ups often required hospitalization and steroid treatments that can trigger psychotic panic and suicidal depression. After 15 years of struggling with this condition, this patient finally decided to have surgery to remove part of the inflamed bowel. The night before the surgery he called panic-stricken and asked me to be available prior to the procedure to help him with his fears about the surgery and its aftermath. We practiced that night focusing on cultivating a caring relationship with his body—the very same body that caused him so much pain. I encouraged him to recognize with kindness and forgiveness any feelings of resentment and hatred toward the body and its betrayal. Then I asked him to let go and trust his decision to undergo the surgery. The next morning we talked while he was on the gurney awaiting surgery. I reminded him that no matter what happened to the body, his heart and who he truly is would remain untarnished and unhurt. Then we did *mettā* practice for the surgeons and nurses. He felt calmer and off he went to the operating room. Will he be free of pain and his life better post surgery? We don't know yet, but one thing for sure, he got a taste of the liberation he has been seeking (Calderón-Abbo, 2013, June 19).

 Life as a Path of Profound Transformation

Steve Jobs, an astonishingly creative and uncompromising man, was a force for technological and cultural transformation. Although Jobs was purportedly a difficult and demanding boss, he was known for inspiring people to reach into their creative depths and strive for excellence in all their endeavors. After his first bout with pancreatic cancer, Jobs delivered the commencement speech at Stanford University and offered the following advice clearly drawn from the Zen Buddhist teachings he had long admired: "Remembering you are going to die is the best way I know to avoid the trap of thinking you have something to lose. You are already naked. There is no reason not to follow your heart" (2005).

To follow the heart of emptiness is the true transformation. Know this is entirely reachable, right here and right now. Why cling to deluded selfing when the truth of identitylessness will set you free? Your heart-mind is utterly naked; your life is nothing less than the groundless ground of unbounded spontaneous creativity.

> What is life? The answer is—there is no ground, just dancing on the stageless stage. . . . To be enlightened means to know how to celebrate life—to embrace your life. The heart of the heart of Buddhism is to love this life with its beauty as well as its messiness. (Thubten, 2012)

Buddhist psychology's open invitation to mindfully drop in and heartfully receive and act is the direct path to knowing that all conditions are the cause of liberation. Since every suffering is the very seat of awakening, you can transform your life by mindfully, joyfully choosing to be a source of liberation.

 Your Action Plan for Transformation

The essence of who we are—the innate mind—is beyond all qualities, including good and bad. Therefore, 'making ourselves better' is just another deluded mental construct that distracts us from *awakened presence*. I propose we renounce all transformations based in clinging to a future 'reformed self' and instead transform suffering by fearlessly becoming aware of all our obscurations and determining to skillfully let them go for the benefit of all beings.

Join me in imagining a treatment plan with the expressed goal of awakening from deluded suffering. Such a plan would certainly include short- and long-term objectives and corresponding therapeutic interventions. However, unlike a standardized treatment plan, its only diagnosis would be humanness. And that condition would be fully embraced as an absolutely necessary starting point rather than an obstacle to liberation from suffering.

The initial step of any treatment plan for awakening would be an investigation into unsatisfactoriness. From there, the possibility of non-suffering can be introduced and understood through inquiry into what mental health means to the patient. Discerning the patient's wants and needs can be facilitated through discussion of the difference between fleeting hedonic happiness and authentic durable happiness. Finally, the therapist and patient work together to define short-term and long-term goals and corresponding mind-heart-body interventions for the cultivation of wisdom, compassion and virtue.

You will now have a chance to create your own plan for awakening. Construct your plan with a sense of deliberateness and an awareness of temporality. It should be regarded as flexible and alterable. Hold with spaciousness the probability of shifting internal and external conditions.

Know Suffering: The Three Marks of Existence

Impermanence

How do the uncertainty and unpredictability of life negatively affect you?

____

____

____

____

____

____

Dis-ease

How do you receive and/or resist painful experience?

____

____

____

How do you cling to pleasurable experience?

____

____

____

How much of your mental time is spent ruminating or worrying?

____

Are you often overwhelmed by your emotional responses?

____

Do you harbor much anger or resentment? ______ Is your life ruled by fear? ______

Do you feel comfortable in your body? ______ Do you live in your mind? ______

How open and loving is your heart? ______ Do you long for connection? ______

Do you struggle with relationship? ______

In what ways do you struggle with meaninglessness, ambivalence or doubt?

____

____

____

What are your main sources of stress?

____

____

Selfing

What percentage of your inner self-narrative is negative, judgmental or critical? ______

What aspects of your identity do you cling to most?

____

____

____

____

In what ways do you emphasize or negate your own wants and needs compared to the wants and needs of others?

____

____

____

____

Which of these destructive self-habits do you want to alleviate?

Self-loathing ____	Self-pity ____	Self-dissociation ____	Self-judgment ____
Self-negativity ____	Self-doubt ____	Self-perfectionism ____	Self-criticality ____
Self-absorption ____	Self-harming ____	Self-woundedness ____	Self-obsession ____

Know your most troublesome cognitive distortions and mental constructions:

Assumptions about the self *("I can't be happy," "I will always be depressed/anxious," "I am unlovable.")*	1. 2. 3.
Assumptions about the world *("No one cares about me," "It's harsh," "It's tough," "It's dangerous and scary.")*	1. 2. 3.
Assumptions about the mind *("It's uncontrollable," "It can't concentrate," "It will always run my life.")*	1. 2. 3.
Assumptions about the body *("It's damaged beyond repair," "I hate it," "It's a prison," "Always in pain.")*	1. 2. 3.
Assumptions about the heart *("Being emotional is showing weakness," "If I feel, the pain will never end.")*	1. 2. 3.

Which of these assumptions are you willing to transform or release?

____

____

____

____

____

What harmful ways of being in the world are you willing to transform or release?

____

____

____

____

What destructive habits/addictions are you willing to renounce?

____

____

____

What else needs to be explored to increase awareness of the contributing causes of suffering?

____

____

____

____

Know Non-suffering: Awareness, Compassion, Virtue and Presence

What is your understanding of emptiness?

Philosophically:

___

___

___

Personally:

___

___

___

Practically:

___

___

___

Which of the informal or formal mindfulness and heartfulness exercises/practices helped you experience the following body states, mind states and awareness?

Focused attention		Calm body	
Sensorial awareness		Tranquility	
Body awareness		Equanimity	
External awareness		Flexibility	
Awareness of awareness		Interest	
Mental clarity		Presence	
Emotional stability		Compassion	

Which of the informal or formal mindfulness and heartfulness exercises/practices helped you experience the following?

Impermanence		Wisdom	
Emotional fallacies		Not-self	
Mental constructions		Virtue	
Dependent nature		Mind	

Right Effort: Right Interventions

To avert the arising of unwholesome mind states	1. Mindfulness of Breath meditation 2. The Four Reflections 3. Vase Breathing 4. Open Monitoring and Objectless *Shamatha* meditation 5. Tonglen, lovingkindness, compassion, equanimity meditation 6. Effortless Mindfulness from within awareness
To release already arisen unwholesome mind states	1. Orienting 2. Resting in physical sensations 3. Noting the feeling tone of experience 4. Kind recognition 5. Inquiry into the constructed nature of thoughts 6. Tonglen, lovingkindness and/or compassion meditation 7. Sympathetic joy 8. Effortless mindfulness from within body, rumination, agitated mentation, craving and aversion
To stimulate and increase wholesome mind states	1. Intention to awaken for the benefit of all beings 2. Mindfulness of Breath meditation Steps 1–16 3. Vase Breathing 4. Tonglen, lovingkindness and/or compassion meditation 5. Sympathetic joy and equanimity practice 6. Open Monitoring and Objectless Shamatha meditation 7. Cultivate practice of one or more *pāramīs/pāramītas* 8. Effortless mindfulness
To maintain already arisen wholesome states	1. Vow to be a *Bodhisattva* in all your activities 2. Work to recognize emptiness and live from wise understanding 3. Commit to virtuous, compassionate conduct 4. Determine to rest effortlessly in awakened presence
To open to the body	1. Resting in physical sensations 2. Noting the feeling tone of experience 3. Vase Breathing 4. Open Monitoring directed toward the body 5. Walking meditation
To heal stress/trauma in the body	1. Orienting 2. Vase Breathing 3. Mindfulness of Breath meditation Steps 1–8 4. Tonglen and compassion meditation toward the body 5. Yoga, chi gong or other mindful movement 6. Effortless mindfulness from within the body

Bodhicitta: Aligning With a Motivation to Awaken Self and Others

Which of these virtuous qualities would you like to cultivate?

Respect ____	Generosity ____	Honesty ____	Responsibility ___	Calm ____
Compassion ____	Kindness ____	Attention ___	Determination ___	Equanimity ___
Forgiveness ____	Restraint ____	Joyfulness ___	Forbearance ____	Virtue ___
Patience ____	Diligence ____	Humility ____	Renunciation ____	Zeal ___

What can you do to bring goodness into this world?

____

____

____

____

How can you lessen or alleviate the suffering of others?

____

____

____

____

How can you align your work with the Bodhisattvic principles of non-harming and selflessness?

____

____

How can you align your relationships with the Bodhisattvic principles of non-harming and selflessness?

____

____

____

Which meditation(s) will you commit to practicing daily?

____

____

____

____

Notes

1 Engler, J. (2003). Being somebody and being nobody. In J. Safran (Ed.), *Psychoanalysis and Buddhism* (pp. 35–79). Boston, MA: Wisdom Publications.
2 If it feels more comfortable, substitute the word 'wise' for the word 'right.'
3 Bodhi, B. (1994). *The noble Eightfold Path: Way to the end of suffering*. Onalaska, WA: Pariyatti Editions.
4 Ibid., p. 45.
5 Saslow, L. R., Willer, R., Feinberg, M., Piff, P. K., Clark, K., Keltner, D., & Saturn, S. R. (2013). My brother's keeper? Compassion predicts generosity more among less religious individuals. *Social Psychological and Personality Science*, *4*(1), 31–38.
6 Zenger, M., Brähler, E., Berth, H., & Stöbel-Richter, Y. (2011). Unemployment during working life and mental health of retirees: Results of a representative survey. *Aging & Mental Health*, *15*(2), 178–185.
7 Davila, E. P., Christ, S. L., Caban-Martinez, A. J., Lee, D. J., Arheart, K. L., LeBlanc, W. G., . . . & Fleming, L. E. (2010). Young adults, mortality, and employment. *Journal of Occupational and Environmental Medicine*, *52*(5), 501–504.
8 Schwingel, A., Niti, M. M., Tang, C., & Ng, T. P. (2009). Continued work employment and volunteerism and mental well-being of older adults: Singapore longitudinal ageing studies. *Age and Ageing*, *38*(5), 531–537.

9

Genuine Mental Health

Offering Up the Illusion of Self

"You *are* going to wait and write the last chapter *after* you return from meditation retreat. Right?" Those were the parting words of the last patient I saw before my week off. As I drove home the unspoken expectation of a revelatory retreat and equally extraordinary ending to this book lingered ominously. Thankfully I remembered my Dzogchen teachers insisting that the extraordinary lies in the ordinary. Or, as Mingyur Rinpoche is fond of saying, "Nothing special *is* the best special."

Although ordinariness is the felt-sense of *awakened presence*, its direct realization can feel extraordinary for a mind accustomed to unawareness. Because the sacred ground of awareness underlies all experiences (including the most devastating ones), unfavorable conditions do not pose an impediment to awakening. So when life unfolds as a depressive nightmare, a substance-abusing hell, or an anxiety-ridden prison, liberation from suffering is a mere wakeful moment away.

We are not helpless, and suffering is not inevitable. Embracing delusion as our precious teacher makes fearless reception of the actuality of self-suffering possible. Courageously know the empty transparency of ego wounding, self-fixation and all forms of discursive narration, and your mind will be freed from cognitive-affective enslavement. Liberation is our birthright. So offer up the illusion of the suffering self on the altar of *awakened presence*!

If genuine mental health is your goal (and I pray it is), then I invite you to liberate yourself from the ego's delusions of specialness. The self is just another phenomenon reflected in the mirror of awareness, and not-self is nothing special. If you still cling to the idea that healing resides in truly being seen, then please do the supreme seeing. *See beyond self-delusion.*

Vow that each time you get lost in self-distracting unawareness—misperceiving thoughts as anything other than just thoughts, emotions as anything other than just emotions, experience as anything other than just experience—you will choose to recognize self-delusion and rest effortlessly in the luminosity of awareness. This human life is precious. Don't waste it living in unawareness. Fearlessly, compassionately live in *awakened presence*!

Doing so will open your heart to you as you truly are—a *Bodhisattva*-in-waiting, one who knows suffering and is fully capable of recognizing the utter emptiness of all affliction and alleviation. You have always been that *Bodhisattva*. You have always been the liberating awareness. You have always been the fearless compassion. You have always been the timeless wisdom of an awakened heart-mind. Courageously love yourself and this life enough to recognize its sacredness and aim to liberate all beings by walking the path of *awakened presence*!

Offer up the illusion of being in the present moment! Awareness is not about being in the present moment. Awareness is beyond manifestation and cannot be contained within any particular moment. *Awakened presence* is the effortless, unperturbed, unelaborated reception of experience—not the effort of trying to be in a present moment.

Right now open your awareness to reading these words—the inner voice, the outer movement of the eyes. Rest in the actuality, the natural flow of these phenomena. Don't hold, fix or push away anything about the experience. If you notice ego narratives about who you are or how you are in the experience, shift your awareness back to reading. Or stop reading and rest in the field of mind, allowing awareness to naturally quiet discursive, habitual self-mentation. Rest effortlessly, abiding in the luminosity of knowing itself.

Ultimately, even the illusion of the enlightened self must be renounced. All forms of self sheathe the diamond sword of awareness in concepts. Encased in conceptualizations, perception remains dull and deluded. To bare the sword of nonconceptual awareness, all our concepts—especially those of enlightenment—must be let go. Question all your definitions and concepts of awareness, and give up the idea that it can be maintained indefinitely. Awareness is just another term for being undeluded. It arrives with the recognition of unawareness. When this occurs, leave your mind as it is, and rest effortlessly, wakefully present for the comings and goings of phenomena. "In the end what we learn on the path is there is only a dance between delusion and non-delusion. Recognizing delusion is the true non-delusion" (Thubten, August 15–16, 2013).

Just before his death, the Buddha implored the monks to be a lamp unto themselves. Each of us is that lamp. Luminous awareness lights the lamp. *Awakened presence* is the recognition of the dreamlike nature of illuminated appearances.

May every mind be liberated from all illusions of self-permanence, self-solidity and self-separateness, and may genuine mental health be a reality for all beings everywhere!

The dreamlike Buddha came to dreamlike beings.
To show them the dreamlike path to dreamlike enlightenment.

The dreamlike Buddha came to dreamlike beings.
To show them the dreamlike path to dreamlike enlightenment.

The dreamlike Buddha came to dreamlike beings.
To show them the dreamlike path to dreamlike enlightenment.[1]

Note

1 Source unknown (referred to by Tsoknyi Rinpoche during numerous retreats).

Exercise and Meditation Lists

Contemplative Exercises and Meditation Instruction

1. Contemplation of the Four Reflections
2. Practices to Develop Presence in the Here and Now

    Orienting
    Just Hearing
    Resting in Physical Sensations
    Noting the Feeling Tone of Experience: Pleasant, Unpleasant and Neutral

3. Mindfulness of Breath Meditation (*Ānāpānasati*)

    Ānāpānasati Group One: Knowing the *Prāna*-Body and Flesh-Body
    Ānāpānasati Group Two: Working With *Vedanā*: *Pīti* and *Sukha*
    Ānāpānasati Group Three: Working With Mind (*Citta*)
    Ānāpānasati Group Four: Knowing Truth (*Dhamma*)

4. Lovingkindness (*Mettā*) Meditation Instruction
5. Compassion Meditation for Self and Loved Ones
6. Compassion Meditation for a Difficult Person
7. Tonglen Meditation
8. *Muditā* Meditation Instruction
9. Equanimity (*Upekkhā*) Meditation Instruction
10. Non-dual Mindfulness

    Open Monitoring Meditation Instruction
    Objectless *Shamatha* Instruction

11. Unfindability: Looking for Mind
12. Gentle Vase Breathing Instruction
13. Effortless Mindfulness: The Refuge of Resting in Awakened Presence

    From Within the Body
    From Within Rumination
    From Within Agitated or Worried Mentation

From Within Craving and Aversion
From Within Awareness Itself

Buddhist Psychotherapeutic Exercises

1. Personal Exploration of Lesser and Greater Happiness
2. Clinician's Exploration of Lesser and Greater Happiness
3. Discovering Pure Desire Exercise
4. Befriending Your Greatest Challenges Exercise
5. Assessing Right View and Right Intention
6. The Seven Principles of Effective Inquiry
7. Your Action Plan for Transformation

Glossary of Pāli, Sanskrit and Tibetan Terms

P = Pāli S = Sanskrit T = Tibetan (Wylie)

afflictive mind states (P: *kilesa* S: *kleśa* (or klesha) T: *nyon mongs*)
aggregates (P: *khandha* S: *skandha* T: *phung po lnga*)
aging and death (P: *jaramarana* S: *jāramarana* T: *rga ba 'chi ba*)
aiming attention (P: *vitakka* S: *vitarkah* T: *rtog pa*)
altruistic joy (P & S: *muditā* T: *dgas ba*)
attention (P & S: *manasikāra* T: *yid la byed pa*)
awakening life force (P: *pīti* S: *kundalini* T: *gtummo*)
becoming (P: *bhava* S: *bhāva* T: *mi srid*)
birth (P & S: *jāti* T: *skye ba*)
bodhicitta (T: *byang chub kyi sems*)
body (P: *kāyā* S: *kāya* T: *lus dran*)
breath of life (P: *pāna* S: *prāna* T: *dbugs*)
Buddhanature (S: *Tathāgatagarbha* T: *rgyal ba'i khams*)
Buddhist teachings (P: *dhamma* S: *dharma* T: *chos*)
clear comprehension (P: *sati-sampajañña* S: *smrti samprajanya* T: *mngon par rtogs*)
clear seeing (P: *sampajañña S: samprajanya T: lhag mthong*)
clinging (P & S: *upādāna* T: *bdag 'dzin*)
cognition-only (S: *vijñapti-mātra*)
compassion (P & S: *karunā* T: *snying rje*)

immeasurable compassion (T: *snying rje tshad med*)
non-referential compassion (T: *dmigs med snying rje*)

conceit of 'I am' (S: *asmimāna*)
concentration (P: *samatha* S: *shamatha* T: *zhi gnas*)
concepts (P & S: *paññatti* T: *rtog tshogs*)
conceptual proliferation (P: *papañca* S: *prapañca* T: *spros bcas*)
conditioned mind (P: *sankhātakhanda* S: *sankhārakhanda*)
consciousness and the mental factors (P: *cittacetasikasankhāta*)
contact (P: *phassa* S: *sparśa* T: *reg pa*)

conventional truth (P: *sammuti sacca* S: *lokasamvrtisatya* T: *kun-rdzob bden-pa*)
craving (P: *tanhā* S: *trsnā* T: *dod sred*)

craving pleasurable experience (P: *kama-tanhā*)
craving becoming (P: *bhava-tanhā*)
craving non-existence (P: *vibhava-tanhā*)

deluded consciousness (S: *klistamanas* T: *nyon-yid rnam-shes*)
Dependent Origination (P: *paticca-samuppāda* S: *pratītyasamutpāda* T: *rten 'brel*)
derived material phenomena (P: *upādāya rūpa*)
derived nature (S: *parabhāva*)
desire (S: *chanda* T: *'dod pa*)
desireless (P: *apanihita*)
discrete cognitive awareness (S: *pravrtti-vijñāna*)
effortless mindfulness (T: *rtsol med kyi dran pa*)
ego (P & S: *manas* T: *bdag*)
Eightfold Path (P: *ariyo atthangiko maggo* S: *āryāstāngamārga* T: *yang dag pa'i lta ba rtog pa*)

right view (P: *sammā ditthi* S: *samyag drsti* T: *yang dag pa'i lta ba*)
right intention (P: *sammā sankappa* S: *samyag samkalpa* T: *yang dag pa'i rtog ba*)
right speech (P: *sammā vācā* S: *samyag vāc* T: *yang dag pa'i ngag*)
right action (P: *sammā kammaññatā* S: *samyag karmānta* T: *yang dag pa'i las kyi mtha'*)
right livelihood (P: *sammā ājīva* S: *samyag ājīva* T: *yang dag pa'i 'tsho ba*)
right effort (P: *sammā vāyāma* S: *samyag vyāyāma* T: *yang dag pa'i rtsal ba*)
right mindfulness (P: *sammā sati* S: *samyak smrti* T: *yang dag pa'i dran pa*)
right concentration (P: *sammā samādhi* S: *samyak samādhi* T: *yang dag pa'i ting nge 'dzin*)

emptiness (P: *suññatā* S: *śūnyatā* T: *stong pa nyid*)
endless rounds (P & S: *samsāra* T: *khor ba*)
equalness (T: *mnyam nyid*)
equanimity (P & S: *upekkhā* T: *btang snyoms*)
essential nature (P & S: *svabhāva* T: *rang-bzhin*)
ethical conduct (P: *sīla* S: *śīla* T: *tshul khrims*)
exalted (P: *mahaggatatā*)
Five Aggregates (P: *khandā* S: *skandha* T: *phung po lnga*)

form/matter (P & S: *rūpa* T: *gzugs*)
feeling (P & S: *vedanā* T: *tshor ba*)
perception (P: *saññā* S: *samjñā* T: *'du shes*)

volition or mental formations (P & S: *cetanā/sankhāra* S: *samskāra* T: *sems pa*)
consciousness (P: *citta/viññāna* S: *vijñāna* T: *rnam shes*)

Five Hindrances (P: *pañca nīvaranāni* S: *pañca nivārana* T: *gribs pa lnga*)

longing (P: *kāmachanda*)
anger (P: *vyāpāda*)
sloth and torpor (P: *thīna-middha*)
restlessness (P: *uddhacca-kukkucca*)
doubt (P: *vicikicchā*)

four elements (P & S: *dhātu*)

air (*vāyodhātu*)
earth (*pathavīdhātu*)
fire (*tejodhātu*)
water (*āpodhātu*)

Four Foundations of Mindfulness (P: *Satipatthāna* S: *Smrtyupasthāna* T: *dran pa nye bar bzhag pa bzhi*)
four immeasurables (P & S: *Brahmavihāras* T: *tshad med bzhi*)
full extinction of defilements (P: *kilesa-parinibbāna*)
happiness (P & S: *somanassa* T: *skyid*)
harmony (P: *samādhāna*)
heedfulness (P: *appamada* S: *apramāda* T: *bag yod pa*)
ignorance (P: *avijjā* S: *avidyā* T: *ma rig pa*)
innate awareness (T: *rigpa*)
insight (P: *vipassanā* S: *vipashyana* T: *lhag mthong*)
joy (P & S: *sukha* T: *bde ba*)
liberation (P: *nibbāna* S: *nirvāna* T: *mya ngan las 'das pa*)
link (P & S: *nidāna* T: *yan lag*)
linking (P: *patisandhāna*)
lovingkindness (P: *mettā* S: *maitrī* T: *byams pa*)
luminosity (T: *gsal ba*)
meditative absorption (P & S: *samādhi* T: *ting nge 'dzin*)
mental consciousness (P: *mano-viññāna* S: *mano-vijñāna* T: *yid-kyi rnam-shes*)
mental factors (P: *cetasikas* S: *caitasika* T: *sems byung*)
mere 'I' (*dak tsam*)
mind and matter (name and form) (P & S: *nāmarūpa* T: *'ming gzugs*)
mind/consciousness (P & S: *citta* T: *tsi ta*)
mindfulness (P: *sati* S: *smrti* T: *dran pa*)
mindfulness and discrimination (P: *sati-nepakka*)
Mindfulness of Breath Meditation (P: *ānāpānasati* S: *ānāpānasmrti* T: *rjes su dran pa*)

mind-only school (S: *cittamātra*)
moral discipline (P: *sīlakkhandha* T: *tshul khrims*)
non-delusion (P: *vijjā* S: *vidyā* T: *rmongs med*)
non-harming (P: *avihimsā* S: *ahimsā* T: *rnam par mi 'tshe*)
obstructions (P: avarana S: *āvarana* T: *gegs*)
one-pointed attention (P & S: *ekaggatā* T: *rtse gcig*)
perfections (P: *pāramī* S: *pāramitā* T: *pha rol tu phyin pa*)

generosity (P & S: *dāna* T: *sbyin pa*)
virtue (P: *sīla* S: *śila* T: *tshul khrims*)
renunciation (P: *nekkhamma*)
transcendent wisdom (P: *paññā* S: *prajñā* T: *shes rab*)
energy/zeal (P: *viriyā* S: *vīrya* T: *brtson'grus*)
patience (P: *khanti* S: *ksānti* T: *bzod pa*)
truthfulness (P: *sacca*)
determination (P: *adhitthāna*)
lovingkindness (P: *mettā*)
equanimity (P & S: *upekkhā* T: *btang snyoms*)
one-pointed concentration (S: *dhyāna* T: *bsam-gtan*)

phenomena (P: *dhammas* S: *dharmas* T: *chos dran*)
physical base or organ (P: *vatthu*)
precious 'I' (T: *dak che dzin*)
proliferation mind (P: *papañca-saññā-sankhā*)
reified or solid 'I' (T: *dak tenpar dzin*)
seeds (S: *bīja-bhāva*)
self-awareness (S: *svasamvitti* T: *rang rig*)
self-cherishing (S: *ātmasneha*)
self-confusion (S: *moha*)
self-existence (S: *satkāya drsti*)
sending and taking (T: *gtong len*)
sense base of mind (P: *mano* S: *manas T: yid kyi skye mched*)
seven factors of awakening (P: *satta bojjhangā* S: *sapta bodhyanga* T: *byang chub kyi yan lag bdun*)

mindfulness (P: *sati*)
investigation (P: *dhamma vicaya*)
energy (P: *viriyā*)
rapture (P: *pīti*)
serenity (P: *passaddhi*)
concentration (P: *samādhi*)
equanimity (P: *upekkhā*)

signless (P: *animitta*)
six sense-bases (P: *salāyatana* S: *āyatana* T: *phyi'i skye mched drug*)
space element (P: *ākāsadhātu*)

spontaneous presence (T: *lhun grub*)
subtle energy channels (S: *nadi* T: *tsa*)
subtle energy hubs (S: *bindu* T: *tigle*)
subtle energy-wind (S: *prāna* T: *rlung*)
suchness (P & S: *tathatā* T: *dharmata*)
suffering/unsatisfactoriness (P: *dukkha* S: *duhkha* T: *sdug bsngal*)

physical, mental and emotional pain (P: *dukkha-dukkha*)
reality of constant change (P: *viparinama-dukkha*)
discomfort underlying all experience (P: *sankhārā-dukkha*)

sustained attention (P & S: *vicāra* T: *chöpa*)
tenderheartedness (P: *anukampā*)
three marks of existence P: *ilakkhaṇa* S: *trilakṣaṇa*

unsatisfactoriness (P & S: *dukkha* T: *sdug bsngal*)
impermanence (P: *anicca* S: *anitya* T: *mi rtag pa*)
not-self (P: *anattā* S: *anātman* T: *bdag med*)

three natures (S: *trisvabhāva* T: *rang bzhin gsum*)

constructed nature (S: *paraikalpitasvabhāva* T: *kun brtags*)
dependent nature (S: *paratantrasvabhāva* T: *gzhan bdang*)
perfected nature (S: *parinispannasvabhāva* T: *yongs gsum*)

true nature of things (S: *dharmatā* T: *chos nyid*)
two truths (S: *satyadvayavibhāga*)
ultimate truth (P: *paramattha sacca* S: *paramārthasatya* T: *don-dam bden-pa*)
unconditioned (P: *asankhata* S: *asankhāra* T: *ma brten pa*)
unconditioned element (P: *asankhata dhātu* S: *asankhāra dhātu*)
unconditioned mind (P: *asankhata-khanda* S: *asankhāra-khanda*)
unconscious or storehouse consciousness (P: *bhavanga-citta* S: *ālaya-vijñāna* T: *kun gzhi'i rnam shes*)
wholesome action (P: *akusalā kamma*)
unwholesome cognitive and emotional states (P: *akusalacitta*)
unwholesome roots (P: *akusala-mūla* S: *akuśala-mūla* T: *dug gsum*)

greed (P: *lobha* S: *rāga* T: *'dod chags*)
hatred (P: *dosa* S: *dvesa* T: *zhe sdang*)
delusion (P & S: *moha* T: *gti mug*)

volitional formations (P: *sankhāra* S: *samskāra* T: *'du byed*)
wholesome action (P: *kusalā kamma*)
wholesome cognitive and emotional states (P: *kusalacitta*)
wisdom (P: *paññā* S: *prajñā* T: *ye shes*)

Resources

For more information on the material presented in this book visit: www.awakenedpresence.com. For information on Lisa and her work visit: www.lisadalemiller.com

Vipassāna Meditation

Cloud Mountain http://cloudmountain.org/index.php?page=about-us
Insight Meditation Society www.dharma.org/
Life Balance Institute www.lifebalanceinstitute.com/
Sitting Groups and Retreat Center listings www.inquiringmind.com/Retreats.html
Spirit Rock Meditation Center www.spiritrock.org/

Dzogchen Meditation

Dharmata Foundation www.dharmata.org/
Dondrubling http://dzogchencommunitywest.org/
Gyalshen Institute http://gyalshen.org/
Ligmincha Foundation www.ligmincha.org/en/
Pundarika Foundation www.tsoknyirinpoche.org/
Rangjung Yeshe Gomde http://gomdeusa.org/
Rigpa Center www.rigpa.org/

Mahāmudrā Meditation

Kagyu International www.kagyu.org/index.php
Nalanda West http://nalandawest.org/
Tergar International http://tergar.org/

Other Buddhist Centers

Land of Medicine Buddha http://landofmedicinebuddha.org/
Tibet House NYC www.tibethouse.org/
Upaya Zen Center www.upaya.org/index.php
Vajrayana Foundation www.vajrayana.org/

Mindfulness and Psychotherapy Training

Certificate in Mindfulness and Compassion in Psychotherapy CIIS www.ciis.edu/Public_Programs/Certificate_Programs/Mindfulness_Certificate.html
Cognitive-Based Compassion Training http://tibet.emory.edu/cbct/
Institute for Meditation and Psychotherapy www.meditationandpsychotherapy.org/
Mindfulness-Based Cognitive Therapy www.mbct.com/
Mindfulness-Based Professional Trainings https://cme.ucsd.edu/mindfulness/index.html
Mindfulness-Based Relapse Prevention www.mindfulrp.com/
Oasis Institute www.umassmed.edu/cfm/oasis/index.aspx
Stanford CCARE http://ccare.stanford.edu/#1
The Mindfulness Solution www.mindfulness-solution.com/Programs.html
Upaya Professional Training Programs www.upaya.org/training/

Contemplative Science

Center for Investigating Healthy Minds www.investigatinghealthyminds.org/
Center for Mindfulness www.umassmed.edu/Content.aspx?id=41252
David Vago, PhD http://contemplativeneurosciences.com/aboutme/home.html
Department of Social Neuroscience Max Planck Institute www.cbs.mpg.de/depts/singer
International Symposium for Contemplative Studies www.iscs2014.org/
Mind and Life Institute www.mindandlife.org/
Yale Therapeutic Neuroscience http://medicine.yale.edu/psychiatry/YTNC/index.aspx

Bibliography

Adler, A. (1927). *Understanding human nature.* New York, NY: Greenberg.

Adler, A. (1931/1998). *What life should mean to you.* Center City, MN: Hazelden.

American Psychiatric Association. (2013). *Diagnostic and statistical manual of mental disorders* (5th ed.). Arlington, VA: American Psychiatric Publishing.

Batchelor, S. (Trans.). (2010). The Pali canon: Source texts for secular Buddhism. *Study tools.* Retrieved April 1, 2011 from http://stephenbatchelor.org/index.php/en/stephen/study-tools

Batchelor, S. (2013, May 4). Interview. (L. D. Miller, Interviewer).

Batson, C. D. (2011). Empathy and altruism. In S. J. Lopez, & C. R. Snyder (Eds.), *The Oxford handbook of positive psychology 2nd edition* (pp. 417–426). Oxford, England: Oxford University Press.

Beck, A. (2005a). Meeting of Minds (His Holiness the 14th Dalai Lama and Professor Aaron T. Beck in Conversation) 9/11. YouTube. Retrieved August 2012 from www.youtube.com/watch?v=j0P2xR_aplE&feature=relmfu

Beck, A. (2005b). Meeting of Minds (His Holiness the 14th Dalai Lama and Professor Aaron T. Beck in Conversation) 10/11. YouTube. Retrieved August 6, 2012 from www.youtube.com/watch?v=JEkf__mlDvs&feature=relmfu

Beck, A. (2010). Aaron Beck meets the Dalai Lama. *Vimeo.* Retrieved August 2012 from http://vimeo.com/12988721

Bentham, J. (1789/1907). *An introduction to the principles of morals and legislation.* Oxford, England: Clarendon Press

Bien, T. (2010). *The Buddha's way of happiness: Healing sorrow, transforming negative emotion and finding well-being in the present moment.* Oakland, CA: New Harbinger.

Bodhi, B. (1994). *The noble Eightfold Path: Way to the end of suffering.* Onalaska, WA: Pariyatti Editions.

Bodhi, B. (1995). *The middle length discourses of the Buddha: A new translation of the Majjhima Nikāya: Translated from the Pali.* Boston, MA: Wisdom Publications Inc.

Bodhi, B. (2000). *The connected discourses of the Buddha: A translation of the Samyutta Nikaya.* Boston, MA: Wisdom Publications.

Bodhi, B., & Thera, N. (1999). *Numerical discourses of the Buddha: An anthology of suttas from the Anguttara Nikaya.* Walnut Creek, CA: Altamira Press.

Boisvert, M. (1995). *The five aggregates: Understanding Theravadan psychology and soteriology.* Delhi, India: India Books Center.

Bokar, R. (1992). *Meditation advice to beginners.* San Francisco, CA: ClearPoint Press.

Brewer, J. (2013). You're Already Awesome. Just Get Out of Your Own Way! YouTube. Retrieved July 5, 2013 from www.youtube.com/watch?v=jE1j5Om7g0U

Brewer, J. M. (1/25/2013). Interview. (L. D. Miller, Interviewer)

Buddhadasa, A. (1988). *Mindfulness with Breathing: A manual for serious beginners*. Boston, MA: Wisdom Publications.

Buddhaghosa. (1975). *The Visuddhimagga*. (B. Nanamoli, Trans.). Kandy, Sri Lanka: Buddhist Publication Society.

Byrom, T. (Trans.). (1976). *The Dhammapada: The sayings of the Buddha*. New York, NY: Random House.

Calderón-Abbo, J. (2013, June 6). Interview. (L. D. Miller, Interviewer).

Calderón-Abbo, J. (2013, June 19). Interview. (L. D. Miller, Interviewer).

Camus, P. (Ed.). (1915). *The gospel of the Buddha*. Warren, H., (Trans.). Chicago, IL: Open Court.

Clark, J. J. (1994). *Jung and Eastern thought: A dialogue with the Orient*. New York, NY: Routledge.

CMU. (2012). How stress influences disease: Study reveals inflammation as the culprit. *Science Daily*. Retrieved November 2, 2012 from www.sciencedaily.com/releases/2012/04/120402162546.htm

Condon, P., Desbordes, G., Miller, W., DeSteno, D., Hospital, M. G., & DeSteno, D. Meditation increases compassionate responses to suffering. *Psychological Science*. [In Press].

Conze, E. (1973). *The perfection of wisdom in eight thousand lines and its verse and summary*. Bolinas, CA: Four Seasons Foundation.

Damasio, A. (2010). *Self comes to mind: constructing the conscious brain*. New York, NY: Vintage Books.

Davidson, R. (2012). *The emotional life of your brain*. New York, NY: Hudson Street Press.

Davis, L. &. (2012). Mindfulness-based treatment for people with severe mental illness: a literature review. *American Journal of Psychiatric Rehabilitation, 15*(2), 202–232.

Decety, J. (2009). *S*. Cambridge, MA: MIT Press.

Decety, J. Y. (2010). Physicians down-regulate their pain empathy response: an event-related brain potential study. *Neuroimage, 50*(4), 1676–1682.

Dunne, J. D. (2005, June 5). Interview. (L. D. Miller, Interviewer).

Dunne, J. (2011). Toward an understanding of non-dual mindfulness. *Contemporary Buddhism, 12*(01), 71–88.

Eliot, T.S. (1968). *Four quartets*. New York, NY: Mariner Books.

Engler, J. (2003). Being somebody and being nobody. In J. Safran (Ed.), *Psychoanalysis and Buddhism* (pp. 35–79). Boston, MA: Wisdom Publications.

Epictetus. (1994–2009). *The Enchiridion*, c. 135. (E. T. Carter, Trans.). The Internet Classics Archive. Retrieved May 4, 2012 from http://classics.mit.edu/Epictetus/epicench.html

Epstein, M. (1996). *Thoughts without a thinker*. New York, NY: Basic Books.

Felitti, V. J., & Anda, R. F. (2010). The relationship of adverse childhood experiences to adult medical disease, psychiatric disorders and sexual behavior: Implications for healthcare. In R. A. Lanius, E. Vermetten, & C. Pain (Eds.), *The hidden epidemic: The impact of early life trauma on health and disease* (pp. 77–87). Cambridge: Cambridge University Press.

Foster, J. A. (2013). Gut–brain axis: how the microbiome influences anxiety and depression. *Trends in Neurosciences, 36*(55), 305–312.

Freud, S. (1908). "Civilized" sexual morality and modern nervous illness. In J. Strachey (Ed. and Trans.), *The standard edition of the complete psychological works of Sigmund Freud* (Vol. 9, pp. 177–204). London, England: Hogarth Press.

Freud, S. (1913). On beginning the treatment (further recommendations on the technique of psychoanalysis). In J. Strachey (Ed. and Trans.), *The standard edition of the complete psychological works of Sigmund Freud* (Vol. 12, pp. 121–144). London, England: Hogarth Press.

Fronsdal, G. (2005). *The Dhammapada: A new translation of the Buddhist classic with annotations*. Boston, MA: Shambhala Publications.

Garfield, J. L. (1995). *The fundamental wisdom of the middle way: Nagarjuna's Mulamadhyamakakarika*. London, England: Oxford University Press.

Garrison K. A., Santoyo J. F., Davis J. H., Thornhill T. A., Kerr C. E., & Brewer J. A. (2013). Effortless awareness: Using real time neurofeedback to investigate correlates of posterior cingulate cortex activity in meditators' self-report. *Frontiers in Human Neuroscience, 7*(440). doi: 10.3389/fnhum.2013.00440

Gethin, R. (2011). On some definitions of mindfulness. *Contemporary Buddhism, 12*(01), 263–279.

Gilbert, P. (2005). Compassion and cruelty: A biosocial approach. In P. Gilbert (Ed.), *Compassion: Conceptualisations, research and use in psychotherapy* (pp. 9–74). New York, NY: Routledge.

Guenther, H. (1976). *The tantric view of life*. Boulder, CO: Shambala.

Gunaratana, H. (1995–2013). The Jhanas in Theravada Buddhism: Introduction. *Access to Insight*. Retrieved April 8, 2013 from www.accesstoinsight.org/lib/authors/gunaratana/wheel351.html#ch1

Gyatso, T. (1990). *Freedom in exile: The autobiography of the Dalai Lama*. New Delhi, India: Rupa & Co.

Gyatso, T. (2002). *Essence of the heart sutra: The Dalai Lama's heart of wisdom teachings*. Boston, MA: Wisdom Publications.

Halifax, J. (2010, September). Compassion and the true meaning of empathy. *TEDWomen 2010*. TED.com. Retrieved 4/13/2013 from www.ted.com/talks/joan_halifax.html

Halifax, J. (2012). A heuristic model of enactive compassion. *Current Opinion in Supportive and Palliative Care*, *6*(2), 228–235.

Hahn, T. N. (2013, September 12). Meditation and Psychotherapy Conference. Unpublished lecture presented at Park Plaza Hotel, Boston, MA.

Hawkins, J. (2004). *On intelligence*. New York, NY: Holt & Co.

Hinton, D. E., Pich, V., Hofmann, S. G., & Otto, M. W. (2011). Acceptance and mindfulness techniques as applied to refugee and ethnic minority populations with PTSD: Examples from "Culturally adapted CBT." *Cognitive and Behavioral Practice, 20*(1), 33–46.

Hixon, L. (1993). *The mother of all the Buddhas: Meditation on the Prajnaparamita Sutras*. Wheaton, IL: Theosophical Publishing House

Hopkins, J. (2008). *A truthful heart*. Ithaca, NY: Snow Lion.

Hoskinson, S. (2013, April 24). Interview. (L. D. Miller, Interviewer)

James, W. (1890). *The principles of psychology Volume 1*. Cambridge, MA: Harvard University Press.

Jinpa, T. (Ed. and Trans.). (2011). *Essential mind training*. Boston, MA: Wisdom Publications.

Jobs, S. (2005, June 14). "You've got to find what you love," Jobs says. *Stanford Review*. Retrieved August 12, 2013 from http://news.stanford.edu/news/2005/june15/jobs-061505.html

Jung, C. G. (1970). Freud and Jung: Contrasts. In *Collected Works of C. G. Jung* (Vol. 4 p. 333–340). Princeton, NJ: Princeton University Press. (Original work published 1929).

Jung, C. G. (1988). (J. Jarrett, Ed.) *Nietzsche's "Zarathustra": Notes of the seminar given (1934–1939)*. Princeton, NJ: Princeton University Press.

Kabat-Zinn, J. (2005). *Coming to our senses: Healing ourselves and the world through mindfulness*. New York, NY: Hyperion.

Kellerman, N. (2009). *"Holocaust trauma" psychological effects and treatment*. New York, NY: iUniverse.

Khyentse, J. (2012). *Not for Happiness: A Guide to the so-called preliminary practices*. Boston, MA: Shambhala Publications.

Kirsch, I. E. (2008). Initial severity and antidepressant benefits: a meta-analysis of data submitted to the Food and Drug Administration. *PLoS Medicine, 5*(2), e45.

Kochanska, G. E. (2009). Early attachment organization moderates the parent–child mutually coercive pathway to children's antisocial conduct. *Child Development, 80*(4), 288–1300.

Kornfield, J. (2008). *The wise heart: A guide to the universal teachings of Buddhist psychology*. New York, NY: Bantam Books.

Levine, P. (2010). *In an unspoken voice: How the body releases trauma and restores goodness*. Berkeley, CA: North Atlantic Books.

Libet, B. (2004). *Mind time: The temporal factor in consciousness*. Cambridge, MA: Harvard Univeristy Press.

Lusthaus, D. (2004). What Is and Isn't Yogacara? *Yogachara Buddhist Research Association*. Retrieved May 1, 2013 from www.acmuller.net/yogacara/articles/intro-uni.htm

Matthews, S. G., & Phillips, D. I. (2010). Minireview: transgenerational inheritance of the stress response: A new frontier in stress research. *Endocrinology, 151*(1), 7–13.

Mingyur, R. Y. (2009). *Joyful Wisdom*. New York, NY: Harmony Books.

Moffitt, P. (2012, December 12). Interview. (L.D. Miller, Interviewer).

Nyanatiloka. (1906). *Word of the Buddha: An outline of the ethico-philosophical system of the Buddha in the words of the Pali Canon*. Kandy, Ceylon: Buddhist Publication Society.

Nyima, C., (2002). *Present fresh wakefulness: A meditation manual on nonconceptual wisdom*. Hong Kong, China: Rangjung Yeshe Publications.

O'Connor, L. E. (2012). Depression, guilt, and Tibetan Buddhism. *Psychology, 3*(29), 805–809.

Paul, K.I. (2009). Unemployment impairs mental health: Meta-analyses. *Journal of Vocational Behavior, 74*(3), 264–282.

Ponlop, D. (2010). *Rebel Buddha: On the road to freedom*. Boston, MA: Shambhala.

Ponlop, R.D. (2006). *Penetrating wisdom: The aspiration of Samantabhadra*. Ithaca, NY: Snow Lion Publications.

Rabjam, L. (2000). *You are the eyes of the world*. (K. Lipman, Trans.). Ithaca, NY: Snow Lion Publications.

Rabjam, L. (2001). *A treasure trove of scriptural transmission: A commentary on the precious treasury of the basic space of phenomena*. (R. Barron, Trans.). Junction City, CA: Padma.

Rangdrol, S. N. (2001). *The life of Shabkar: The autobiography of a Tibetan yogin*. (M. Ricard, Trans.). Ithaca, NY: Snow Lion.

Ricard, M. (2013, May 3). Teachings on compassion par Shabkar Tsok Druk Rangdrol 1781–1851. *Mattieu Ricard Blog*. Retrieved July 2013 from www.matthieuricard.org/en/blog/posts/teachings-on-compassion-par-shabkar-tsok-druk-rangdrol-1781-1851

Rogers, C. (1951). *Client-centered therapy: It's current practice, implications and theory*. London, England: Constable.

Rogers, C. (1961). *On becoming a person: A therapist's view of psychotherapy*. London, England: Constable.

Salzberg, S. (1995). *Lovingkindness: the revolutionary art of happiness*. Boston, MA: Shambala.

Santikaro. (2008, July 18). *Anapanasati*.Unpublished lecture presented at Cloud Mountain, Castle Rock, WA.

Saraha. (n.d.). Saraha's Song for a King (translation). *Natural Awareness*. Retrieved May 27, 2013 from www.naturalawareness.net/mahamudra.html#_Toc119661362

Schneider, K. (2013). *The polarized mind*. Colorado Springs, CO: University Professors Press.

Shantideva. (1997). *A guide to the Bodhisattva way of life*. (V. W. Wallace, Trans.). Ithaca, NY: Snow Lion.

Singer, T. (2012). The past, present and future of social neuroscience: A European perspective. *Neuroimage*, *61*(2), 437–449.

Stcherbatsky. (1968). *The conception of Buddhist Nirvana*. Varanasi, India: Bharatiya Vidya Prakashan.

Stcherbatsky. (1970). *The central conception of Buddhism and the meaning of the word Dharma*. Dehli, India: Motilal Banarsiddas.

Teasdale, J. D., Moore, R. G., Hayhurst, H., Pope, M., Williams, S., & Segal, Z. V. (2002). Metacognitive awareness and prevention of relapse in depression: Empirical evidence. *Journal of Consulting and Clinical Psychology*, *70*(2), 275.

Thanissaro, B. (2012). Rājan Sutta: The King. *Access to Insight*. Retrieved March 10, 2013 from www.accesstoinsight.org/tipitaka/kn/ud/ud.5.01.than.html.

Thompson, E. (2013, February). *Consciousness*. Unpublished lecture presented at Upaya Zen Center, Santa Fe, NM.

Thubten, A. (2011, August). Unpublished lecture presented at Vajrapani, Boulder Creek, CA.

Thubten, A. (2012, July 29). Unpublished lecture presented at Dharmata Foundation, Richmond Point, CA.

Thubten, A. (2012, December 23). Unpublished lecture presented at Dharmata Foundation, Richmond Point, CA.

Thubten, A. (2013, March 13). Unpublished lecture presented at Dharmata Foundation, Richmond Point, CA.

Thubten, A. (2013, April 8). Unpublished lecture presented at Dharmata Foundation, Richmond Point, CA.

Thubten, A. (2013, May 26). *Dharma talk*. Unpublished lecture presented at. Dharmata Foundation, Richmond Point, CA.

Thubten, A. (2013, July 7). Unpublished lecture presented at Dharmata Foundation, Richmond Point, CA.

Thubten, A. (2013, July 21). Unpublished lecture presented at Dharmata Foundation, Richmond Point, CA.

Thubten, A. (2013, August 15–16). Unpublished lecture presented at the Angela Center, Santa Rosa, CA.

Vago, D. (2013, February 27). Interview. (L. D. Miller, Interviewer).

Waldron, W. (2003). *The Buddhist unconscious: The ālaya-vijñāna in the context of Indian Buddhist thought*. London, England: RoutledgeCurzon.

Wallace, A. B (1999). *The four immeasurables*. Boulder, CO: Snow Lion.

Wallace, B. (2007). *Contemplative science: Where Buddhism and neuroscience converge*. New York, NY: Columbia University Press.

Wallace, V. W. (1997). *Shantideva: A guide to the Bodhisattva way of life (Bodhicaryavatara)*. Ithaca, NY: Snow Lion.

Williams, P. (2008). *Mahayana Buddhism: The doctrinal foundations*. New York, NY: Routledge.

Index

CPSIA information can be obtained
at www.ICGtesting.com
Printed in the USA
FSOW02n2149300617
35891FS